BoB WAGGONER

Understanding Crime Prevention

National Crime Prevention Institute

Butterworths
Boston London Durban Singapore Sydney Toronto Wellington

All references in this book to personnel of male gender are used for convenience only and shall be regarded as including both males and females.

Library of Congress Cataloging-in-Publication Data

Understanding crime prevention.

Previously published as v. 1 of: The practice of crime prevention.
Bibliography: p.
Includes index.
1. Crime prevention. 2. Crime prevention–United States. 3. Crime prevention–Citizen participation. 4. Crime prevention–United States–Citizen participation. 5. Buildings–Security measures. I. National Crime Prevention Institute (University of Louisville)
HV7431.U52 1986 364.4 86-11799
ISBN 0-409-90075-3

Butterworth Publishers
80 Montvale Avenue
Stoneham, MA 02180

10 9 8 7 6

Printed in the United States of America

Table of Contents

Preface

The National Crime Prevention Institute (NCPI), a Division of the University of Louisville's School of Justice Administration, College of Urban and Public Affairs, was established in 1971. Since then, it has served as the nation's educational and technical resource for the development of comprehensive crime prevention programs at the local, state and national level.

Crime prevention through criminal opportunity reduction, defined as *the anticipation, recognition and appraisal of a crime risk and the initiation of some action to remove or reduce it*, is a practical and cost-effective approach to the reduction and containment of criminal activity. The wide-ranging knowledge and skills of crime prevention have been taught by NCPI, to over 22,000 crime prevention practitioners, criminal justice administrators, planners and trainers, public and private officials, and citizen leaders from communities and agencies in every state and from many national agencies and organizations.

Understanding Crime Prevention is a major milestone in NCPI's continuing efforts to stimulate the most rapid possible expansion of the ranks of professional crime prevention practitioners. This volume is addressed to the crime prevention practitioner. However, it is also designed to be directly relevant to the **needs** of the police chief; sheriff; director of public safety; mayor or city manager; institutional or corporate administrator; regional, state or federal criminal justice administrator; service club member; professional, volunteer, trade or labor organization administrator; primary, secondary or college-level educator; private security company executive; insurance underwriter, agent or loss prevention engineer; and many others for whom crime and its impact are an area of major responsibility or civic concern.

Although high-quality practical and academic learning experiences for criminal justice professionals is stressed, the principle that the control and management of crime cannot occur through the efforts of criminal justice professionals alone is recognized and emphasized. Only through the active participation of every sector of community interest can crime reduction be achieved. *Understanding Crime Prevention* can do much to advance this partnership idea, as well as provide specific guidance to crime prevention practitioners and their citizen-colleagues.

It is recognized that this volume is not the final word but, rather, the start of a continuing process by which the staff of the National Crime Prevention Institute will strive to organize and disseminate the knowledge and technologies of crime prevention. Your comments, criticisms and new ideas will aid in accomplishing this objective.

Acknowledgments

Publication Staff

National Crime Prevention Institute

Timothy D. Crowe, Director
Barbara R. Bomar, Assistant Director
Richard W. Mellard, Manager, Education & Technical Assistance Programs
Joe A. Mele, Loss Prevention Specialist

Contributors

The Publication Staff wishes to acknowledge the special contributions to the development, review, and production of this book made by the following:

Leon Bauer, Assistant Vice President, United Jersey Banks
Roy W. Dixon, Writer
James Edgar, Writer
O.C. Foster, Director of Loss Prevention, Taylor Drug Company
Dr. Irving F. Franke, Researcher

Douglas Frisbie, former Director, Minnesota Crime Watch
B.M. (Mac) Gray, II, Director of Marketing, NCPC
C. Ray Jefferey, Professor, Florida State University
Harry Keeney, Consultant
Carl Kellem, Group Security Administrator, IBM Corp.
John C. Klotter, Professor, School of Justice Administration
John McKay, former Associate Director, Criminal Justice Projects, National League of Cities
D.W. Rogers, Editor
George Sunderland, Senior Coordinator, Criminal Justice Program, AARP
Doyle Shackelford, Deputy Warden, Kentucky Reformatory-LaGrange
Larry Vardel, Chief of Police, Williamsburg, VA

1

Introduction to Crime Prevention

Crime is a costly and demoralizing problem affecting all of us. The victims of crime suffer injury, financial loss and intimidation. Everyone is affected by higher prices for products, taxes, insurance premiums, and the sense of insecurity and fear that result from criminal acts. Those who live or work in "high crime" areas can be deprived of some of life's normal opportunities and pleasures by the social and economic impact of crime and by the alienation and despair that accompanies the fear of crime.

Can we hope to eliminate the crime problem? Probably not, but it is reasonable to believe that crime and the fear of crime can be reduced and controlled. What has been lacking in our society is a systematic and effective crime control strategy. Crime prevention appears to be a major part of this needed strategy.

Crime prevention is an elegantly simple and direct approach that protects the potential victim from criminal attack by anticipating the possibility of attack and eliminating or reducing the opportunity for it to occur—and the possibility for personal harm or property loss should it occur.

Crime prevention programs have been developed in many parts of the United States and have attracted the participation of thousands of law enforcement professionals; public and private officials; leaders of voluntary service, professional and and labor organizations; and millions of citizens.

The purpose of *Understanding Crime Prevention* is to bring together for the first time the ingredients of crime prevention practice, thus to provide a roadmap for those who may wish to take part in this fascinating and demanding field.

THE MEANING OF CRIME PREVENTION

The phrase *crime prevention* has been loosely applied to any kind of effort aimed at controlling criminal behavior. However, as used here, crime prevention applies only to before-the-fact efforts to reduce criminal opportunity. Crime prevention is a direct crime control method, in contrast to all other types of crime reduction methods. As C. Ray Jefferey points out: *Direct controls of crime include only those which reduce environmental opportunities for crime. Indirect controls include all other measures, such as job training, remedial education, police surveillance, police apprehension, court action, imprisonment, probation and parole...*

Our current method of controlling crime is predominantly through indirect measures after the offense has been committed. The failure to control crime is in no small measure due to the strategies we select to deal with crime. It is obvious that we do not control crime if we allow it to occur before taking action. We may attempt to treat offenders or rehabilitate them after they have become criminals, but we should not confuse the treatment of criminals with the prevention of crime. The polio vaccine prevents polio; polio victims are treated via physical therapy after they have contracted polio.[1]

The formal definition of crime prevention as adopted in several countries is: *The anticipation, recognition and appraisal of a crime risk and the initiation of some action to remove or reduce it.*

Crime prevention can also be operationally explained as **the practice of crime risk management**. Crime risk management involves the development of systematic approaches to crime risk reduction that are cost effective and that promote both the security and the socioeconomic well being of the potential victim. Managing crime risks involves:

- Removing some risks entirely;
- Reducing some risks by decreasing the extent to which injury or loss can occur;
- Spreading some risks through physical, electronic and procedural security measures that deny, deter, delay or detect the criminal attack;
- Transferring some risks through purchase of insurance or involvement of other potential victims; and
- Accepting some risks.

HOW CRIME PREVENTION WORKS

Opportunity Reduction

Three ingredients must be present for a crime to be committed:

- Desire or motivation on the part of the criminal;
- The skills and tools needed to commit the crime; and
- Opportunity.

Crime prevention aims to reduce criminal opportunity rather than to attack either criminal desire or criminal skills. The reason for this emphasis is that reduction of opportunity (by making a potential target of attack inaccessible or unattractive and by making the attack itself dangerous or unprofitable to the criminal) is a practical approach that has proven its value.

Criminal Desire

Working to directly reduce criminal desire before-the-fact is anything but practical. In the first place, we would need some way to immunize people against criminal intent. But, we have been unable to develop such a "cure" even for those offenders whom we catch, imprison, and try to rehabilitate (we might change their attitudes while they are in prison, but we have no way to sustain that change once they are back on the streets). And, even if we had such a cure, how could we identify even a fraction of the potential offenders in the general population? How many have committed crimes without ever having been caught? How many others might steal, assault or kill, given the temptation and the opportunity? Then, if we had both a cure and a means to identify all actual and potential offenders, how would we administer the cure without violating civil rights? At present, preventing crime to any significant degree by directly reducing criminal desire and motivation is, from a practical standpoint, impossible.

Criminal Skills

It is also impractical to try to deny people the right to own and use tools which might be applied to criminal activities (except for those few implements legally defined as burglary tools) or to try to deny criminals from associating with—and thus learning from each other. A criminal, like anyone else, learns by doing. He does not necessarily learn his trade at the feet of a more experienced colleague. Such an enormous variety of tools can be employed in criminal activity that to outlaw the tools could be to paralyze large sectors of legitimate activity (the plastic credit card can be used to open spring bolt door locks), and the criminal would presumably develop unlawful ways to obtain his tools anyway.

Criminal Opportunity

Even if we could somehow greatly improve our ability to identify and treat criminals or manage effectively to remove both the tools that contribute to crime and the personal associations that teach crime skills, opportunity reduction would still be the most practical approach.

The reason for this is that criminal opportunity is controllable to a large degree at its end point—within the victim's environment. Potential victims can reduce their vulnerability to criminal attack by taking proper security precautions. It is not necessary to identify the criminal, to take any action to directly affect his motivation or his access to skills and tools. What is necessary is that potential victims reduce criminal opportunity by understanding criminal attack methods and taking precautions against them.

The Community Response

Does this mean that potential victims must turn their homes, businesses and neighborhoods into fortresses? Not at all. But we must admit that as a society we currently encourage impulsive, opportunistic crime by our carelessness. We put inadequate locks on our doors that even the unskilled amateur can easily get through. Then we neglect to use even those poor locks. We let large amounts of cash accumulate in our stores because we would rather not take the trouble to go to the bank. We don't report suspicious activity around our neighbor's house because we think "it's none of our business." We tolerate physical and social environments which invite criminal attack. So, the task of crime prevention is simply to convince each member of society to take a few basic precautions and to then convince those who build our homes and our cars, design our communities, and otherwise create the community environment to take some basic precautions.

An easy way to gain a quick appreciation for crime prevention is to look at its successful application (in the United States) to the crime of skyjacking. Most of us remember how a lone gunman was able to take over a commercial airliner, demand and receive several hundred thousand dollars, and then leap out of the airplane over the Pacific Northwest never to be heard from again. This was the start of an epidemic of skyjackings and a corresponding epidemic of so-called preventive measures. For example, psychiatric profiles of skyjackers were developed and distributed to airlines personnel. Squads of "Sky Marshals" were put aboard airlines. Low-velocity handguns were developed for use by peace officers aboard aircraft.

All of these efforts concentrated on the skyjacker himself and proved to be ineffective or dangerous or both. The approach that finally worked, and continues to work, totally ignores the offender and attempts instead to identify the weapons (guns, knives, bombs) used in skyjacking before they can be brought aboard. Now every person boarding a commercial aircraft in the United States must undergo a screening of self and carry-on luggage. When this screening process became operational at all airports, skyjacking in this country virtually ceased. The crime of skyjacking has been prevented in this country by a straightforward (opportunity-reduction) technique, and will continue to be prevented to the extent that detectable weaponry is needed for a successful skyjack.

Skyjacking, admittedly, is a rather dramatic crime far removed from the crimes that citizens and police confront in day-to-day life. But the principles of analytic thinking and strategic planning which led to successful prevention of skyjacking can be applied just as well to preventing most crimes that involve a victim.

The Crime Prevention Program

The specific techniques of crime prevention are, in many ways, not new at all. Alert individuals and groups have always been able to find ways to protect themselves against criminal attack to some degree. In the private sector, crime risk management techniques have been used for many years to protect specific facilities, operations or valuables. What is new and most promising about crime prevention is the idea of managing crime risks on a jurisdiction-wide scale through a crime prevention program so that everyone, not just those who are sufficiently affluent or clever, can enjoy higher levels of security and, equally important, freedom from fear.

It is assumed that criminals, like everyone else, learn through experience. Successful experience strengthens the criminal motivation, and unsuccessful experience weakens it—whatever the reason for the criminal motivation in the first place. If criminal opportunity is reduced, the criminal's "experience-learning curve" is inhibited. However, there is no net effect on successful criminal experience if the criminal, frustrated at one house, simply goes next door to attack a less cautious neighbor. So, security measures must be applied as universally as possible, and social groups must assume a collective responsibility for watching out for each other's safety and security. If crime prevention programs are established in all cities, towns and rural areas, we will see major national reductions in the impact of crime.

As the governmental arm responsible for public security, law enforcement agencies must learn to take a major role in the development of effective community-wide programs and serve not only as crime prevention consultants in existing community affairs but also participate in the planning of future community developments.

Finally, the law enforcement role, though pivotal, is by no means the only role to be played in a crime prevention program. All significant elements of the public and private sectors must join in the common effort and fully cooperate with each other.

The crime prevention program is carried out through a crime prevention organization, which is usually established in or by a unit of government (often the law enforcement agency itself). The purpose of the crime prevention organization is to plan, implement and manage a comprehensive crime prevention program within its jurisdiction. The program typically develops a wide range of projects and services involving three levels of operation:

- At the **client** level, the objective is to design crime risk management systems for application to the needs of specific homes, businesses, institutions, or other facilities which are owned or managed by individuals or organizations.
- At the **multiple client** level, the objective is to design crime risk management projects through which the many occupants and users of a neighborhood, shopping center or industrial area, or the members of a special population group, can collectively improve the security of the area or group.
- At the **public policy** level, the objective is to design crime risk management activities which units of government can carry out to improve the security of everyone within jurisdictions and, where appropriate, across jurisdictional lines.

The strategies used by the crime prevention program include:

- Public awareness—to make citizens aware of crime problems and the services available to them through the program;

- Crime risk management recommendations—involving services to individual clients;
- Teaching and counseling services—for specific groups;
- Group projects—through which organizations and agencies are helped to develop useful crime prevention activities;
- Environmental design—through which efforts are made to modify the existing and future physical environment to both discourage criminal activity and encourage citizen activity in the environment;
- Surveillance and reporting—through which citizens are encouraged to watch for criminal activity and report observations to police;
- Law enforcement—through which all law enforcement personnel are trained in and encouraged to support and promote crime prevention in all contacts with the public; and
- Private security—to expand the efforts of private security organizations to provide reliable and cost-effective security products and services.

THE CRIME PREVENTION PRACTITIONER

The crime prevention practitioner must possess a wide general knowledge of crime prevention theory and practice. He becomes skilled in applying this knowledge to individual client needs and to the design, development and management of projects which serve geographic areas and population groups. He works within the context of a jurisdiction-wide crime prevention program.

The typical crime prevention practitioner is a career law enforcement professional with several years of police experience prior to becoming involved in crime prevention. Either directly, through crime prevention training, or indirectly, through exposure to other practitioners, he or she has become convinced that criminal opportunity reduction is the crime control approach of the future.

A significant number of criminal justice planners, administrators and instructors have also been trained in crime prevention. A smaller number of trained practitioners operate within agencies and organizations which are outside the criminal justice field.

The private security field includes a large number of security and loss prevention specialists. Many private security specialists may also be classified as general practitioners because they have obtained appropriate training. These specialists primarily concentrate their efforts at the individual client level.

Law enforcement crime prevention practitioners have caused a shift away from traditional police methods toward the crime prevention approach. This is one of the most significant developments in the history of American law enforcement, and like most radical changes in established professional fields, it has not come without difficulty. Thanks to the pioneering efforts and support of a small group of police chiefs, sheriffs and criminal justice administrators, the National Crime Prevention Institute (NCPI) was able to train its first few groups of students.

The work of those early practitioners showed their own and neighboring agencies the value of the crime prevention approach, and the demand steadily increased. Not only has the demand for NCPI's training increased greatly since 1971, but also many states have developed their own crime prevention training programs.

Today's practitioner is part of a growing new professional field. Great opportunities exist for professional growth and advancement. It is no coincidence, for example, that many of NCPI's early graduates are now high-level law enforcement and criminal justice administrators as well as private security managers.

The person who enters the crime prevention field today has an even better chance for professional growth. The training now available, for example, is both of better quality and is more comprehensive than during those early days. Support for the idea of the practitioner as a professional is growing rapidly as more and more state governments establish statewide crime prevention programs, and as increasing numbers of state crime prevention associations are formed.

CONCLUSION

Crime prevention is a practical method for the direct control of crime. It involves analyzing criminal attack methods and designing specific actions within the environments of potential victims to reduce criminal opportunities and manage crime risks.

The mechanism through which crime prevention operates is the community-wide crime prevention program. This program serves as a planning and management setting through which a range of strategies is developed. The strategies of crime prevention basically aim to stimulate appropriate crime prevention attitudes and behavior on the part of individuals and groups and to work toward physical environment changes which promote crime prevention.

The key actor in crime prevention is the crime prevention practitioner, who is typically a law enforcement officer. The wide and diverse body of skills and knowledge needed by the practitioner is described in the following chapters.

2 The Evolution of Crime Prevention

In this chapter, we will deal with the emergence of modern crime prevention from—and in contrast with—offender-oriented crime control approaches.

Crime, defined by Webster's dictionary as "an act committed in violation of a law prohibiting it, an act omitted in violation of a law ordering it, or an offense against morality," is as old as mankind, and so is mankind's interest in eliminating, reducing or preventing crime.

Victim-oriented, opportunity-reduction crime prevention, though relatively recent in terms of widespread practice, grows out of a varied history of society's efforts to control and reduce wrongdoing.

Societies have practiced crime prevention of some crude sort throughout history.[1] The use of natural and man-made barriers and military or vigilante forces and a variety of needed mutual protection activities by members of each community to defend against attack by enemies or outlaws has occurred in every culture up to and including modern times. The tradition of a crime prevention approach that went beyond walls, gates and armed reprisals, however, had its beginnings in 17th Century England.[2]

ANCIENT TRADITION

Society's response to crime has been characterized by a range of approaches as varied as man's cultures and the historical periods from which they sprang.[3]

Punishment of the offender, either to "correct" him or to serve some other social purpose has been but one response. In preliterate cultures, in contrast, we find:

> *. . . certain motives and attitudes which apparently preceded the punitive reaction to lawbreaking but were not, in themselves, punishment: desire to annihilate an enemy of the group, sacrifice to appease or fend off the wrath of the gods, social hygiene measures to rid the community of pollution, self-redress in cases of private injury, and surprise and disgust at the person who injured his own family. Deliberate and "just" infliction of pain by the group in its corporate capacity was not invented until later.*[4]

It was only with the rise of the king or other central authority figure that duly authorized officials took on the task of dealing with wrongdoers on behalf of the society, or state, as a whole. The state's reaction to crime tended to be punitive, but the punishment inflicted did not necessarily reflect a belief that the offender's pain itself had some redeeming value. Instead, the purposes of punishment were often very pragmatic. In many cultures a criminal might be fined, mutilated or killed. The fine was levied to repay the victim's loss. Mutilation served to show others that the offender was untrustworthy. Execution was used to settle a family feud or remove a "wild-beast" offender from society.[5]

On the other hand, at certain times in history, crime control by the state consisted of seemingly vengeful acts against criminals. More often than not, the guilty one was given an added measure of punishment to ensure that he did not repeat the act, that he "properly" atoned for it, and that he provided a horrible example for others who might be tempted. Public spectacles of flogging, amputation of limbs, branding and a variety of forms of painful death were the order of the day, even for trivial criminal offenses and for moral offenses such as adultery, heresy and witchcraft.

The most famous early attempt to establish a legal basis for an orderly and just approach to crime control is Hammurabi's Code, dating from about 1800 B.C. Hammurabi, King of Babylon, was an enlightened administrator, and his schedule of penalties for infractions was restrained, compared to the usual punishment standards of the day.[6] Hammurabi's Code stated, among other things, the first approach to crime prevention through environmental design.

- If a builder builds a house for a man and does not make its construction firm and the house collapses and causes the death of the owner of the house—that builder shall be put to death.
- If it causes the death of a son of the owner—they shall put to death the son of the builder.
- If it causes the death of a slave of the owner—he shall give to the owner a slave of equal value.
- If it destroys property he shall restore whatever is destroyed and because he did not make the house firm he shall rebuild the house which collapsed at his own expense.

The Mosaic Code,[7] or Law of Moses, set down about a thousand years later, provided a lengthy and elaborate guide to the conduct of Hebrew affairs, and stipulated, for example, that:

> *If a person hears a solemn adjuration to give evidence as a witness to something he has seen or heard and does not declare what he knows, he commits a sin and must accept responsibility.* Leviticus, Chapter 5, Verse 1.
>
> *When one man strikes another and kills him, he shall be put to death. Whoever strikes a beast and kills it shall make restitution, life for life. When one man injures and disfigures his fellow-country-man, it shall be done to him as he had done; fracture for fracture, eye for eye, tooth for tooth; the injury and disfigurement that he has inflicted upon another shall in turn be inflicted upon him.* Leviticus, Chapter 24, Verses 17–20.

Wide and vigorous administration of "just" punishment based on a body of criminal law has prevailed until modern times, despite the fact that whether "just" or not, punishment's effectiveness as a primary crime control measure has always been dubious at best.

Over the past several hundred years, the modern European and American states have attempted to control crime by moving from punishment and reprisal to appeals to man's better nature to attempts at reform and rehabilitation of offenders and, finally, to the beginnings of the pragmatic, scientifically-based management approach to before-the-fact crime reduction, which we now call crime prevention.[8] This evolutionary process has left its traces in the complex and conflicting patterns which still characterize our criminal justice system.

THE ENGLISH TRADITION

A departure from the purely punitive or defensive approaches occurred when Oliver Cromwell, in 1655, attempted to set up a professional police force. He established 12 police jurisdictions in England and Wales, and the forces were organized and operated along military lines. When strong popular opposition forced Cromwell to abandon the plan, crime control reverted to the hands of the judicial system and its enforcers, and, for a time, punishment was once again supreme.[9]

In 1729, Thomas deVeil of Westminster organized a group of Thief Takers and Informers in an attempt to provide a police-like alternative to the corrupt, inefficient and self-serving judicial system. Unfortunately, little improvement was noted. Because these agents were only paid upon conviction of criminals, they tended to choose their victims carefully, and they left organized criminal gangs alone because of the danger of reprisals. They were not above planting evidence on innocent persons in order to maintain their incomes.

The appointment of Henry Fielding as a London Magistrate in 1748 set the stage for the first coherent development of police forces in England. Fielding set forth two objectives for himself. The first, *to stamp out existing crime,* was hardly original. but the second, *to prevent outbreaks of crime in the future*, was truly revolutionary.[10]

In Fielding's view, his objectives could not be achieved without:

- A strong police force;
- The active cooperation of the public; and
- The removal of the causes of crime and the conditions in which it flourishes.

Among his efforts to develop the necessary conditions for crime control and prevention, Fielding attempted to replace the corrupt or inefficient Parish Constables under his jurisdiction with hand-picked men of proven ability and good character. He appealed directly for public cooperation through newspaper advertisements such as the following:

> *All persons who shall for the future suffer by robberies, burglaries, etc., are desired immediately to bring or send the best description they can of such robberies, etc., with the time and place and circumstances of the fact to Henry Fielding, Esq. at his house in Bow Street.*[11]

Fielding also started a publication called *The Public Advertiser* to make people aware of the kinds of crimes being committed. He published lists of stolen property to encourage people to help recover the stolen items. Just before he died in 1754, he received funding to expand the distribution of *The Public Advertiser*, to establish a register of criminals, and to recruit more hand-picked "runners." These were to be on call at all times, ready to investigate and prevent crimes.

John Fielding, Henry's half-brother, took over as Magistrate, and for 26 years John tried to further his brother's plans. He obtained regular budget payments for street patrols, and published pamphlets about police—emphasizing their prevention role: "It is much better to prevent even one man from being a rogue than apprehending and bringing forty to justice."

The Fieldings must be credited with planting and nurturing the idea of a preventive police force, even though there were only a few small organized units at the time of John's death. Various attempts were made to establish a formal police force in London thereafter, but it was another 50 years before the Home Secretary, Sir Robert Peel, succeeded in influencing Parliament to pass the Metropolitan Police Act of 1829. As the first squads of Metropolitan Police marched out into the streets of London, the idea of preventive full-scale police forces became a reality.[12] The first Order of the Metropolitan Police was a triumph of clarity, simplicity and vision:

> *INSTRUCTIONS:*
>
> *The following General Instructions for the different ranks of the Police Force are not to be understood as containing roles of conduct applicable to every variety of circumstances that may occur in the performance of their duty;*

> *something must necessarily be left to the intelligence and discretion of individuals; and according to the degree in which they show themselves possessed of these qualities and to their zeal, activity and judgment, on all occasions, will be their claims to future promotion and reward.*
>
> *IT SHOULD BE UNDERSTOOD, AT THE OUTSET, THAT THE PRINCIPAL OBJECT TO BE ATTAINED IS THE PREVENTION OF CRIME.*
>
> *To this great end every effort of the police is to be directed. The security of person and property, the preservation of public tranquility, and all the other objects of a Police Establishment, will thus be better effected, than by the detection and punishment of the offender, after he has succeeded in committing the crime. This should constantly be kept in mind by every member of the police force, as the guide for his own conduct. Officers and Police Constables should endeavor to distinguish themselves by such vigilance and activity, as may render it extremely difficult for anyone to commit a crime within that portion of the town under their charge.*
>
> *When in any Division offences are frequently committed there must be a reason to suspect that the Police is not in that Division properly conducted. The absence of crime will be considered the best proof of the complete efficiency of the Police. In Divisions, where this security and good order have been effected, the Officers and Men belonging to it may feel assured that such conduct will be noticed by rewards and promotion.*

In other handbooks of police duties developed during the next few years, prevention was usually emphasized as the essence of police duty.[13] Detection of crimes was considered important, but only if it supported and did not replace the principles of crime prevention, namely:

- To prevent crime and disorder, as an alternative to their repression by military force and severity of legal punishment;
- To maintain at all times a relationship with the public that gives reality to the historic tradition that the police are the public and the public are the police. The police being only members of the public who are paid to give full-time attention to duties which are incumbent on every citizen, in the interests of community welfare and existence; and,
- To recognize always that the test of police efficiency is the absence of crime and disorder and not the visible evidence of police action in dealing with them.

Thus, the great tradition of an organized police force was established. It grew steadily through the whole of Great Britain. By 1856, the process was completed.

The initial emphasis on prevention did not last. Police gradually became more and more occupied with investigating crimes and apprehending criminals, and prevention efforts decreased accordingly.

It was not until after World War II that attention in Great Britain once again turned to the crime prevention concept, through local campaigns at first. (Ironically, renewed interest in crime prevention efforts at the national level was triggered by reports that Sweden had established a permanent Crime Prevention Advisory Bureau, supported by insurance companies and the police.) A national crime prevention campaign was held during 1950 and 1951, featuring films, exhibits and printed material. By 1956, a number of other national-scope activities had appeared, such as standardized techniques for publicizing crime hazards and for recommending crime prevention tactics, and formal liaison between police and insurance companies.

In 1963, the Home Office Crime Prevention Training Centre was established at Stafford, offering formal training in crime prevention to members of all police forces in the United Kingdom. In subsequent years, a comprehensive national crime prevention program was built, featuring not only a wide variety of training activities but also the coordination of insurance, private security and police efforts and mass media campaigns. Through this process, crime prevention has finally become an integral part of police activity in the United Kingdom.[14]

CRIME PREVENTION IN AMERICA

In most respects, the development of police forces in the United States has not been uniform. The British model of a national police force with local subdivisions did not develop here, nor did the early British emphasis on preventive policing.[15]

While crime prevention and loss reduction has been a key activity of the private security field in the United States since its beginning over 100 years ago, the crime prevention concept only recently has entered the field of law enforcement in a formal way. However, as law enforcement developed in the United States, there were sporadic attempts to introduce opportunity reduction principles. Early examples include the branding of cattle and the assumption by citizens of law enforcement responsibilities in such forms as the sheriff's posse, the vigilante group and the town watchman. Later, there developed within law enforcement a strong emphasis on juvenile delinquency prevention. Finally, in the early 1960s, opportunity reduction projects such as Operation Identification began to emerge in a few police departments. Beyond these limited efforts, little need was felt for police-based before-the-fact prevention programs until 1968. In that year, John C. Klotter, Professor at the University of Louisville's School of Justice Administration, undertook a Ford Foundation-funded program of research in burglary prevention.

Professor Klotter's admiration for the success of the English system led him to suggest that the establishment of crime prevention units within police departments in this country could become a significant factor in crime control. To stimulate the development of such units, he recommended that:

Crime prevention schools, such as those in England, should be started on a national or regional basis. At these schools, police personnel should be

> *trained in the methods of preventing crime. When returning to their respective departments, the specially trained officers should be assigned exclusively to crime prevention work.*[16]

As a result of the Klotter study, the National Crime Prevention Institute (NCPI) was established as a Division of the School of Police Administration at the University of Louisville in 1971, under the initial sponsorship of the University, the Kentucky Crime Commission, and the Law Enforcement Assistance Administration (of the U.S. Department of Justice). By December 1977, NCPI had trained over 4,000 police officers, criminal justice planners and administrators, local government officials, volunteer leaders, national association officials, and private industry representatives in the principles and practices of crime prevention, and provided continuing information, post-graduate training and technical assistance to them.

NCPI has become a national educational and technical resource for the development of local, state and national crime prevention programs in both the public and private sectors and continues to provide crime prevention training, information and technical assistance to ever-increasing numbers and kinds of individuals, agencies and organizations.[17] However, there has yet to emerge a comprehensive and coordinated national crime prevention campaign in the United States. The federal government has funded a separate organization, the National Crime Prevention Council (NCPC), to undertake this task. It is now coordinating a national media campaign and the activities of the Crime Prevention Coalition which includes nearly 150 organizations.

The growth of crime prevention has been significant since 1971. It is currently estimated that over 85% of the cities in this country have a crime prevention specialist in their police departments or other city agencies.[18] Twenty-five states have, or are developing, statewide crime prevention campaigns, and some states have developed statewide training centers modeled after NCPI. The Texas Crime Prevention Institute is the leading example, and there are also training programs in California, Washington, Minnesota, North Carolina, and Florida.

At the federal level, the Federal Bureau of Investigation established a Crime Resistance program involving all of its field offices.[19] The U.S. Department of Housing and Urban Development developed systematic crime prevention programs within federally-sponsored public housing projects.[20] The Department of Defense (DoD) and the separate military services designed a coordinated crime prevention program for all DoD installations. The Department of Commerce is active in cargo theft reduction, airport security, the development of standards for security devices and the prevention of crime against small businesses. The National Institute of Justice, through program grants and research and information services, is a major contributor to crime prevention program development at all levels.

National service, voluntary, and public interest organizations are rapidly entering the ranks of crime prevention proponents. The pioneers in this sector are the American Association of Retired Persons, which has done much to organize citizen participation and law enforcement activity; the National Exchange Club, which has sponsored a National Crime Prevention Week for over 30 years; and the National Sheriff's Association, which has helped organize large numbers of Neighborhood Watch programs through its members.[21] The International Society of Crime Prevention Practitioners (ISCPP) is now emerging as a professional association for crime prevention specialists.

Private business and industry is also manifesting a rapidly increasing level of interest in crime prevention. The private security field has grown enormously in the past decade, and the insurance industry focuses increasing attention on crime prevention and crime-related loss reduction.[22]

The current status of crime prevention programming in the United States is discussed in more detail in Chapter 11. Meanwhile, suffice it to say that the establishment of the National Crime Prevention Institute has led to explosive growth of interest and activity in crime prevention—reaching levels unimaginable in 1971.

From this brief historical discussion, one can see that crime prevention has arrived—not only as an important component of police work, but also as a significant area of activity for every kind of public and private interest in the United States.

CRIME PREVENTION AND CRIMINOLOGY

No discussion of the evolution of crime prevention would be complete without mention of the evolutionary patterns of the science of criminology and their impact on crime prevention.

From its inception, criminology has had a conflicting and controversial effect on society's responses to crime. A young discipline, dating back only to the early 1700's, criminology concerns itself with what causes people to commit crimes, the social conditions which affect criminal activity, and the methods that can be used to control crime. As is inevitable in any field of study, several schools of thought have developed in criminology, including the Classical School, the Positive School, the "Sociological" School, and the "Contemporary" School.

The Classical School

As a reaction to the arbitrary practices which characterized criminal law prior to and during the 1700s, there developed a movement to reduce and standardize the severity of punishments. This Classical school of thought holds that punishment should be used to discourage criminals and prevent crimes instead of to retaliate against convicted offenders. Proponents contend that crime should be defined in legal terms, with specific punishment assigned to each unlawful act, and with prohibitions against torture, limits on the admission of evidence, and other protections of the rights of the accused. Thus, it is held, people will select their behavior on the basis of reward and punishment, pain and pleasure, and persons will decide whether or not to commit criminal acts based on their degree of willingness to accept the prescribed punishment. (As Gilbert and Sullivan's Mikado says, "Let the punishment fit the crime.") The Classical School believes that considerable prevention is achieved from the deterrent effect of fear of punishment.[23]

The Positive School

In another movement, which developed in the early 1800s, law was seen not as a means to deter criminals but, rather, as a way to protect society on the one hand and reform the criminal on the other. The Positive School does not believe in strict definitions of crimes or predetermined sentences. Instead, this school advocates broadly defined criminal laws and sliding scales of punishment, taking into account whether the offender is "responsible" for his acts.[24] Justice can thus be exercised in terms of the particular circumstances at hand, and sentences passed from the dual viewpoint of protecting society and rehabilitating the offender. Indeed, the offender, rather than the offense, is the thing of importance, and all acts performed by society against the offender (including punishment) are to be taken out of a desire to treat his social pathology. To the Positive School, law or punishment has little effect as a means of social control. Rather, treatment and rehabilitation are the issues. The creation of juvenile court is perhaps the clearest, most tangible reflection of this school.[25]

The "Sociological" School

Sociological criminology emerged in the 1920s, primarily at the University of Chicago, as a way of explaining the origins of criminal behavior. Its proponents hold that adverse social conditions stimulate criminal learning experiences and anti-social attitudes.[26]

There are two important theories flowing from this approach:

- The weakening of family, ethnic and community traditions weakens society's ability to informally control criminal behavior; and,
- A state of social and economic deprivation causes people to create a criminal subculture.

An outgrowth of the criminal subculture theory, which was popular during the anti-poverty program years, is that delinquency is caused by the blocking of legitimate social and economic opportunity. In general, reduction in crime means modifying the social and economic conditions which foster crime.[27]

- Apprehension of offenders (to discourage others and to permit society to punish offenders);
- Recovery of property;
- Regulation of non-criminal conduct (such as traffic control, sanitation, and general public order); and,
- Miscellaneous services (such as emergency aid, driver licensing, and a wide variety of assistance to citizens, including "police-community relations"—an activity developed in recent years to improve communication patterns between the citizenry and the police).

The amount of effort devoted by police forces to these functions varies, but knowledgeable observers agree that the regulation of non-criminal conduct and the provision of miscellaneous services may make up as much as 80 percent of the average police department's workload.[32] This leaves scant resources available for crime-related duties, and it is easy to understand how the necessity for responding to crimes already committed leaves little or no time available for crime prevention, prevention of delinquency, or recovery of property.

Thus, it is probably accurate to say that many traditional police administrators do not view crime prevention with enthusiasm. To them, it can only represent an additional manpower drain in the short term.

It is for this reason that a considerable sum of money was made available through the Law Enforcement Assistance Administration and through state and municipal budgets to add manpower for the specific purpose of developing crime prevention programs.[33] Through this kind of support, crime prevention got started in many communities, and this led to a recording of police priorities by community leadership.

In the long term, however, crime prevention effort must pay for itself if it is to become a significant permanent part of the police mission. For this to occur, police must be given the opportunity to be trained in and to practice crime prevention techniques for a long enough period of time to demonstrate the merits of crime prevention on a cost-effective basis in comparison with traditional law enforcement methods. Fortunately, such opportunities are rapidly increasing among the nation's law enforcement units, and the results so far are encouraging.

THE ASSUMPTIONS OF CRIME PREVENTION

Let us summarize the important operating assumptions of crime prevention practitioners as taught by the National Crime Prevention Institute.

1. Potential crime victims or those responsible for them must be helped to take action which reduces their vulnerability to crimes and which reduces their likelihood of injury or loss should a crime occur.

2. At the same time, it must be recognized that potential victims (and those responsible for them) are limited in the action they can take by the limits of their control over their environments.
3. The environment to be controlled is that of the potential victim, not of the potential criminal.
4. Direct control over the victim's environment can nevertheless affect criminal motivation in that reduced criminal opportunity means less temptation to commit offenses and learn criminal behavior and, consequently, fewer offenders. In this sense, crime prevention is a practical rather than a moralistic approach to reducing criminal motivation. The intent is to discourage the offender.
5. The traditional approaches used by the criminal justice system (such as punishment and rehabilitation capabilities of courts and prisons and the investigative and apprehension functions of police) can increase the risk perceived by the criminal, and thus have a significant (but secondary) role in criminal opportunity reduction.
6. Law enforcement agencies have a primary role in crime prevention to the extent that they are effective in providing opportunity-reduction education, information and guidance to the public and to various organizations, institutions and agencies in the community.
7. Many skill and interest groups need to operate in an active and coordinated fashion if crime prevention is to be effective in a community-wide sense.
8. Crime prevention can be both a cause and an effect of efforts to revitalize urban and rural communities.
9. The knowledge of crime prevention is interdisciplinary and is in a continual process of discovery, as well as discarding misinformation. There must be a continual sifting and integration of discoveries as well as a constant sharing of new knowledge among practitioners.
10. Crime prevention strategies and techniques must remain flexible and specific. What will work for one crime in one place may not work for the same crime in another place. Crime prevention is a "thinking person's" practice, and countermeasures must be taken after a thorough analysis of the problem, not before.

Thus, crime prevention is concerned with protecting people and property. Its focus is the potential victim and his environment, and it works by analyzing the vulnerabilities of potential victims and taking countermeasures through which victim behavior and the immediate social and physical environment are altered so as to reduce those vulnerabilities.

Crime prevention focuses on the offender only to the extent that a knowledge of criminal characteristics and attack methods is relevant to the design of effective countermeasures.

Crime prevention holds that each individual is responsible to avoid becoming a victim, and neighbors are responsible to and for each other. The citizenry, business sector, and the government sector are responsible for the allocation of resources and the development of comprehensive programs, and the police are responsible for, at the very least, emphasizing prevention in all aspects of their contact with the public.

CONCLUSION

Despite the rapid development of a crime prevention movement in this country, the potential power of crime prevention is still held back by conflicting criminological theories, confused criminal justice system missions, scarce public resources, and traditional police priorities. Nevertheless, some of the power and much of the appeal of crime prevention are already evident in the thousands of law enforcement units that now practice crime prevention at the local level and in the hundreds of other organizations (and millions of Americans) that practice, advocate or support crime prevention at the local, state and national levels.

Understanding the specific conditions under which a particular crime takes place leads directly to specific strategies by which a potential victim can improve his or her security against that crime. Crime prevention thus protects person and property in the most practical way—the reduction of criminal opportunity in the potential victim's own environment.

The creative promise which this idea of controlling crime by reducing criminal opportunity held for such pioneers as Henry and John Fielding and Sir Robert Peel is finally becoming a reality. The theory that crime prevention **should** and **can** work is now being tested in many places around the country.[34]

3

Roles in Crime Prevention

In the first two chapters, we presented the general dimensions of crime prevention and its historical development as an organized approach to crime control.

In this chapter, we concern ourselves with the central role of the crime prevention practitioner as the teacher, counselor and catalyst of individual action, group action and public policy action within the community. We also briefly sketch the range of community energies which the practitioner can mobilize. Finally, we suggest that the goal of the practitioner's efforts is the establishment of a comprehensive, community-wide crime prevention program.

By analogy to a wheel, the practitioner's activities can be represented as the hub, the various community efforts can be looked upon as the spokes, and the community-wide program can be considered as the rim. Like the wheel, all of these components must be assembled properly for the crime prevention "system" to work.

To look at the practitioner as the "hub" emphasizes his vital and central role in developing and sustaining crime prevention efforts, but also acknowledges that he is primarily a stimulator and coordinator of the efforts of others. It is ironic but true that the crime prevention practitioner, by himself, does not prevent crime (except for those crimes that might befall his own home or family). Instead, he enables other people to reduce criminal opportunity in their own environments.

The practitioner works with individual potential victims, because they have a vital role to play in crime prevention. This role, at the start, may be no more complicated than the reduction of carelessness. In no sense should we make the mistake of blaming the victim for the crime, yet how often does utter carelessness lead to assault, homicide, burglary and robbery? Acceptance of personal responsibility by potential victims is a key issue.

The practitioner also works with the groups and organizations that make up the community, because self-protection by potential victims is only part of the totality of crime prevention. Each segment of society also has a role and a responsibility, because the individual is always limited in what he can do. At some point, a person or a business needs the help of neighbors, and at a further point governmental help is required. Crime prevention is most effective when there is a comprehensive and cooperative sharing of opportunity-reduction responsibility among individuals, social groups, and economic and political units.

The following discussion of the crime prevention practitioner's roles, and the roles of others with whom he works, is necessarily brief. Its purpose is to provide a framework for understanding how the knowledge and skills of crime prevention, as discussed more extensively in the following chapters, fit into the operational roles of the practioner.

THE ROLES OF THE PRACTITIONER

The crime prevention practitioner's purpose is to serve as the hub of crime prevention activities in his community. Carrying out this purpose involves a set of complementary and interacting roles in which he:

- Supports individual action;
- Supports group action;
- Guides public policy decisions; and
- Develops the comprehensive crime prevention program.

Supporting Individual Action

It is relatively easy for the head of a household, the proprietor of a business or any person to reduce risk of criminal attack in daily life. **This role of the crime prevention practitioner is to serve individual clients by observing, analyzing, recommending and teaching.** Just as one person might teach safe driving habits to another person, so the crime prevention practitioner tries to teach individuals, families, businesses and others how to reduce their own crime risks. For the client it is a matter of learning and applying new skills. For the practitioner the issue is knowing how to teach these skills so as to achieve maximum impact on the client.

Efforts to improve security at the individual level usually start with public education programs and public awareness campaigns. Pamphlets and brochures are developed and distributed which show the home owner or the businessman how to apply security devices and procedures. Distribution of brochures may be coupled with exhibits in shopping centers or other public places, TV and radio public service announcements, newspaper articles, and personal presentations in schools and at group meetings. These general education approaches are typically followed up by a variety of specific efforts to teach crime risk management.

Teaching Crime Risk Management

Teaching the proper use of elementary security devices and procedures to a home owner or business person is really only the first step in sensitizing that individual to the concept of crime risk management. The crime prevention practitioner who thinks that security devices and simple procedures are the be-all and end-all of crime prevention has missed the fundamental point that even the most "normal" and "routine" daily life is a constantly shifting and changing situation in which good habits of attitude and judgment are more important in reducing the risk of criminal attack than are the rote application of simple devices and procedures. The practitioner must become knowledgeable in helping clients to make the needed "judgment calls" in their daily lives.

Having said that, it should also be pointed out that the rigorous application of devices and procedures has a basic and important role. Properly ingrained in a person's life, good individual risk management consists mostly of judgment. But it also consists of some very basic and essential *nevers* and *always*. (Always lock your car. Never leave your home unlocked. Never leave large amounts of cash lying around your store.) These kinds of absolutes are like the unfailing use of a checklist by a good pilot. He never takes the chance that memory might fail him as he inspects the various parts of the plane before flying in it. The use of a checklist does not guarantee him a safe flight. What it does is guarantee that he won't carelessly omit checking that one defective item on that one fatal occasion.

The individual action support role of the practitioner is to teach people not only the proper application of security devices and procedures but also the essential habits of judgment which permit them to routinely avoid crime risk.

The crime prevention practitioner will engage in a wide range of formal and informal teaching and counselling activities aimed at helping individuals and organizations to develop crime risk management approaches.

For example, people may be counselled concerning such general behavior as locking their cars, and avoiding parts of town where street crime is rife. Women and older people will be particularly counselled concerning their risk of exposure to violent crimes. Parents are counselled concerning the risks their children face. Children are taught how to be careful of their possessions, themselves, their homes and their neighbors, and even how to teach their parents.

The principle behind all of these counselling and teaching efforts is that just as people expose themselves to crime risks by their behavior, so they can reduce that exposure by modifying their behavior. Very much the same principle is involved in safe driving. The driver who is skilled in defensive driving is able to identify potential accident situations while there is still time to avoid those situations, and take the necessary avoidance action. The unskilled driver, on the other hand, may not be aware of an accident hazard situation until it is too late to avoid the situation. And, if he does manage to identify the hazardous situation in time, he may not have the skills to avoid it.

The crime prevention practitioner, to be effective, must learn how to motivate as well as to teach practical knowledge.[1] He must learn that new ways of doing things, once taught, must be reinforced time and time again before they become habitual actions. The crime prevention practitioner must not only teach proper security actions to people in the first place, he must continually remind people to make use of their new knowledge and skills.

His viewpoint needs to be analytical in nature. In other words, he must be concerned that some minimum percent, at least, of the people he talks with not only comply with his suggestions and recommendations, but also enjoy improved security as a result. If he is aware of and concerned for his own batting average, he can develop techniques to improve it. If, on the other hand, he is merely interested in the number of people with whom he has made contact, he has no way of knowing how he is performing in terms of improved client security. He measures his success statistically—by the degree to which his client group *as a whole, over time, benefits from the application of his teachings.*

His concern must be that individuals learn to routinely take the action that reduces or avoids the risk rather than to worry about whether the risk would have actually developed into a harmful situation. An individual may never know whether or not his actions have prevented a crime, just as the good defensive driver may never know whether an accident would have occurred if he had not acted to avoid it.

As the teachers of fire prevention, disease prevention, and defensive driving know only too well, risk is an abstract concept that is hard to teach. The incautious driver says, "It will never happen to me" and ignores the risk. The overly cautious driver says, "It's going to happen to me" and magnifies the risk. The concept of risk implies that there is an appropriate preventive response to be made in each situation, and that what is appropriate in one situation may not be appropriate in another. The person who is skilled in managing the risks associated with driving knows instinctively that safe travel on a given road may require very different speeds at night than during the day, in dry weather as opposed to wet weather, in heavy traffic as opposed to light traffic, and even in one car as opposed to another.

Security Survey (See sample survey guides in Chapter 5.)

A specific form of crime risk management counseling is the security survey, an on-site examination of a physical facility (home, business, industrial plant, hospital, for example) and its surroundings.[2] In a security survey, a trained crime prevention practitioner inspects a home or business and advises the client (occupant, owner or manager) of the risks and weaknesses observed and the measures that may be taken to improve overall security. The facility is analyzed as a system, and recommendations for improved security are also systematic. The basic idea is to help the client to design and implement a crime risk management system which uniformly protects him to some desired level and leaves no weak links for easy attack.

If the practitioner succeeds in his efforts to support individual action, the individual will have been helped to develop a risk management system which is appropriate to his lifestyle or type of business, the value and type of property within his facility, and the existing crime patterns in his area.

Supporting Group Action

At this level of crime prevention action, the practitioner becomes primarily concerned with actions of a group nature which tend to reduce the risk of each member of a given population **whether or not that person is willing to, or capable of, taking appropriate individual action.**[3]

By analogy to traffic safety, if most drivers on the road are good defensive drivers, then there is also less chance that a careless driver will have an accident. Should he have an accident anyway, there is less chance that others will be injured. Or, if by law we require all cars built after a certain year to be inherently safer than older cars, then all people who purchase and drive the new car will enjoy a reduced risk of accident, whether they are skilled drivers or not. This doesn't mean that a drunk or careless driver can't have an accident. We have simply, through collective action or public policy action, reduced the likelihood of injury or death should a crash occur.

The practitioner's role at the group action level is to stimulate action which will not only be of great help to the careful individual in reducing his crime risk, but also will be of some help to the individual who cannot or will not take appropriate action on his own behalf.

Examples

One of the more popular group action approaches is the Neighborhood Watch[4] program. With the help of the crime prevention practitioner, residents in a given neighborhood organize themselves to watch for suspicious circumstances and to report these circumstances to police. Participants are encouraged to take improved security precautions in their homes and in their daily lives.

At first, the surveillance and reporting function of a Neighborhood Watch does not prevent crimes as much as it helps police do a better job of detecting and apprehending criminals.[5] However, over time, the fact that neighbors are watching out for neighbors and reporting to police, and the fact that police are responding, will become known to the local criminal population. If a would-be criminal believes that his activities are likely to be seen, reported and produce a police response, he may feel that the risk is unacceptably high for him in the project neighborhood.[6]

This presence of a credible threat of observation, reporting, and apprehension for the neighborhood as a whole is sufficient to reduce the level of criminal opportunity for each resident in the neighborhood, despite the fact that it is extremely unusual to find a case where **all** residents of a neighborhood participate in the program. Thus, if only a fraction of the residents are observing and reporting suspicious activities for police response, all residents may be protected to some degree, even those who carelessly expose their own homes and persons to criminal attack.

On the other hand, Neighborhood Watch cannot completely protect the neighborhood. If the would-be thief, burglar, vandal, or assailant is not aware of the surveillance program, it will not affect his decision to attack. If he is drunk, under the influence of drugs, or otherwise operating in an irrational manner, even knowledge of the threat may mean nothing to him.[7] Thus, a Neighborhood Watch project, like a safe automobile, is no guarantee of safety. It merely reduces the probability that a given resident will be attacked. Each resident (like the defensive driver) can further reduce his vulnerability through individual security actions.

Neighborhood Watch is but one example of the wide variety of ways in which the practitioner can stimulate action by—or on behalf of—a group. The well-lighted parking lot at the shopping center does not guarantee that shoppers will not be assaulted, robbed or have their cars broken into. But it does increase the probability that a criminal will be seen by someone during the course of his attack. That increased probability for surveillance will deter some number of attackers, however, and the opportunity for crime will be reduced by the lighting program. If we design a new neighborhood so that commercial and residential structures are intermingled rather than separated, we create a situation in which people are more likely to be on the streets day and night, which in turn increases the probability that a criminal will be observed in the act.[8] If we build a small grocery store as part of our high-rise residential development for older people, we reduce the probability for robbery and mugging of residents as they go to and from a more distant grocery store.

A very good demonstration of the combination effects of individual and group actions occurred in El Paso, Texas.[9] The El Paso Police Department's Crime Prevention Unit selected a particular high-crime patrol district adjacent to the Rio Grande River, where numerous burglaries were committed by people crossing the virtually dry river by night to attack and escape quickly back into Mexico. The strategy of the El Paso Crime Prevention Unit was to place crime prevention officers in the district full-time for a period of nine months.

Starting with the homes and businesses of previous crime victims, the practitioners moved from door to door, providing advice and recommendations to residents and business people, and offering to perform security surveys. They also organized block groups and conducted general public education. The effect of this activity was to substantially increase the level of individual action within the district and to create the credible appearance of high levels of crime prevention effort throughout the district. This combination of individual and group approaches produced dramatic declines in burglary rates compared to the previous year. It also apparently produced significant increases in burglary in other parts of El Paso as the criminals were forced to find other targets. Whether or not the increases in city-wide rates were equivalent to the decrease in target district rates could not be determined. However, during that year, El Paso enjoyed a slight overall decrease in burglary, compared to the increase which had typically occurred from year to year in the past.

The El Paso experience emphasizes an extremely important potential effect of individual and group action—called displacement.

Understanding Displacement

It is important for the practitioner to understand that by helping individuals and groups to reduce their risk of becoming crime victims, however successfully, he may not reduce the incidence of crime for the community as a whole. The reason for this lies in the phenomenon of displacement.[10]

One of the problems associated with the crime prevention approach is that while it affects criminal behavior, it does not have a direct effect on criminal motivation. The criminal who perceives opportunity to be reduced below an acceptable level in a given situation will probably simply seek a better opportunity. Thus, we have displacement. If your home is adequately secured, the would-be criminal may simply go next door. If all the homes in your block are adequately secured, the criminal may simply go to the next block.[11] If all opportunities for a particular kind of criminal act are effectively denied him, he may try another kind of crime.* Or, if all opportunities for any kind of crime are denied him at a particular time, he may simply wait until another time. At first glance, this might seem to present a hopeless situation. There are, however, some factors which tend to offset the displacement phenomenon.

It has been observed, for example, that many—if not most—opportunistic, impulsive criminals (particularly the younger, less experienced individuals who appear to be responsible for the great bulk of criminal incidents) will only displace their activities to a limited degree. They operate most comfortably within their "home turf." If opportunity is denied them within that familiar area, they may go somewhat beyond it to commit crimes. However, there seems to be strong relationship between distance from immediate home area and desire to commit crimes. By the same token, it appears that the impulsive, opportunistic criminal who is denied opportunity for "low-skill" crimes (for example, random burglary or vandalism) is unlikely to tackle more difficult crimes.

The exact nature of limits on displacement and the exact degree to which the limits may be expected to operate in a given situation are not yet known. That they do operate has been shown time and time again in the practical

*There is some evidence to indicate that the type of offender who engages in burglary does not engage in robbery and vice versa.

experience of crime prevention practitioners. There have even been a few well-documented research projects which demonstrate the operation of these limits. For example, a three-year study of a neighborhood crime prevention project in Seattle[12] indicated that if a fairly large percentage of the residents in a given neighborhood took appropriate security measures, crime rates decreased both for those protected homes and neighbors who chose not to participate. Moreover, the study indicated that the net decrease of crime in the project neighborhoods was not offset by net increases of crime in surrounding neighborhoods.[13]

It is therefore apparently safe to assume (though this cannot yet be absolutely proven) that in addition to displacement of time, place, and type of crime, there is also a phenomenon which we might call absolute displacement. When absolute displacement operates, some percentage of the crimes that might statistically be expected simply do not occur at all. Absolute displacement is the same as net crimes prevented.

We will discuss displacement in a more practical sense later. For now, it is enough to know that as long as crime prevention practitioners are dealing strictly with individual action crime prevention, crime displacement may occur. Thus, even though the practitioner has helped selected individuals avoid victimization, he may have had no effect on the victimization potential of the community as a whole.

On the other hand, the fact that displacement has occurred should not be considered as entirely negative. In fact, the displacement of crime means that the practitioner has at least partially succeeded in managing crime patterns.

Sustaining Group Action

Group action can be useful in reducing crimes against people in a geographic area or population group, whether or not each person in the area or group chooses to participate, and whether or not displacement results. But, such reduction, once gained, may not remain in effect.

Increases in physical security do have the advantage of remaining in place, at least until attack methods are developed which can overcome a particular defense. On the other hand, a group activity, such as Neighborhood Watch, may retain its opportunity reduction effect only as long as it continues to operate.[14]

Clearly, it is more difficult to sustain than to establish any kind of significant change in the behavior and action patterns of people. One need only look at the experience of the disease prevention field to realize this. For several generations Americans have been taught and urged to adopt good health habits. Yet, it is still possible for epidemics to occur anytime that public health agency pressure on the public diminishes. Venereal disease, for example, was brought largely under control during the 1950s and early 1960s. But it flared up again in the late 1960s and early 1970s as public health programs turned their attention elsewhere. More recently, local and regional flare-ups of childhood diseases such as measles and mumps have occurred because public officials have slacked off in their insistence that children be immunized before entering school.

There is much evidence to indicate that crime prevention efforts by individuals and groups are not necessarily self-perpetuating. Once people feel that they have achieved some success, their efforts may dwindle or cease altogether. If this occurs, it is logical to expect that, sooner or later, criminal activity will revert to its original levels or higher. Thus, the practitioner must help sustain collective action.

The short-lived project may even have a negative effect in the long range. It is relatively easy to induce significant numbers of people to participate in crime prevention activities. But if the activities cease, and crime thereafter returns to its former levels, people may become disillusioned (whether rightfully so or not) and it may become difficult to obtain positive responses to crime prevention projects in the future and practitioners may be led to conclude, erroneously, that citizens are apathetic.

The lesson to be learned by crime prevention practitioners is that there can be no such thing as a time-limited effort. There is no question that the crime prevention approach **can** work, but there is also no question that it must be built into the fabric of the community and made a permanent program if it is to have continuing success.

The primary way in which this "building-in" occurs is through a process called informal social control.

Informal Social Control

Group action works best if it stems from, or grows into, a stable pattern of social interaction and a stable tendency for members of the social group to enforce constraints on criminal behavior within the group. In general, the higher the levels of social interaction, the lower the criminal opportunity.[15] All other things being equal, the neighborhood where people are in constant friendly contact with each other will have a lower level of criminal activity than the neighborhood in which people do not tend to interact socially. The first neighborhood tends to create for itself a naturally hostile environment for criminal behavior, and the second neighborhood does not.[16]

Where some level of informal social control already exists, the practitioner's role is to strengthen it. Where little or no informal social control exists, the practitioner needs to bring to bear a variety of community organization skills—primarily through other people who are able to influence the behavior and attitudes of the group. The practitioner needs to be very sensitive to informal social control, because the presence or absence of formal social organizations is not the same as the presence or absence of informal social control.

Guiding Public Policy Decisions

The practitioner's role at this level is to identify the ways in which public policy action can support and extend individual and group action, and to guide the decision-making process leading to appropriate public policy action.

Just as the individual must turn to the group if he is to increase his security beyond a certain point, so must the group turn to a larger entity at some subsequent point. For instance, a homeowner can take reasonable security precautions for his own home, but it takes the cooperation of neighbors to begin to make the streets and playgrounds secure, and to reduce the crime pressure on the neighborhood as a whole. However, the neighborhood acting collectively can only go so far. For example, the neighborhood group cannot improve street lighting by itself, and it cannot force closure of a neighborhood bar which serves as a crime magnet. For these types of action, it must turn to appropriate branches of local government.[17]

The same kind of cycle repeats itself from the local level to the state level, and from the state level to the national level. Local government can, for example, install additional street lighting, close the bar, and organize a comprehensive crime prevention program for the whole community, but it cannot establish a specialized training center for crime prevention practitioners. State government can do this, but it cannot create a national network for identification and return of stolen property. And so on.

To more clearly understand the relationship of public policy to crime prevention, let us consider again the matter of skyjacking. If the installation of security screening devices and procedures at airports had been left to the discretion of individual airlines or individual airport management, only those people who flew out of some airports on some airlines would have enjoyed a reduced risk of becoming skyjack victims. And this is exactly what happened during the initial phases of airport security screening. Then, a national public policy decision was made to require all airlines and all airports in this country to set up security screening. Now, all people flying on commercial flights that originate in the United States enjoy an extremely low skyjacking risk compared to people flying in other countries.[18]

Another type of example is the widespread interest in establishing municipal building security codes. The goal is to require builders to install adequate security devices and materials during construction. In pursuit of this desirable goal, many towns hastily developed their own codes without intercity or interstate coordination. This has created a great deal of confusion for manufacturers of equipment and materials, building contractors, and others who were forced to live with code requirements which differed from one town to the next.

The solution to this problem is the development of a uniform national security building code which can be adopted with minor changes by all communities. Such an effort is now in final phases of development. Once model codes become approved and accepted, a community can use them to establish a building security code consistent with that of any other community.

A final case in point is that appropriate physical design changes in streets, shopping complexes, neighborhoods, public housing projects and other major community components can directly or indirectly discourage criminal activity. In most cases, the occupants of such areas lack the ability to change the major features of their physical environment, and must rely on the public sector (or a large non-government entity such as an apartment complex owner) to energize or at least approve and coordinate changes in street lighting patterns, roadway configuration, structural alterations in building complexes, and other major environmental alterations.

The practitioner serves as the true intermediary between the crime prevention-related needs of individuals and groups in the community and the development and coordination of action by government on behalf of groups and individuals. In performing this role, he is led to the design of a community-wide program.

Developing a Comprehensive Crime Prevention Program

It is not until the practitioner is capable of working in a coordinated, community-wide crime prevention program that he really begins to function as the hub of community crime prevention efforts.

Any local government can make a public policy decision that can have great impact on crime: that is, the decision to establish a comprehensive jurisdiction-wide crime prevention program. Such a program must have a permanent public agency organizational base (for example, the crime prevention unit of the local police department, the mayor's council on crime prevention, a citizens' crime prevention task force, and so on), and should provide for:

- Jurisdiction-wide crime prevention responsibility;
- Capacity to formulate objectives and strategies;
- Ability to establish and sustain projects;
- Capacity to target projects to appropriate citizens groups; and,
- Capacity to assess results.

It is only from the position of jurisdiction-wide program scope and responsibility that specific programs and projects can be developed which complement each other, relate productively to all interests, do not create more problems than they solve, and lead rationally to the ultimate reduction of crime on a community-wide basis. It is also only from this position that the full range of community skills and resources can be mobilized.

The establishment of such a program should be the ultimate goal of all of the practitioner's efforts. This means that he must look beyond his own resources and capabilities and those of his parent organization, to the wealth of resources and support that can be provided by others.

THE ROLES OF OTHERS

Each significant social, economic, institutional and political segment of the community has a number of potential resources which can be brought to bear on crime prevention through the efforts of the practitioner. One of his major responsibilities is to identify the specific roles that others can play in the community-wide programs, and stimulate the various actors to develop and carry out those roles. Some of the major potential actors and the types of roles which they might play are described below.

The Police Role

Active participation by law enforcement organizations is essential to the success of the community crime prevention program. If the practitioner is a member of a law enforcement agency, he must see to it that such participation is developed and sustained throughout the agency. If he is not a member of a law enforcement agency, he must work with police and other community officials to ensure that proper participation does develop.

As the public agency responsible for responding to and investigating reported crimes and for conducting a wide variety of peacekeeping activities, it is up to the police to create and maintain the threat that a criminal will be identified and arrested. This threat is a basic part of most crime prevention strategies.

As a primary source of information on crime patterns, police agencies can provide guidance to the community on prevailing kinds of crime and the specific attack methods used by criminals.

As the group charged with maintaining the public safety and security, police are the logical public source of technical expertise for the anticipation, recognition and appraisal of crime risks and for the design of actions to remove or reduce crime risks. Equally important, police can be the primary source of public education campaigns in crime prevention and the communications hub that coordinates all crime prevention activity in a given jurisdiction.

Many police departments now have crime prevention units or crime prevention bureaus. In some cases, the activities conducted are jurisdiction-wide and comprehensive in scope. In other cases, they are limited to individual client counselling services and a few special projects. In any case, each police department should develop an organizational unit with specific crime prevention responsibilities.

However, outside of their normal law enforcement and public service roles, police agencies have limited powers. A trained police crime prevention officer can recommend that a homeowner, businessman, neighborhood, developer, public housing authority, industrial plant or school take action to improve security and can, if asked, provide detailed guidance as to what action to take. In most cases, he has no legal authority to require that such action be taken (although he might be called upon to enforce a building security code or a false alarm ordinance or arrest a motorist who, contrary to local or state law, leaves the keys in his car).

Police crime prevention programs, therefore, must rely on the cooperation and voluntary participation of individuals and groups. The police role, though pivotal in effective crime prevention programming, is that of an educational, technical and supportive resource—an "enabler" rather than a primary "doer".[19]

The Private Security Role

Although police and other public law enforcement agencies (such as institutional police forces, sheriff's departments, state highway patrols, state bureaus of investigation, the Federal Bureau of Investigation and other federal agencies) are the most visible means by which society maintains public safety and public order, there is also a vast and diverse security industry in this country which performs many of the same functions on a private basis.[20] The elements of the private security industry are:

- Guard, patrol, armored car, and other protective services;
- Security analysis, consultation and management; and,
- Manufacture, distribution, sales, and installation of physical and electronic security devices and materials.

Historically, the private security industry in the United States has been more involved in asset protection and loss reduction than the public law enforcement sector.[21] This is a natural consequence of the fact that people and organizations which contract for private security services and purchase security equipment expect their crime risks to be reduced directly as a result. The major sectors within the private security industry are not well coordinated in their efforts, and until quite recently there has been little in the way of minimum performance standards within or affecting most of the industry. Nevertheless, many of the specific skills and most of the security devices in the "tool kit" of today's crime prevention practitioner have been adopted or adapted from private security.

The role of private security in comprehensive crime prevention programming is generally to supplement and extend the crime prevention practitioner's role in supporting individual action, and to perform services which the practitioner cannot, such as management of security programs for private facilities, the installation of security devices, and the provision of a wide variety of security services for private customers.[22]

The Role of the Building Professions and Trades

Architects, engineers, construction contractors, land developers, carpenters, electricians, plumbers, and the wide variety of other building professionals and skilled trades need to become knowledgeable of appropriate aspects of crime prevention practice. Street design, building site layout, building design and techniques of construction all have relevance to the possibilities for victimization in or near a given structure.[23]

The practitioner relates to these individuals as a teacher and advisor.

The Role of Local Government Agencies

There is a significant crime prevention role inherent in the activities of most types of public agencies, and some types of agencies can play a crucial role. The following suggests some of the possibilities.

- Planning, zoning, community development, public works, and traffic engineering units can stress criminal opportunity reduction principles in both their general and specific urban development activities.
- Housing and building inspection units can stress the need to develop and apply good building security codes;
- Human service agencies can advise clients as to proper security precautions, help organize interest in group crime prevention action, and serve as a link between client population groups and crime prevention practitioners;
- Schools can provide courses of instruction and other educational programs in crime prevention;
- Fire departments can integrate crime prevention services with their current building inspection services;
- Public information units can promote crime prevention; and,
- Legislative and executive units (Council, Mayor, etc.) can provide political and financial support for crime prevention programs, can supervise comprehensive programming, can direct other public agencies to participate, and can take the lead in public policy development.

The practitioner can serve as the stimulus for these and other actions by local government.

The Insurance Industry Role

Insurance companies and their affiliated and independent agents have a major potential role to play in crime prevention. Their estimates of crime costs can, if supplemented with risk management knowledge, make insurance representatives excellent sources of advice to clients on proper security measures. Also, they can use premium discounts as an incentive for clients who practice good self-security. On the other hand, they can use premium increases or denial of coverage as a penalty for clients who do not.

The practitioner and his counterparts can work with insurance agents at the local level and through them with state and national insurance regulatory agencies, associations and corporations. The Insurance Commissioner in each state is the primary agent for stimulating this insurance company role.

The practitioner will usually find such groups very receptive to specific project suggestions.

The Role of Civic Groups

Service clubs, voluntary organizations, professional associations, labor unions, trade organizations and other civic groups can develop crime prevention education programs for members and can develop a wide variety of crime prevention service projects for the community.

The Communications Industry Role

Radio and television broadcasters, newspapers, magazines, book publishers and other public communicators can be instrumental in developing public information and education programs in crime prevention.

The practitioner can serve to educate, inform and advise these groups.

The Role of the Business Community

Businessmen of all kinds can help in the development of comprehensive crime prevention programming by taking proper security precautions at their own establishments, cooperating with other business people in group efforts, and providing financial and political support for comprehensive programs and the development of appropriate public policy decisions.

Because business people can be shown that participation in crime prevention activities is both good business and good public relations, the practitioner can usually obtain major support from this area.

The Role of the Citizen Organization

The many different types of formal and informal neighborhood groups, community action groups, religious groups, youth groups, women's groups, senior citizen groups, ethnic groups, fraternal groups and others provide a ready-made base for collective action in crime prevention. These groups can develop a wide variety of projects and programs in crime prevention for their members, their geographic areas, their group (older people and women, for example) or, through coordination and political activity, for the community as a whole.

Like the civic groups, these groups are usually receptive to appropriate projects suggested by the practitioner.

The State Government Role

State agencies with local counterparts can develop statewide emphases on crime prevention within those local units. State Insurance Commissions can work with insurance companies to develop premium discount programs. State Police agencies can develop statewide education and advisory programs, particularly for small towns and rural areas which may lack crime prevention-oriented local law enforcement. Attorneys-General and criminal justice agencies can provide both political and programmatic sponsorship of coordinated statewide education and information programs, as well as training programs in crime prevention for local law enforcement personnel. Legislatures can provide political and financial support, as can Governors, and both can be instrumental in key public policy decisions.

The practitioner may find it easier to relate to state government through a statewide association of crime prevention practitioners or through local public officials than through his own individual efforts.

A specific exception is the state crime prevention program. Many states have developed, or are developing, such a program to support the efforts of local practitioners. The practitioner should be sure to take full advantage of services provided by such a program in his state.

The Role of Practitioners' Statewide Associations

In a growing number of states, practitioners are banding together to form crime prevention officer's associations. Such associations usually concern themselves with coordinating efforts to improve crime prevention training throughout the state, with providing problem-solving assistance to members, and with rallying state government support efforts. They can also work usefully with other statewide associations (business, professional, labor, etc.) to build communication networks affecting every community.

The practitioner should join such an organization, where it exists, or help in efforts to develop one.

The Federal Government Role

While the activities of federal agencies at the national level are beyond the ability of the individual practitioner to stimulate or influence, he may find a number of local representatives of those agencies who will be only too glad to work with him.

For example, public housing authorities, federal reservations (military bases, health care institutions, national parks and recreation areas, federal office complexes, local post offices, to name a few), may have both needs which the practitioner can meet and resources which they can make available to the community program.

The National Association Role

Each of the multitude of national associations with a local constituency can develop crime prevention service programs for that constituency and urge constituents to participate in local programs.

The practitioner should become aware of those associations which have active crime prevention projects and work closely with their local clubs or affiliates (see Chapter 11 for a listing of such associations).

The National Corporation Role

Major corporations and national industry groups can, acting by themselves or in cooperation with government, develop crime prevention emphases for their products (a good example is the use of steering column locks in all American cars manufactured after 1971), establish good security programs in their own facilities, and encourage local subdivisions to participate in local crime prevention programs.

The practitioner should develop close relationships with any such corporations with facilities in his area.

The National Crime Prevention Institute Role

The NCPI, by virtue of its wide-ranging knowledge of crime prevention practices and its nationwide communications network of crime prevention practitioners, is in an excellent position to provide national crime prevention strategy guidance to federal agencies and the Congress, as well as to continue serving as the collector and synthesizer of new information and as the national training resource in crime prevention.[24]

Practitioners should arrange to receive NCPI publications, obtain training, or otherwise ensure that they can benefit from the knowledge and information which NCPI has to offer.

CONCLUSION

With appropriate support of the public and the governmental structure, the crime prevention practitioner functions as teacher and advisor to individuals and groups carrying out their responsibilities to protect persons and property in their neighborhoods. This function has the greatest impact when the practitioner works out of a city-wide crime prevention program, where a variety of skills and resources can be brought to bear with respect to crime prevention projects, including the potential to obtain funds from local, state, and federal levels. **The practitioner must have the structure and the resources to perform his enabling role in crime prevention.**

However, he must also have the right perspective. First, he must realize that his job is to guide the individual to protect persons and property within his span of control. But there is a limit as to what the individual can do about environmental conditions outside of his sphere of control. In some cases, practitioners must guide government to take action on behalf of its people. In other cases, such as Neighborhood Watch, people can act in behalf of themselves, but the crime prevention practitioner is needed to provide guidance, the police are needed to respond to reported crime, and other kinds of municipal support (as discussed previously) may be required.

Second, crime prevention requires a broad range of effective resources, skills and relationships from and among elements in the community. The practitioner must be able to assist those elements in planning, mobilizing and coordinating their skills and resources.

Finally, and most importantly, crime prevention is a "thinking person's" game. The practitioner has to know how to analyze crime problems before making recommendations for solutions. The solutions have to fit the problems, but he must understand the problems first, and he must understand that as the problems change, so must the solutions. This relationship between problems and solutions is more fully explored in subsequent chapters.

4

Designing Crime Risk Management Systems

Beginning with this chapter, we examine the specific areas of knowledge and skill needed by the crime prevention practitioner. The first of these areas, Designing Crime Risk Management Systems, involves the practitioner's services to—and relationship with—individual clients. The ability to design cost-effective crime risk management systems which are also acceptable to a client is the single most important skill to be developed by the crime prevention practitioner. And, it is the primary building block for all other practitioner skills.

In this chapter we are concerned with defining risk management, discussing the client-practitioner relationship and describing the tasks that the practitioner performs on behalf of the client.

UNDERSTANDING CRIME RISK MANAGEMENT

The concept of risk management[1] is exemplified by the old saying, "nothing ventured, nothing gained." If we wish to receive some benefit, we must take some risk. The risk can involve either cost, loss, or both. Risk management attempts to reduce the possiblities for cost or loss in order to derive the highest possible net benefit.

For example, we might wish to operate a jewelry store in order to benefit financially from the sale of jewelry. There are numerous risks associated with attaining this benefit—the cost of our merchandise, the cost of operations, the possibility that we might not be able to sell the merchandise at a high enough price to cover our costs, and the possibility that we might lose the merchandise through robbery, burglary or theft—to name a few.

Through application of risk management techniques, we would seek to reduce these possibilities for cost and loss. Cost of merchandise might be reduced through arrangements for quick delivery with a wholesaler, which permit us to purchase and maintain a minimum inventory of jewelry. Also, the lower the inventory, the less the total loss potential in the event of criminal attack. On the other hand, low inventory levels might also cost us some sales from customers who don't want to wait a few days for delivery.

We might install physical and electronic security devices to reduce the probability for loss in case of a criminal attack. Such installation would carry some cost. Yet, that cost might be less than the cost of fully insuring the merchandise against criminal attack, or, it might be offset by the reduced insurance premiums which would accompany installation of a security system.

Thus, risk management in general and crime risk management in particular always involves a variety of specific cost or loss reduction actions taken in some appropriate relationship with each other so as to assure a maximum possibility for benefit. This can be a rather complex undertaking because, as the example suggests, each risk reduction action may involve a cost or loss in and of itself. Crime risk management, like crime prevention itself, must be understood as a "thinking person's game," and its essential basis is the idea of cost effectiveness.

Risk management refers to our efforts to exercise some control over each of the various dynamic and pure risks we face. NCPI defines risk management as *the anticipation, recognition and appraisal of a risk and the initiation of some action to remove the risk or reduce the potential loss from it to an acceptable level*. (Note that this is also the basic definition for crime prevention.) A risk management system, however, implies that we are trying to control our risks in a systematic fashion, so that all related risks are controlled to about the same degree and our efforts to reduce one risk (or maximize its benefit) do not create, or increase, another.

Any risk situation which carries the potential for both benefit and cost or loss is called a **dynamic risk.**[2] The manufacturer faces dynamic risk in deciding whether or not to launch a new product line. The retail merchant faces dynamic risk in deciding how much stock to purchase in advance for the Christmas season. The family faces dynamic risk in deciding whether or not to purchase a more expensive home. Here, the decision is based on the relationship between benefit and cost or loss.

A **pure risk**[3] situation, on the other hand, is one in which there is no possibility for benefit, only for cost or loss. The risks of fire, flood or other natural disaster and, in many cases, the risk of crime are all pure risks. Here, all we can do is minimize the potential for loss. The issue is simply how much we are willing to pay or sacrifice to reduce the risk and what method of risk reduction we prefer or can afford.

It has been contended that all criminal activities represent pure risks.[4] However, in a risk management systems approach, the countermeasures used against pure crime risks may improve overall benefit or profitability because the countermeasure (a cost item) both reduces potential loss and creates a potential benefit. For example, television surveillance cameras were installed in a New Jersey shoe store as an anti-shoplifting measure. To the owner's surprise, the flow of customers and purchases actually increased following the installation. Interviews with customers convinced him that the cameras not only discouraged shoplifters, they made honest customers feel more secure against purse snatching or other personal attacks, and thus more interested in shopping at his store.

In the above illustration, the benefit derived from the countermeasure was accidental. But, the practitioner who understands both the client's interest and the ways in which crime risk management systems are designed can often produce such benefits deliberately. One practitioner tells the story of a small grocery store in an urban neighborhood which was plagued with shoplifting almost to the point of bankruptcy. At the practitioner's suggestion, the store owner replaced much of his conventional food stock with open displays of inexpensive items preferred by the people who lived in the neighborhood. This attempt to cater to local tastes had the effect of increasing his business and reducing the incidence of shoplifting, with the added benefit of reducing his costs.

In the case of a family living in a home or apartment, development of a cost-effective crime risk management system can not only reduce potential loss, it may also have a beneficial influence on lifestyle. If the family feels more secure, levels of crime-related fear and anxiety may be reduced accordingly. With the stress of fear and anxiety reduced, life may become more comfortable and relaxed, with associated benefits for the entire family.

Thus, the practitioner must not only stress the reduction of potential loss, but also (and at least as important) the use of security measures which translate potential losses into potential benefits or gains. Such a perspective allows the practitioner to truly serve the interests of the client and increases the likelihood that the client will comply with the practitioner's recommendations.

A crime risk management system, therefore, is a systematic effort to maintain a balanced level of control over all crime-related risks.

WHO IS THE CLIENT?

A crime risk management system can only be designed on behalf of an individual client, and a client must have the ability to manage the facilities and activities for which a crime risk management system is to be designed. A home owner, a businessman or an institutional administrator could be a client, but a group of homes in a neighborhood or stores in a commercial strip could not.

The reason for this restricted definition of "client" is that the crime risk management system is but one consideration in overall management, and is closely related to the management of funds, staff, production, sales, facilities and even, in the case of a home, of lifestyle.

In the absence of a central management focus, a crime risk management system cannot be considered, let alone designed.

The practitioner can and should apply the principles of crime risk management throughout his practice of crime prevention. However, he can only perform the specific task of crime risk management system design on behalf of an individual client, as defined above.

THE CLIENT-PRACTITIONER RELATIONSHIP

Technical expertise alone is not a sufficient basis for a successful practitioner-client relationship. The practitioner must, first and foremost, be able to recognize that each potential client has a unique set of interests and will not knowingly violate those interests, nor tolerate advisors who press him to violate them. The practitioner will be ineffective if he insists on suggesting crime risk management approaches which, whatever their merits from a security viewpoint, violate the client's interests. For example, putting all retail stock behind counters or in display cases might discourage shoplifting, but it would also eliminate the self-service feature which many merchants find to be very attractive to customers.

To be accepted, trusted and therefore to effectively render service, the practitioner must be perceived as a professional who understands and respects the client's needs and wants.

To be effective in serving clients, one must care about them, and caring means understanding and at least emphathizing with (if not totally accepting) their needs, problems and viewpoints. Does this mean that we should tell clients whatever they want to hear? Absolutely not. The doctor does us a disservice if he fails to point out the health hazards associated with smoking and overeating. The accountant and lawyer may land us in jail if they condone our income tax cheating. But one must first gain the client's respect and trust if one is to serve him, and this may mean putting off the hard-to-follow or unwanted advice until a relationship of understanding has been built. On the other hand, there may be matters that can't wait and force one, like the mule trainer, to "lumber" the client in order to get his attention. In general, however, the crime prevention practitioner should develop a professional relationship in which the client's needs and desires, rather than the practitioner's, are used as the building blocks in the relationship.

The practitioner must also become familiar with the basics of his client's operations. What kind of business is he in? Who are his customers? How does he prefer to conduct operations? In the case of a resident, what kind of lifestyle does the family prefer? In the case of a school or other institution, what methods of operation and client groups are required by policy, tradition and law? Accurate answers to these questions are crucial to the practitioner, because they help him relate to the client's unique situation in his crime risk management analysis.

It is crucial for the practitioner to understand the client's perceptions and attitudes toward crime, because the threat perceived by the client can be very different from the actual threat as determined by the practitioner through his crime pattern analysis. On the one hand, the client's fear may be higher than is justified, in which case the practitioner may have to accommodate that fear in his crime risk management system design. On the other hand, the client's concern may be less than the level suggested by the crime pattern analysis, in which case the client may be unwilling to accept the level of security recommended by the practitioner. In either case, the client's perception of the crime threat will greatly influence all of his decision-making in connection with crime risk management systems, and the practitioner must take this into account as he works with the client.

As part of understanding the client's perception of crime, the practitioner must also become aware of the client's previous victimization experience, because this will be a significant factor in his perception of crime and will underlie whatever security precautions the client has already taken.

CRIME PATTERN ANALYSIS

Before he can begin to provide effective services to clients, the crime prevention practitioner must understand prevailing crime patterns. Given the type of client (home jewelry store, bus depot, service station, etc.) and the client's location, the practitioner must be able to determine **what** crimes may impact the client, **who** is likely to commit them, **how** they are likely to occur, and **when** they are likely to occur. This analysis provides the practitioner with a picture of the *crime pressure* to which the client is subject.

A convenient way to understand crime pressure is the **crime rate by opportunity**, which compares the number of crimes of a particular type with the number of potential targets of that particular crime over a defined period of time.

For example, if there were 1,500 residential burglaries in a given jurisdiction last year, and the number of residences in that jurisdiction was 15,000, then the crime rate by opportunity for residential burglary was 0.1 (1,500 divided by 15,000). This rate can also be expressed as the number of crimes per thousand targets (100 in this example) or as the probablity that any given target would have been attacked (1 chance in 10, in this example).

The crime rate by opportunity is thus usable in a very direct way to inform both the practitioner and the client as to the probability that the client will be victimized by particular kinds of crime this year. This rate can be calculated for each kind of crime for the jurisdiction as a whole (as in the above example) or for specific parts of the jurisdiction such as a residential neighborhood or a commercial strip. All that is required is knowledge of the number of incidents of each crime and the number of targets potentially exposed to each crime.

As another example, the crime rate by opportunity for commercial burglary—by type of commercial establishment—in Minneapolis for the period July 1974 through June 1975 is shown below.

Type of commercial establishment	Number of units in city	Number of reported victimizations	Rate per 1,000 units	Chances of victimization
Hotel or Motel	139	135	971	1 in 1
Gas Station	299	240	802	1 in 1
Drug Store	60	35	583	1 in 2
School	223	129	578	1 in 2
Grocery	275	123	447	1 in 2
Bar or Restaurant	545	173	317	1 in 3
Department Store	82	20	244	1 in 4
Factory	772	180	233	1 in 4
Bank	98	9	91	1 in 11
Office	2,889	260	90	1 in 11
Other	7,038	754	107	1 in 9
All Establishments	**12,420**	**2,058**	**164**	**1 in 6**

Source: Adapted from Frisbie, *et al.*, **Crime in Minneapolis.**[5] Table 6.3, page 101.

One can easily see from this table that there may be a substantial difference at the jurisdiction-wide level among client types as to their chances of victimization from a particular type of criminal attack. A similar analysis performed at the neighborhood level would probably reveal an even wider variation in victimization chances.

There are other dimensions of crime pressure which should not be ignored. For example, what specific attack methods are most commonly used? What is the likelihood that crimes in progress will be observed and reported? These and other aspects of crime patterns are discussed more fully in subsequent chapters. Suffice to say for now, that the practitioner's understanding of crime pressure should include the following, at a minimum, for each client type and location and for each type of crime:

- Crime rate by opportunity;
- Typical and preferred attack methods;
- Typical and preferred times of attack (day, week, month);
- Suspect characteristics;
- Crime reporting patterns; and
- Typical types and amounts of loss.

CONDUCTING THE SECURITY SURVEY

Armed with his knowledge of crime patterns, client perceptions of crime and client interests, the practitioner is ready to undertake a security survey of the client's premises. The purpose of the survey is to examine the client's physical features, procedures, activities and possible targets of criminal attack in order to recognize and appraise the specific risks which are present.

The purpose of the security survey is to provide the practitioner with sufficient knowledge so that he can map out crime risk management strategies for recommendation to the client. Note the use of the word *strategies*. Although the practitioner must be concerned with detail in his survey, his overall objective is to achieve a balanced crime risk management system design. For this reason, his method of approach to the survey should also be strategic in nature.

The traditional approach to the security survey is to start with the exterior of the client's premises and work inward. The reasoning behind this approach is that the practitioner thus puts himself in the place of the attacker and assesses the effectiveness of each layer of security as he works his way in.

The strategic approach recommended by the National Crime Prevention Institute is completely the opposite. NCPI holds that the practitioner should start at the very heart of the client's operation by identifying the specific targets of possible criminal attack, whether they be cash, property, or person. His first focus of concern then becomes the targets themselves, not the security devices and procedures which are being (or might be) used to generally secure the premises.

For each specific target of criminal attack, the practitioner makes two impact-related determinations:

- The possible maximum loss; and,
- The probable maximum loss.

Possible maximum loss is the maximum loss that would be sustained if a given target or combination of targets were totally removed, destroyed, or both. In a retail store, for example, the possible maximum loss would be the store's entire stock.

Probable maximum loss, on the other hand, refers to the amount of loss a target would be likely to sustain. For example, a merchant might have equivalent value in his inventory of toilet paper and transistor radios. But it is unlikely that a criminal would remove dozens of cases of toilet paper when he could acquire merchandise of the same value by removing a single case of radios. In this simplistic example, the possible maximum loss would be the combined value of paper and radios. The probable maximum loss would be the value of the radios alone. The importance of the probable maximum loss calculations is that they permit the practitioner to assign priorities to the targets at risk. They also permit him to establish realistic limits on the cost basis for the final crime risk management system design, because it is almost always uneconomical to secure a client beyond the probable maximum loss level.

DETERMINATION OF PROBABLE MAXIMUM LOSS

Starting with the identification of specific targets and their possible maximum loss, the practitioner systematically works toward the outside of the premises, examining each physical or procedural barrier to access to—or removal of—the target, and each feature that would permit observation or detection of the criminal in the act of approaching or removing the target. This may involve assessment of several rings of protection: for example, the safe, the room where the safe is kept, the surface of the building itself, intrusion detection systems near the safe and at the building's surface, and any perimeter barriers (or multiple combinations of these). It may also involve only one ring of protection—the stock in a retail store which is only protected by the building shell.

For each component in the existing security system, the practitioner estimates its effect on probable maximum loss. Upon completion of his assessment of existing security levels, he is able to estimate the net probable maximum loss for each target. These estimates then become the driving force in his efforts to design the crime risk management system.

DESIGNING THE SYSTEM

When all crime risks have been identified as to their probable maximum loss through the use of the security survey, the practitioner is ready to consider methods for managing those risks. He is always careful not to make the mistake of jumping to solutions before this time, because he is aware of the need to design a rational security system rather than a patchwork quilt of expedient security measures. Knowing the targets of attack and their probable maximum loss—both separately and together—makes it possible for him to apply the five principal methods of risk management:

- Risk avoidance;
- Risk reduction;
- Risk spreading;
- Risk transfer; and,
- Risk acceptance.

All crime risks can be managed to a desired level through application of one or more (and in some cases, all) of these methods.

Risk Avoidance

This is always the first alternative to be considered. If the target can be removed altogether, the risk can be completely avoided. For the homeowner, this might mean keeping his valuable coin collection in a safe deposit box. For the merchant, it might mean depositing his cash in a bank. For a gun dealer, it might mean eliminating display stocks. Unfortunately, the application of the risk avoidance method may often create additional problems which prohibit its use. The gun dealer would soon lose customers if he eliminated his display stock. The merchant would be unable to conduct business if he completely eliminated the use of cash. The coin collector would probably be most unhappy if he could only work with his collection in a small cubicle near the bank's safe deposit vault.

Thus, relatively few significant risks can be altogether avoided, because such avoidance is likely to be extremely incompatible with the client's method of doing business or his lifestyle. However, it is well worth the practitioner's energy to conscientiously apply this method as far as it will go. For example, the merchant or homeowner may needlessly keep negotiable securities on the premises when a bank vault would be just as convenient. Also, risks involving personal injury (such as carrying large amounts of money) can be avoided by changing personal behavior, even if the risk of property loss remains.

Risk Reduction

If a risk cannot be avoided without creating severe operational difficulties, the next step is to reduce it to the lowest level which is compatible with the client's operations. For example, the merchant can reduce his maximum probable loss by keeping only enough cash on hand for immediate business needs during the hours his store is open, and by removing all cash to a bank each night. The coin collector could schedule himself to work with the collection at home one evening each week, and keep the collection in the bank's vault the rest of the time. The gun dealer could set up an inventory control system based on his average sales rate for each type of weapon and on the time delay between ordering and receiving additional inventory, and thus have on hand at any given time only the minimum stock needed.

Risk reduction is probably the most fertile single method the practitioner can use. Most clients needlessly expose themselves to risk in some significant ways. Risk reduction is usually an easy and inexpensive way to take up the slack before applying the more costly and difficult measures. It is also the area in which the practitioner's knowledge of the client's interests and ways of doing things pays the biggest dividends. For example, the neighborhood grocery store owner referred to earlier in the chapter needlessly exposed himself to the risk of shoplifting by displaying expensive products that his clientele seldom could afford. By converting to a less expensive, more frequently used type of stock, he reduced his maximum probable loss and attracted more customers.

Thus, risk reduction offers a good chance of not only reducing maximum probable loss at little or no cost, it also offers the practitioner a way to provide improved profits, feelings of personal security or other benefits valued by the client.

Risk Spreading

Probable maximum losses which remain after the fullest possible use of risk avoidance and risk reduction methods can be further reduced through risk

MAKING RECOMMENDATIONS TO CLIENTS

In the course of his survey, the alert practitioner will have taken advantage of every possible opportunity to develop further rapport with the client and to discuss his methods of crime risk reduction. Thus, by the time the practitioner has finished his work and submitted a report of findings and recommended actions (always prepared neatly and logically in writing), the client should have an emerging inclination to start complying with the recommendations. Like the crime risk management system which the practitioner has developed in his mind as the survey has proceeded, the recommendations to the client should be arranged systematically and logically, each with adequate justification (i.e., with each client expenditure there is a reduction of risk). To present a brief "laundry list" of miscellaneous recommendations is to virtually insure that the time of both the practitioner and the client has been wasted.

Ideally, the practitioner's report should not simply be mailed to the client, it should be personally presented so that the practitioner has the opportunity to fully explain and even to modify his own recommendations should discussion with the client produce new information, or should more creative approaches suggest themselves.

This meeting with the client also permits the practitioner to immediately reinforce the concept of crime risk management in the client's mind, and increase his level of motivation to comply with the recommendations. But primarily, it provides the opportunity for both the practitioner and the client to re-examine the recommendations and fine-tune them as needed with respect to cost effectiveness, order of priority, and applicability.

It is usually wise for the practitioner to re-visit the client after some time has elapsed (30-60 days, for example) since the recommendations were made and discussed. During this visit, the practitioner can actually observe the extent to which his recommendations have been carried out, and determine the reasons for any observed non-compliance. Second thoughts on the feasibility and desirability of the various security provisions can be discussed and modified again as needed, and the practitioner can once again stimulate the client and reinforce the risk management idea.

Thereafter, the practitioner should continue to visit the client periodically to perform routine check-ups. During these visits, he can not only continue to reinforce the client, he can also provide new information on changing criminal attack patterns in the area and answer questions that may have arisen in the client's mind. Perhaps most importantly, he can provide feedback to the client on the actual effectiveness of similar security programs in other homes or businesses around town. To perform this task properly, the practitioner must maintain good statistical records on crime incidence and attack patterns.

Finally, the practitioner should always immediately re-visit any client who is victimized. The purpose of this visit is to analyze the attack pattern used and the types of losses which occurred in order to yet again adjust the client's risk management system as necessary, and to obtain full knowledge of the reason for failure of that particular security system.

The practitioner's performance in the area of service to individual clients should always be measured by his "batting average" of client compliance with his recommendations, and by the subsequent victimization experience of clients who do comply. He should not only be concerned with compliance rate but level of effectiveness of the crime risk management system as well.

CONCLUSION

In summary, the design of crime risk management systems is concerned with serving the individual client so that the environment for which he is responsible is both secure and consistent with his interests and lifestyle. This requires the practitioner to look systematically at targets of attack and existing security elements in relation to profit, in the case of business, and lifestyle, in the case of a residence.

It also requires that the practitioner by as concerned with improving the profitability, comfort and convenience of the client as with reducing his risk. But reducing the vulnerability of individual clients is not the end-of-the-line for the practitioner, because the criminal may simply displace his efforts to more attractive targets. Thus, the practitioner must also develop group action and public policy action approaches, as will be discussed in Chapters 6 through 10.

5

Security Devices and Procedures

The preceding chapter was a review of the basic skills involved in designing crime risk management systems. In this chapter we present a summary of the security devices and procedures that can be used in the **risk spreading** method of crime risk management. The purpose of this chapter is to provide an understanding of security devices and procedures rather than to equip anyone with immediately applicable skills. Accordingly, we caution you not to attempt to apply the devices and procedures discussed in this chapter until you master the far greater detail presented in Volume III of *The Practice of Crime Prevention* series.

OVERVIEW

Risk spreading involves physical, electronic and procedural measures used either alone or in combination to directly oppose a possible criminal attack. Specifically, such measures are intended to:

- **Deter** the criminal from attacking;
- **Detect** him if he does attack so that a police (or other) response may be initiated;
- **Delay** him so that he may be apprehended before achieving his objective; and
- **Deny** him access to particular targets.

Physical security places barriers in the path of the potential attacker to deter him from attacking, delay him if he decides to attack, and deny him access to high-value targets even if he succeeds in penetrating the security system. A barrier may be either physical or perceptual. A solid building wall or a steel safe is a physical barrier. A boundary fence, a row of shrubbery or even a "beware of the dog" sign can serve as a perceptual barrier. Perceptual barriers can be quite effective in deterring attackers but must rely for effectiveness on the possibility that the attacker will believe them to be effective. They will only deter and will not delay or deny should the criminal decide to attack. Physical barriers, on the other hand, can deter, delay and deny the attacker.

Electronic security permits a criminal attack to be detected, will usually not delay or deny, but can deter to the degree that the attacker is aware that he may be detected. (In this sense, electronic security systems serve as perceptual barriers.) Electronic security measures are basically extensions of the human senses (with the exception of electronic locking devices, which more properly belong in the physical security category). Surveillance systems provide direct or indirect visual observation, and intrusion detection systems provide the ability to detect attackers in the absence of visual observation.

Procedural security measures can deter, delay, detect or deny by restricting authorized access to targets; by requiring that several persons cooperate in any effort to reach a target; by providing for formal or informal observation of targets; by reducing, dividing and spreading, or eliminating the targets themselves; and by many other similar approaches.

The best overall protection results from the interaction of an appropriate combination of physical, electronic, and procedural measures (Figure 5-1). Where such interaction is systematically developed, the resulting levels of security can be far greater than would be provided by any of the parts of the system. The following diagram illustrates the interaction effects of physical, electronic and procedural security. Where three interact, security is greater than where two interact, and so on.

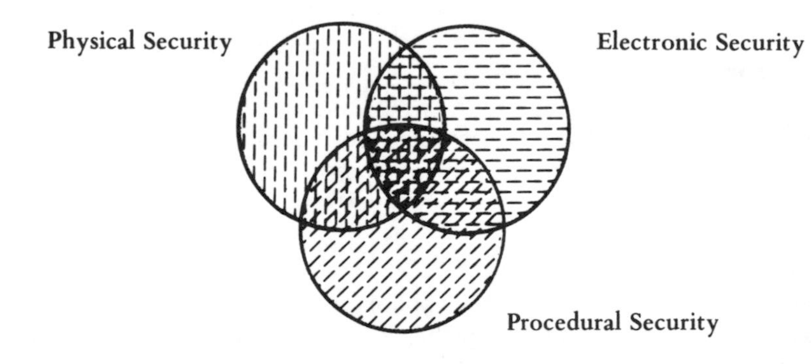

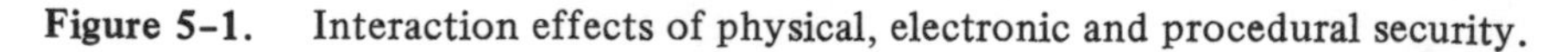

Figure 5-1. Interaction effects of physical, electronic and procedural security.

For example, a relatively secure perimeter barrier system (walls, doors and windows of a structure) may be equipped with an intrusion detection system, and procedural controls may be used to restrict access to door keys and the vital parts of the intrusion detection system. Thus, the physical and procedural measures protect both the building's contents and the intrusion detection system, and the intrusion detection system ensures that unauthorized attempts to break through the physical security system will be detected.

PHYSICAL SECURITY SYSTEMS

Although there is a wide variety of natural and man-made physical and perceptual barriers which can be part of physical security systems, we will only concern ourselves here with the most common types, namely:

- Boundary markers as barriers;
- Perimeter barriers;
- Perimeter access systems; and
- Internal barriers.

Before addressing these barrier types, let us consider some of the general and specific functions of barriers.

General Functions

Most barriers have several functions. Building walls and roofs, for example, are designed to provide shelter against weather, to provide an insulated enclosure for heat and air conditioning, to provide internal light, to create a pleasing appearance, and to be cost effective with respect to these functions. In many (if not most) cases, walls and roofs are not primarily designed to provide security, although they may be relatively secure as a coincidental by-product. Sometimes, security is a primary consideration in building and wall design. Even so, security factors must compete with other functional and cost considerations.

Inevitably in barrier design, some sort of balance must be struck among the various needs for security, convenience, utility, illumination, access, climate control and pleasing appearance. The objective is to design the barrier so that security features are compatible with all other considerations, are cost effective, and provide the needed degree of protection.

Security Functions

The use of barriers for protection against unwanted intrusion predates recorded history. Primitive tribesmen fortified hilltops. These later evolved into elaborate strongholds with high stone walls surrounded by moats or built on the top of sheer cliffs. Castles were deliberately built in inaccessible places, and usually consisted of a maze of small, dark rooms with few windows. They were hard to heat and impossible to clean, but, they were also difficult to invade. The castles successfully overcome were almost always starved into submission after a long seige or betrayed by internal complicity.

Modern technology, however, can overcome any passive barrier, no matter how formidable. Any barrier can be penetrated given time, opportunity, skill and desire.

But absolute protection is seldom required of barriers. Unlike an invading army, the criminal rarely approaches with overwhelming force. In fact, the overwhelming force is almost always on the side of police and other security forces. The criminal, therefore, usually tries to attack quickly and quietly, so as not to attract the attention of reaction forces. This need for stealth necessarily limits both the techniques he can use and the amount of time he is willing to spend making his attack. Thus, the primary functions of a barrier are to delay the intruder as much as possible and to force him to use methods of attack that are highly conspicuous or noisy.

Deterrence

Ideally, a barrier should discourage most potential intruders from trying to penetrate it. It should also improve the likelihood of detection by requiring that the attacker make himself conspicuous while attempting his penetration.

A barrier should be at the very least resistant enough to deter casual, opportunistic, or impulsive intrusion. The unplanned, impulsive attack by the relatively unskilled intruder is the type that most often plagues residential and commercial establishments. Here, a single stout barrier may discourage the opportunist.

As the value of the target increases, however, the strength of the barrier must increase proportionately. High-value targets tend to attract more determined attackers who can often bring considerable expertise to the attack. This type of attacker can only be deterred if the barrier is strong enough to convince him that the attack is not worth the risk. In general, the more formidable the barrier appears, the more potential intruders will be deterred by it.

Delay

Given an attacker with sufficient time, the proper tools, and the necessary skills and determination, any barrier can be breached. Therefore, if it does not discourage the attack, the barrier must delay him long enough so that he can be detected and apprehended before he reaches or removes his target. The amount of delay a barrier must provide is partially a function of the value of the property to be protected but, more importantly, it is a function of the likelihood of detection of (and response to) the attack. If provision can be made for quick detection and rapid response, a barrier need not provide for extensive delay. On the other hand, if the attack is not likely to be detected or responded to rapidly, then substantial delay must be built into the barrier. This trade-off between delay time and detection time is perhaps the single most important consideration in designing a barrier.

Conspicuousness

Good barrier-design not only delays the attacker, it also forces him to use attack methods which can call attention to his presence. Thus, the fact that an intruder must use bulky and conspicuous tools and make a lot of noise in order to gain entrance has its own deterrent potential, even though the barrier design that forces the conspicuous behavior may have been intended primarily to delay him.

Intrusion Versus Escape

Barriers not only make it difficult for an intruder to gain entrance, they should also increase the difficulty of removing valuable property from the premises. For example, if the first floor exterior design of the building is such that an intruder can only gain entrance through second floor windows, and if the first floor barrier design is as impenetrable from the inside as from the outside, then the intruder is forced to remove only that property which can be safely handled through the second floor window. Such anti-removal designs also reduce the attacker's escape route options.

Circles of Protection

Seldom is there a situation in which only one barrier is used. In most cases, even where security is not a consideration, there are likely to be at least two layers of barrier protection around a target. The first barrier might be a fence. The second might be the walls and roof of the structure itself. Or, the first might be the surface of the structure, and the second might be a secure interior room.

In security design, the concept of concentric barrier circles should be extended in depth as much as possible. Not only might there be an outer protective ring (such as a fence) at the property line and a second ring consisting of the building shell, but also within the building there might be one or more additional barriers to protect specific targets. For example, a truck terminal might have a boundary fence, an inner fence protecting the area where trucks are parked, a building within which freight is stored, an inner secured area for high-value freight items, a separate secure room for valuable records, and a safe within that secure room for the storage of cash. Thus, an intruder intent on reaching the cash would have to overcome several barriers of increasing difficulty before reaching his target.

The same idea might be used in a home; a fence around some or all of the property, the shell of the home itself, a secure storage closet, and a money safe inside that closet.

A single barrier ring (particularly in the case of commercial or industrial establishments) may be both ineffective and dangerous, because once an intruder penetrates it, he may be free to do as he wishes, screened from observation by the barrier that was intended to keep him out in the first place.

Boundary Markers as Barriers

In the past, it has been customary to treat as barriers all physical objects used to define the limits of protected property and then to classify as perceptual barriers those boundary barriers which were less difficult to penetrate (for example, low fences and hedges). The growing weight of evidence, however, suggests that **no boundary barrier can serve as anything more than a perceptual barrier**, because it has been demonstrated that even the relatively unskilled attacker can go over, under or through any boundary barrier in a matter of seconds.

Hence, fences, boundary walls, hedges and other such obstacles are referred to by NCPI as **boundary markers**, to make it clear that boundary marking is their major function. If boundary markers can also provide a degree of perceptual security, so much the better, but in no event should they be considered as physical security systems.

Boundary markers generally take the form of wood or metal fences and concrete and masonry walls. Of these, the concrete or masonry wall is the most substantial, but it is also the most costly. Chain link, barbed wire and wood stockade fencing provide less overall security, but they are usually much less expensive.

Boundary markers may attempt to provide perceptual security while serving other functions. Particularly in residential applications, fences and walls are often used for privacy purposes. They also enhance the appearance of the property, define its boundaries, prevent casual trespassing, and confine small children and pets. They are ordinarily low, insubstantial, and simple to climb.

If a boundary marker is to provide any significant degree of perceptual security it must be designed and built with that purpose in mind. Generally, security fences or walls are stronger, more substantial, higher, and with fewer projections to aid in climbing than fences and walls built for other purposes.

Concrete and Masonry Walls

Poured concrete, laid-up concrete building blocks or bricks may be used to build a solid wall. Poured concrete walls are more expensive than concrete block walls, as well as more difficult to penetrate, but current tests indicate that any wall can be penetrated in minutes.

To discourage climbing attacks, such barriers can be topped with broken glass set in concrete or with barbed wire, often on outriggers, and leave no projections on the external side to make the wall easier to climb. Even with such provisions, however, a concrete or masonry wall does not provide much protection against climbing. For example, an eight-foot high masonry wall topped with glass and/or barbed wire can be climbed in under five seconds.

An important deterrent aspect of concrete and masonry walls is that the unskilled intruder cannot look through to see what might await him on the other side.

Fences

Three types of boundary marker fencing are currently used; the wood stockade fence, the barbed wire fence, and the chain link fence. All provide about equal protection, and all cost less than concrete or masonry walls.

Certain guidelines apply to all. For example, the fence should be relatively high to discourage climbing (7-8 feet). Sharp projections, such as barbed wire, barbed tape and metal or pointed wooden stakes installed along the top of the fence provide additional defense against climbing. The exterior surface of the fence should be free of projections that can serve as hand- or foot-holds. Fence posts should be placed in concrete. The fence should extend to within two inches of the ground to discourage those who might crawl under it. Concrete curbs or buried wire mesh should be used to discourage easy underneath entry.

Maintenance is a very important factor with perimeter security fences, because an improperly maintained fence can quickly lose its effectiveness. Objects that can serve to reduce the effective height of the fence (such as cartons, crates and trash stacked in such a way that they can be used for climbing) should be kept away. Provisions should be made to prevent vehicles from being driven alongside the fence to aid the climbing attacker. The fence should be visually inspected often for breaks and evidence of tampering. This reduces the chance that an intruder will weaken the barrier one day and return later to complete his attack. Additional maintenance items include the regular clearing of brush and grass and the regular testing of any alarm systems or surveillance devices used in conjunction with the fence.

Wood fences are intended only to discourage the relatively unskilled opportunist. Against skilled and determined intruders, they provide little real protection, because an attacker can climb the fence quickly, remove portions of the fence, or even attach a chain to the fence and pull it down with a vehicle.

Barbed wire fences offer no more protection than other fences. Specifically, the barbed wire fence is quite vulnerable to an intruder equipped with heavy-duty wire cutters or bolt cutters.

However, barbed wire fences cost less to build than wooden or chain link fences, and thus may be the preferred type of boundary marker in some situations (agricultural fencing, for example).

Chain link is by far the most common type of fencing used for boundary marking. It is relatively attractive, low in maintenance cost, simple to erect, and less of a safety hazard than barbed wire. Vinyl and wood strips can be inserted into any standard mesh to restrict visual penetration. However, the best chain link fence can be climbed or penetrated by determined attack in less than a minute.

Gates

Gates are often the weakest part of the boundary marker. The usual reason for this weakness is improper design or installation. Gates should fit tightly between posts (and between each other in the case of double gates) because a gap of only six inches is sufficient to permit the entry of an intruder. Built-in locks are preferable to padlocks and chains, because the padlock is totally exposed and subject to a variety of attacks.

It is particularly important that the gates remain secure from the inside as well as outside. If target items are so large that they cannot be carried over or through the fence, a secure gate may foil the attack.

The Boundary Marker-Barrier System

Boundary markers of any kind can be defeated by climbing, tunneling, or breaking through in less than a minute. A wall or fence used without additional security measures is merely intended to pose a psychological deterrent to the opportunistic intruder. For this reason it is important to choose a fence or wall that has a formidable appearance and to avoid a flimsy appearance that would invite attack.

However, it should again be emphasized that no boundary barrier will deter a skilled and determined intruder. The purpose of the barrier is to delay him until an appropriate response can take place. But since only a limited delay can be provided, the ability to quickly detect an attack in process becomes crucial. Surveillance and intrusion detection systems, (lighting, visual monitoring, alarms) can dramatically increase the risk to the intruder if they are combined with quick response capability by police or security forces.

Perimeter Barriers

A perimeter barrier is any obstacle which defines the physical limits of a controlled area and impedes or restricts entry into the area. It is the first line of defense against intrusion. In a planned, in-depth security system, it may be only the first of several obstacles the intruder must overcome before reaching the target area. At a minimum, a good perimeter barrier should discourage an impulsive attacker. At the maximum, when used in conjunction with other security measures, it can halt even the most determined attack.

A variety of obstacles may serve as perimeter barriers, but for our purposes here, building surfaces (floors, roofs, walls) are the only type of perimeter barrier that need be considered.

Floors

Floors are the least likely point of entry in most buildings. Ordinarily, the floor is either a concrete slab or a wooden surface protected by an enclosed basement or foundation. Weak spots or openings in foundation walls make it possible for an intruder to get under the floor where he might work for an extended period of time without visual detection, as do pilings or other openwork foundations, underground sewers and other utility passages. No matter how strong the floor is, it can be penetrated by a determined intruder who has access to the underside of it and time to employ tools in an unobserved fashion.

Roofs

Sloping roofs (of whatever style) are unattractive to intruders because anyone on a sloping roof is usually visible from ground level. The slope itself poses a risk of falling, and the necessary tools must be held in place while not being used. However, sloping roofs should be analyzed with respect to ventilating ducts, skylights, or other possible access points.

The flat roofs most often found on commercial buildings can, on the other hand, be very attractive to intruders. Because the walls on many commercial buildings extend a few feet above the roof line, they may provide excellent concealment for any intruder attempting to penetrate the roof. Large, sophisticated tools can be used for an extended period of time, and a considerable amount of noise can be made if the building is unoccupied. Given such favorable attack conditions, no flat roof except one made out of thick reinforced concrete offers any real resistance to penetration. However, penetration of the roof itself is seldom required, because the typical flat commercial roof offers numerous skylights, ventilation openings, trap doors and other maintenance accessways which are more convenient points of penetration than the roof itself. Such access points can and should be strengthened to the point of at least being as penetration resistant as the rest of the roof.

Walls

Wood frame and masonry are the two basic materials used in most wall construction. Most single family residences have wood frame exterior walls, with or without a surface layer of masonry. The rest have solid masonry walls. For commercial structures, masonry or concrete is usually the material of choice because of its durability and resistance to fire.

Wood frame walls are relatively inexpensive, easy to build, durable, and provide good insulation against noise, weather, and heat loss. But they do not provide much penetration resistance unless additional protective measures are taken to strengthen them. However, even frame walls can deter the impulsive intruder. His points of attack will almost always be doors, windows and other accessways, and if these are secure he will move on to an easier target unless there are high-value items inside the structure. But because a determined intruder can break through an ordinary frame structure in just a few minutes, a frame wall is insufficient protection for high-value property, unless coupled with an intrusion detection system.

Masonry and concrete walls, more expensive than frame walls, are used especially in commercial and institutional structures because of their durability and resistance to fire and insulation against weather, noise and heat loss. They usually consist of either poured concrete or concrete block.

As has been mentioned, poured concrete walls are relatively difficult to penetrate. However, concrete block walls which have not been filled with concrete or reinforced with steel can be as vulnerable to attack as wood frame walls. On the other hand, any masonry walls can be penetrated by a determined attack.

Perimeter Access Systems

The most vulnerable points in any building surface are the gaps in the wall, floor or roof which can permit entry of an intruder or tool into the protected space inside. Doors and windows are the most obvious types of access openings, but there are many others, such as vents, ducts, mail slots, coal chutes, skylights, sewer mains, utility tunnels and so on. Any opening of 96 square inches or more, providing that one side is at least 6-8 inches, is big enough for an intruder to wriggle through. Even smaller openings can be used to open a larger access barrier from the inside, or to extract target items using a suitable tools.

Doors

The door system includes the door itself, the hinges, the lock, the strike, the locking bolt, the door frame, and the structure of the supporting wall. All of these elements (as shown in Figure 5-2) must be designed to work together, because a weakness in any one element can compromise the security of the entire system. Door systems can be made as strong as necessary (vault doors, for example, can be built to withstand highly sophisticated attacks for extended periods of time). For most purposes, door systems used in residential and commercial applications provide adequate security if they can resist an intruder's strength supplemented by a limited variety of tools. Unfortunately, many (if not most) door systems currently in use cannot provide this degree of protection.

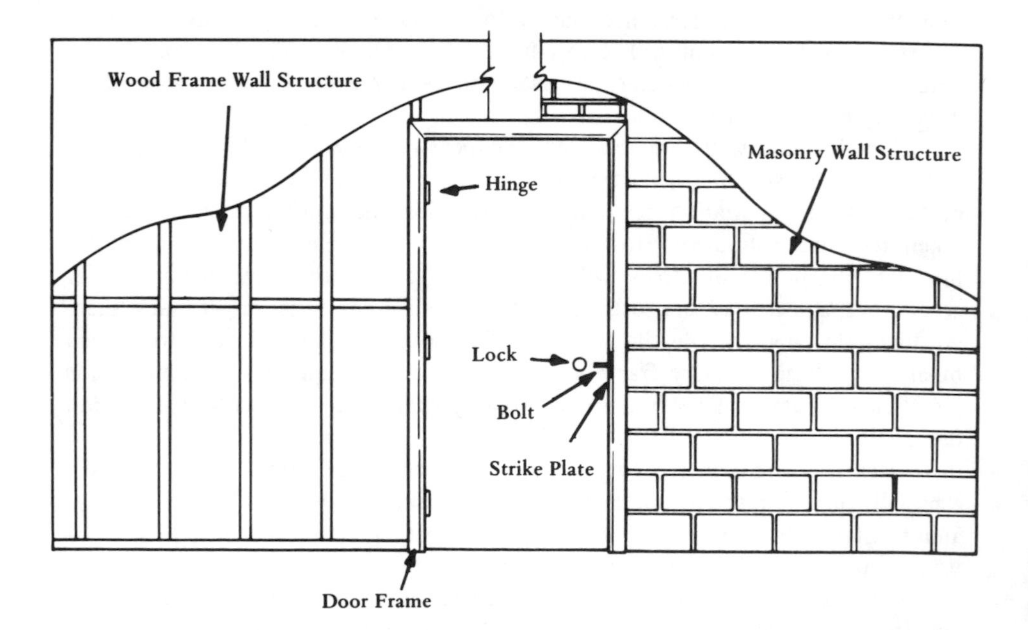

Figure 5-2. Door system components.

Wood Doors (See Figure 5-3). Two types of wooden doors are used for security purposes: flush doors and panel doors. Screen doors, storm doors, jalousie doors and other types of doors used for weather-proofing or decorative purposes are not suitable as security barriers without substantial reinforcement.

A flush door has flat interior and exterior surfaces and no glass panes, panels, louvers or grills, and may have a variety of filler materials.

Hollow core doors are not at all suitable as security barriers. The average man can kick a hole through the door with one or two blows, since the thin wood skin offers little resistance to penetration. With a hammer or other suitable tools, passageway can be made to allow direct intrusion, or a smaller hole can be made to permit the intruder to reach in and unlock the door from the inside. Although the hollow core door can be reinforced to some degree, the cost of a reinforced hollow core door would (at best) be little less than the cost of a solid door.

In the solid, woodblock core door, blocks of wood of varying lengths are usually glued together and glued to the face panel. This results in a door which is as substantial as a solid wood plank door, if not more so. Wood block core doors are the most expensive of the solid core type but are quite resistant to tool and muscle power attacks, although they can be breached given sufficient determination and time.

The particle board core consists of wood particles or sawdust bonded and formed under pressure. Particle board offers less penetration protection than solid wood, but such a door is usually much less expensive than the wood block

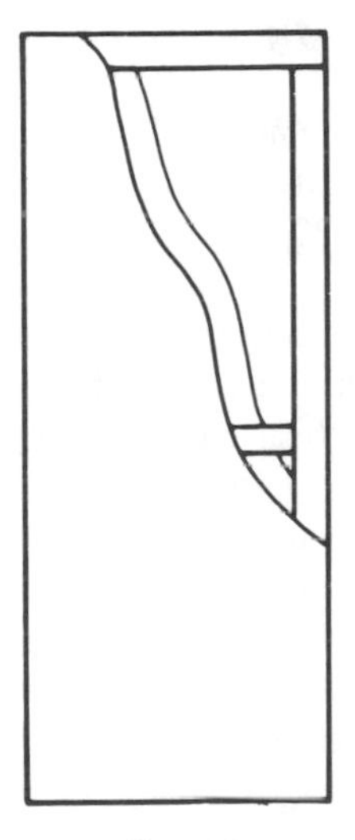

Hollow Core

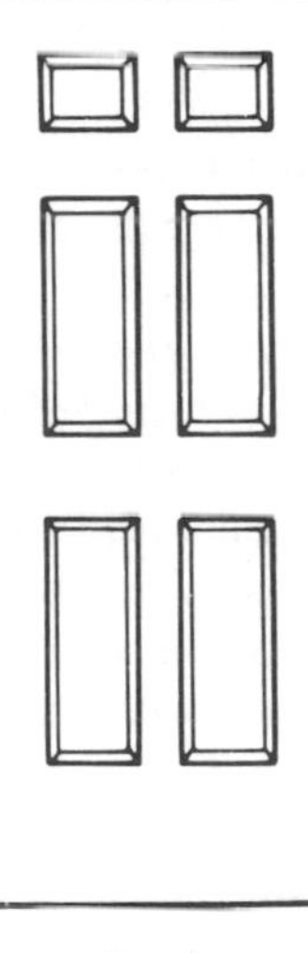

Panel

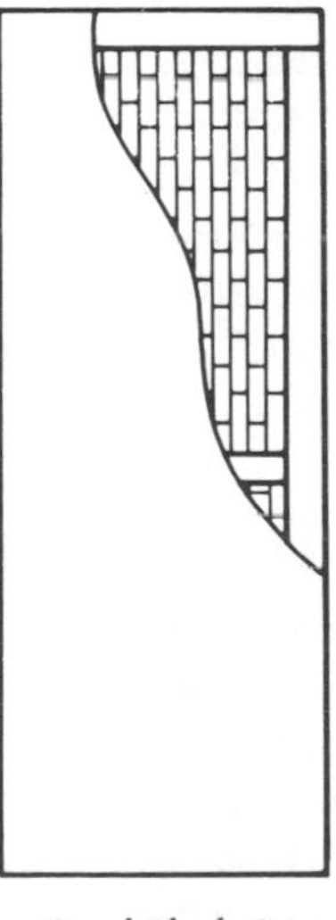

Wood Block Core

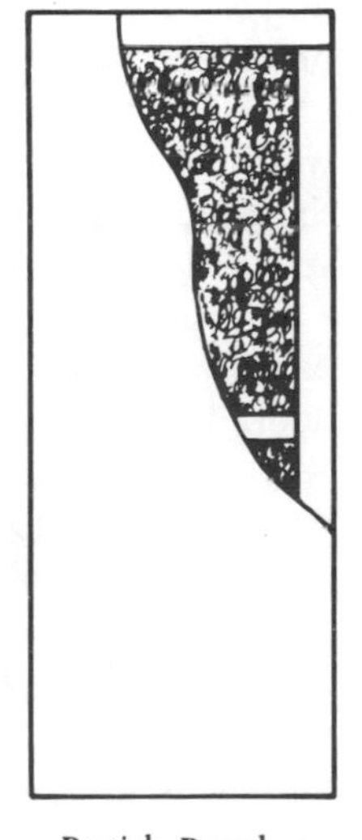

Particle Board or Insulation Core

Figure 5-3. Types of wood doors.

core door, and certainly provides, on an average, significantly more protection than a hollow core door.

The mineral or insulation core door contains fire resistant materials. The degree of security provided by such doors is only slightly better than that provided by a hollow core door, because the insulation material can easily shatter or crumble under a determined attack.

Among the solid core flush doors, the wood block core is easily the best choice for security application. The particle board door (given a high enough density of the particle material), while significantly less secure than the wood block core, nevertheless provides a distinctly higher level of security than the mineral core or the hollow core door. The mineral or insulation core door is only slightly more secure than the hollow core door, and neither one should be considered appropriate for security applications.

The panel door is the only other common type of wooden door. The basic weakness of the door is the panels themselves. Any panel can be kicked or knocked out of the door, permitting ready access to the protected interior. The use of glass in a panel door further compromises its security unless impact resistant glazing material is used. Thus, a panel door can have special security problems. However, if the panels are too small to permit entry if knocked out, an inside keyed cylinder will prevent the intruder from reaching in and unlocking the door. In addition, the panels or vision lites may be backed by break-resistant glazing material or expanded steel mesh.

Steel Doors (See Figure 5-4). The hollow steel door is generally stronger, more durable, less susceptable to damage and deterioration, and usually provides better protection against forced entry.

The standard steel door consists of a steel grid frame or core material around which is wrapped sheet steel in various thicknesses. For security purposes, the sheet steel used to face the door should not be thinner than 20 gage. Common standard steel doors currently in use are described below.

Full flush doors use an enclosed grid type of steel frame and the steel face panel is wrapped around this grid, but no seams are visible on either face of the door. In the seamless variety, no seams are visible on the vertical edges either.

The recessed panel door has a panel or panels made of a shingle sheet of steel. Because of the single sheet panel, it is not ordinarily suitable for security application.

The kalomein door is made by rolling two face panels of light steel around a soft wood frame and filling the interior cavity with injected plastic. Such doors are vulnerable to a variety of attacks unless specially reinforced, but can provide more protection than a wood panel door, although not as much as a solid wood block core door, and not nearly as much as a standard steel door.

Core materials used within steel doors have a range of security implications. The best security barrier is provided by a heavy gage steel grid frame in which the framing members are closely spaced. The second best type of core is one which contains horizontal sheet stiffeners of heavy gage steel. Foam and mineral insulation cores have no security value.

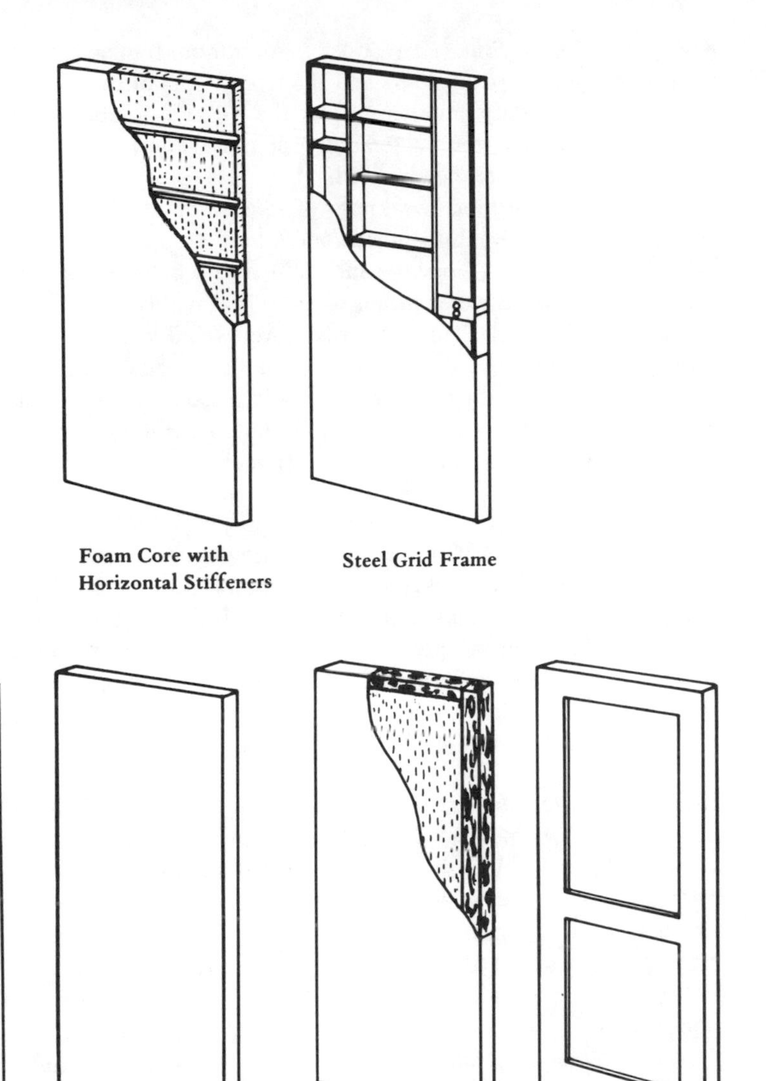

Figure 5-4. Common types of standard steel doors.

Reinforcement should be used around the hinges and the locks for increased protection and durability. All locks should be mounted in a reinforced lock bracket designed for the type of lock used. Grills should be fabricated of heavy steel, and applied so that no fastener is exposed on the exterior (security side) of the door. Glazing should be a material which resists breaking such as laminated glass, acrylic or polycarbonate glazing material.

Aluminum Narrow Stile Glass Doors. Aluminum framed glass doors such as those used on residential patio doors and the front doors of business establishments have always posed security problems. Over the years a number of measures have been developed to reduce the vulnerability of these doors, but basic problems remain which cannot be entirely eliminated.

The most obvious weakness of the door is the large glass panel itself. Although crime prevention practitioners tend to agree that intruders will usually avoid breaking glass if possible, an intruder who believes that the risk is small will break the glass if no easier means of entry is available. Glass doors in business store fronts located in well lighted, heavily traveled and well patroled commercial areas may be fairly safe. But glass patio doors in unlighted residential areas almost invite attack. Perhaps the single most important reason why more glass panels are not broken by intruders is that aluminum-framed glass doors are so easy to open that breaking the glass is seldom necessary. If such doors are to provide any protection at all, special hardware must be used.

Swinging Narrow Stile Glass Doors. Swinging store front aluminum glass doors have traditionally been locked by a short throw horizontal dead bolt which engaged the slot cut into the aluminum door jam. However, aluminum is very soft, and the frame can either be spread to disengage the bolt, or the aluminum around the strike area can be quickly peeled back to expose the bolt. A partial answer to this type of problem is new door hardware designs including long-throw pivoting dead bolts and armored reinforcement fittings around the strike area.

Sliding Narrow Stile Glass Doors. Sliding glass doors, such as those found in patio installations at homes are difficult to secure. Most residential sliding glass doors are too narrow to use the locks demanded for swinging doors. As a result, the primary lock on residential sliding doors is often a hooked spring-loaded latch, which may be sprung or the frame peeled back and the bolt exposed. Also, it is often possible to lift the entire door out of its track. Lifting of the door out of the track can be made more difficult by mounting adjustment screws in the top track so that in its closed position the door cannot be lifted far enough to clear the bottom track. A number of supplementary locks for sliding glass residential doors are available which also may help in preventing prying and lifting attacks.

However, nothing will prevent an intruder from breaking through the glass on the door except replacing the glass with one of the available break-resistant glazing materials such as acrylic or polycarbonate or by mounting expanded metal over the glass. These solutions are either expensive or unsightly or both, but they may be less expensive than replacing the sliding door with some other type of access door. If this degree of protection is needed, other glass access openings in the building should also be reinforced to provide the same level of security.

Door Frames and Strikes

No door is any more secure than the frame in which it is mounted. Weak door frames and improperly designed and mounted locking bolt strikes have consistently been problem areas in door security. There are two distinct problems in the strike-frame relationship. First, if the frame is weak, the strike, no matter how strong by itself, can easily be split out unless the mounting screws extend through the frame and into the internal structure of the wall. Second, there is normally about one-eighth-inch clearance between the door and the frame on either side of the door. This means that there is a potential gap of one-fourth inch available for spreading or prying. Since the ordinary bolt extends into the strike for a maximum of three-eighths inch, if the frame has any "give" to it at all, the door and frame of an in-swinging door can easily be spread and any door can be pried enough to pop the bolt out of the strike. The obvious solution to the strike-frame spreading problem is to use a longer bolt. Crime prevention specialists normally recommend that the bolt extend into the frame/strike at least five-eighths inch.

Wood Frames. There are several basic security defects in wooden door frames themselves. First, frames are usually made of soft lumber which is easily cracked and splintered. Second, the frame unit is installed in a rough wall opening which is usually deliberately oversized for ease in installing the frame. Thus, there is usually a gap on one or both sides between the frame and the supporting structure, which permits the frame to be deflected with a suitable pry bar, separating the bolt from the strike. The basic remedy to this problem is proper construction involving a tight fit between the edges of the rough door opening and the door frame. Stopgap remedies, such as filler plates, interlocking deadbolt locks, and security strikes, can be used on existing construction to mostly offset the problem. (See Figure 5-5.) It is almost impossible to mount a conventional strike securely on a soft wood frame unless the screws used to mount the strike are long enough to extend solidly into the supporting studs. Reinforcement metal brackets are also available (see Figure 5-5) which spread the mounting strain across the width of the frame such that the whole frame would have to be ripped out before the strike could be removed by force.

Steel Frames. When properly installed, hollow steel frames avoid most of the problems of wood frames. Steel frames should be made of 18-gage or heavier steel, reinforced at the corners and around the hinges and strike. When the frame is installed, the hollow portions inside should be filled with concrete resulting in a rigid structure which will resist attempts to spread it. (See Figure 5-6.) Steel frames should also be properly anchored to the supporting wall. If an appropriate anchor is not used, the entire door and frame assembly can sometimes be pushed out of the wall. If these precautions are taken, however, a steel frame provides excellent protection against attacks directed against the frame and strike. New wrap-around replacement 18-gage frames are now available on the market.

Aluminum Frames. As was pointed out above, aluminum door frames are susceptible to peeling and prying attacks. However, they may be strengthened through the use of multiple layers of aluminum or by the addition of an armored strike.

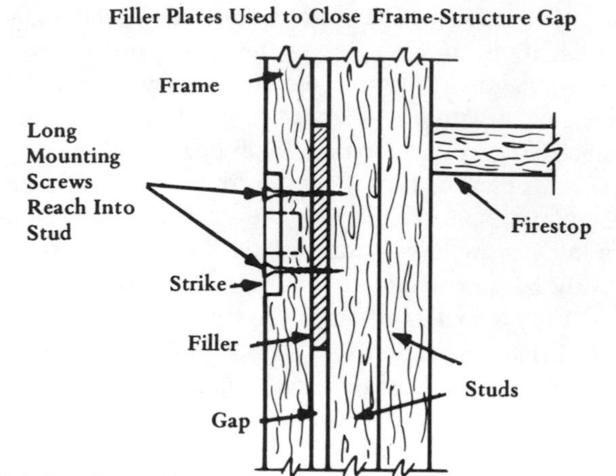

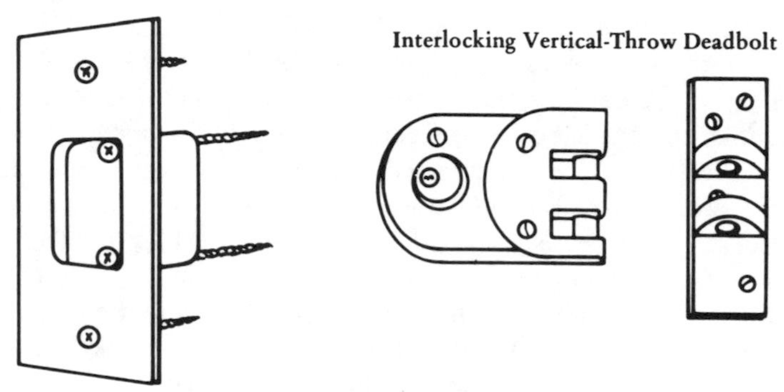

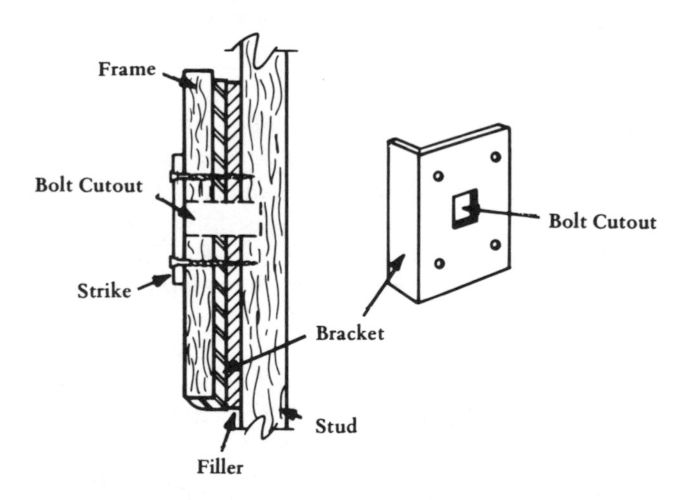

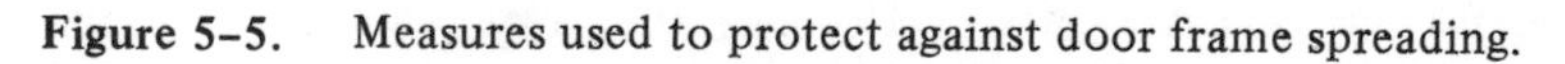
Figure 5–5. Measures used to protect against door frame spreading.

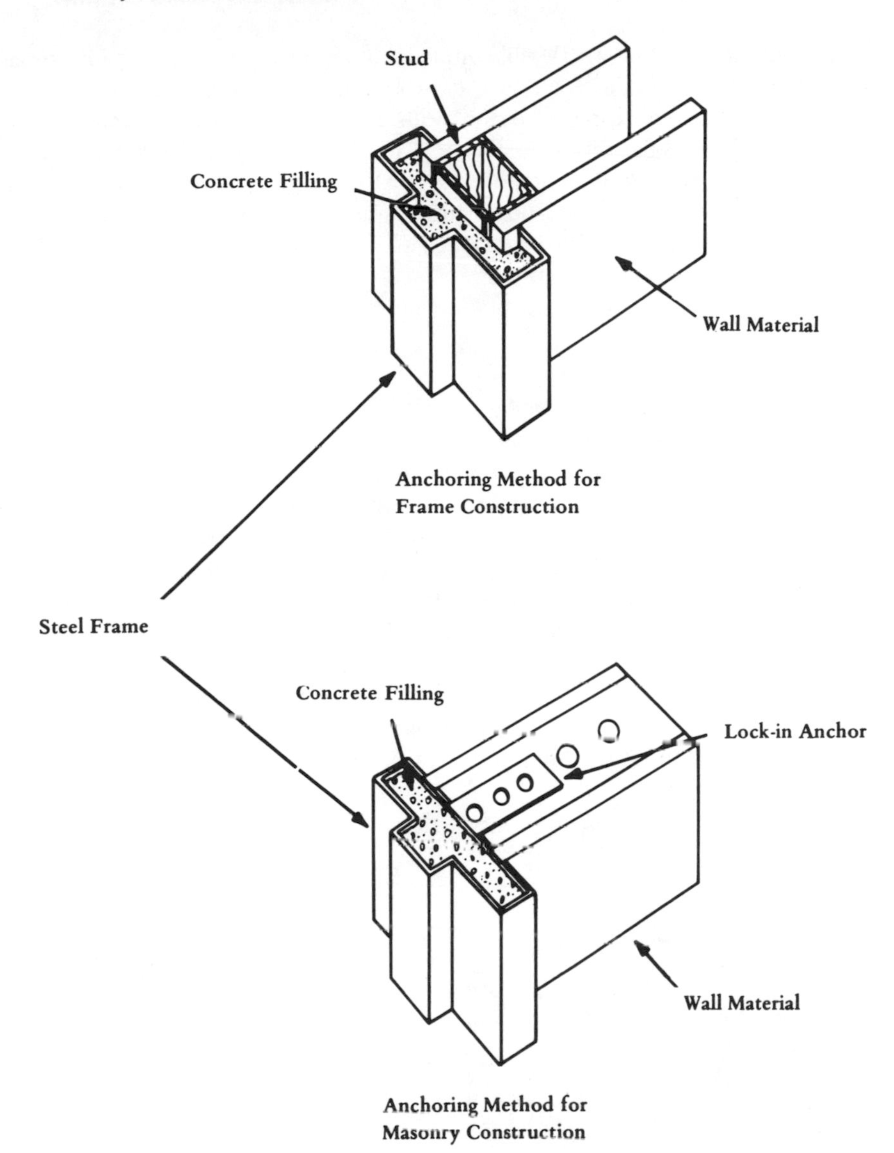

Figure 5-6. Steel door frames filled with concrete.

Supporting Wall Structure

Concrete and masonry walls provide rigid support for door frames when the frames are properly mounted. A steel frame properly mounted in a concrete wall will resist almost any amount of pressure that is possible to apply in an attempt to spread the frame of an in-swinging door. This is not the case with a wood frame construction, which may be flexible enough to permit a door frame to be spread even when it is solidly fastened to the structure. For example, a two-thousand-pound horizontal load applied to the door frame with an automobile bumper jack will produce a deflection at the bolt of about one-half inch—sufficient to spring a normal five-eighth-inch bolt. A pry bar can also produce this amount of deflection. However, if additional horizontal reinforcement is built into the wall frame, the deflection can be reduced to almost nothing unless enough force is applied to actually break the structure.

Hinges

Doors are secured to their frames by hinges. When any force (either of a spreading or penetrating variety) is placed on these fasteners, they must be strong enough to absorb the stress without distorting or pulling loose in such a way as to release the door from the frame. If hinges are appropriate to the size and weight of the door and installed correctly, they will usually provide sufficient resistance to attack. However, when possible, hinges on wood frames should always be mounted with fasteners long enough to go through the jamb and securely into the supporting structure. Attention should also be given to the pins which hold the leaves of the hinge together. On an outward opening door, this pin is exposed. If the pin is of a removable type, it can easily be knocked out by an intruder and the door opened on the hinge side. This weakness can be eliminated by using hinges with fixed pins or using a steel stud which penetrates each side of the hinge leaf set. (See Figure 5-7.)

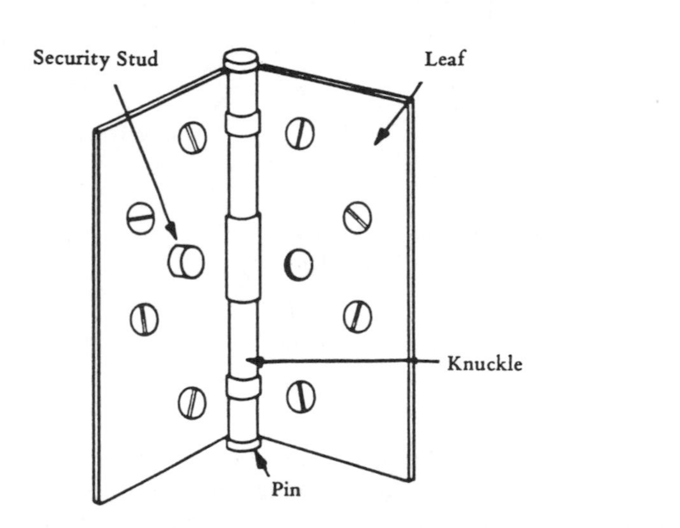

Leaf Hinge With Security Stud

Fixed Pin Leaf Hinge

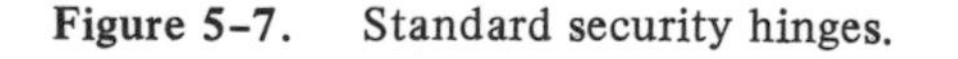

Figure 5-7. Standard security hinges.

Locks

The subject of locks is vast and complex. In this discussion we will touch only on the few points needed for an initial understanding locking. The lock is often the most vulnerable point on the door, and the first place attacked. Unfortunately, most exterior spring bolt type door locks currently in use in the United States are quite vulnerable to forceful attack. The common key-in-knob lock, for example, is extremely susceptible to attack by a pipe wrench or similar tool which simply breaks off the knob and exposes the bolt to manipulation by hand. Such locks have no security value and should, without exception, be replaced or supplemented with good deadbolt locks.

The three components of any lock are the bolt mechanism, the cylinder and the strike. The bolt mechanism moves the bolt in and out of the strike. The cylinder controls access to the bolt mechanism. The strike engages the bolt and prevents it from being moved in any manner other than in and out.

There are three basic types of bolt mechanisms (see Figure 5-8):

- Spring bolt—bolt is extended into the strike and held in place by a spring;
- Dead bolt—bolt must be moved in and out of the strike mechanically; and
- Interconnected bolt—consists of a spring bolt and a dead bolt which are released with one motion.

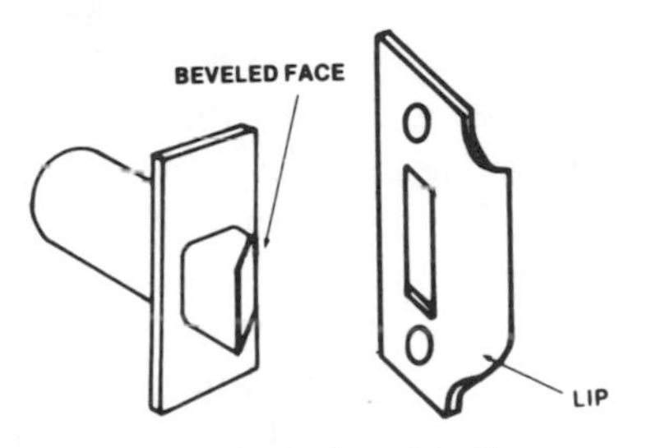

Spring Bolt and Strike

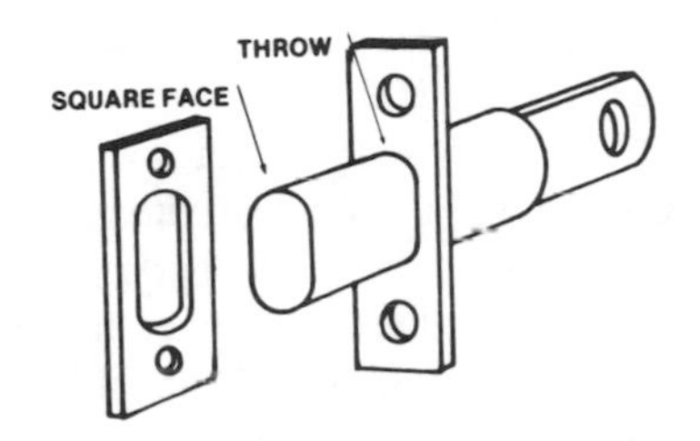

Horizontal Long-Throw Dead Bolt and Strike

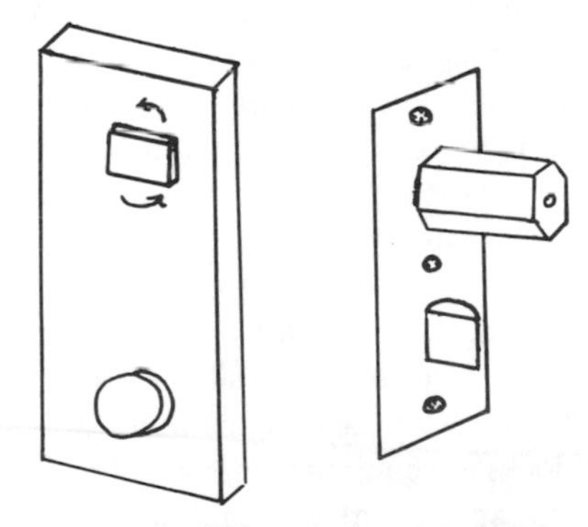

Interconnected Spring Bolt and Dead Bolt

Figure 5-8. Basic types of bolt mechanisms.

There are only two types of cylinders which need to be understood in connection with door locks in the United States:

- Warded locks (cylinders) and
- Pin tumbler locks (cylinders).

Warded Locks (See Figure 5-9). The simplest type of mechanical cylinder is known as the warded lock. On door applications it is easily recognizable by its large, see-through key hole and a long cylindrical key with a slotted tab. Still in use in older buildings and in many inexpensive padlocks, the warded lock has a bolt which is held in position by a steel spring. Inserting and turning the key releases the spring tension and moves the bolt. However, in order to turn at all, the key must pass through a series of obstacles called wards that are built into the lock case. Not only is it fairly easy to obtain or create a key which will open a warded lock, the lock action can be rotated by a bent coat hanger or other similar improvised device. Warded locks are therefore no longer considered as security locks unless specially redesigned.

Pin Tumbler Locks (See Figure 5-10). The oldest and most effective cylinder is called the pin tumbler. It was invented by the ancient Egyptians. The current pin tumbler was mass produced for the first time in the 19th Century and has become the most widely used lock in this country for exterior and interior doors. As currently designed and manufactured, it can provide a very high level of lock security. As Figure 5-10 shows, pin tumbler locks consist of a plug which rotates with the key to throw or withdraw the bolt. Surrounding the plug is the shell, a fixed assembly into which the plug fits. A series of pins fit into matching cylindrical holes in these two lock parts. With the key withdrawn, the pins extend through the surface between the plug and the shell so that the plug cannot turn. Insertion of the correct key lines up pins in such a way that the outer end of each one matches the surface separating the plug from the shell (shear line), so the plug can turn to withdraw the bolt.

More often than not, the pin tumbler lock is attacked with attempts to twist, punch, or pull either the plug or the entire cylinder out of the locking assembly. Good metal-to-metal through-bolting of both the lock case and the cylinder and the use of tapered guards to keep the plug from being pulled out of the cylinder (as well as punched inward) and the use of a one-inch-throw deadbolt can make the pin tumbler lock a very secure type of lock.

Any type of lock equipped with a spring bolt without an anti-shim device can be defeated by inserting a credit card or a thin, flexible piece of metal (both referred to as "shims") between the bolt and the strike. This simple action presses against the wedge-shaped outward face of the bolt, exerts pressure on it, and easily retracts it. Some such locks are equipped with small supplemental deadbolts which, when properly engaged, can prevent a "shim" attack. However, it is very easy to

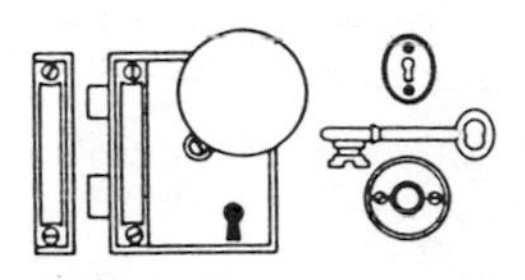

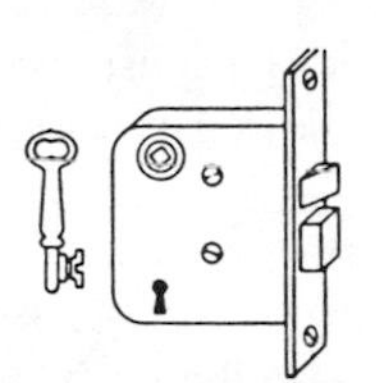

Figure 5-9. Typical warded locks.

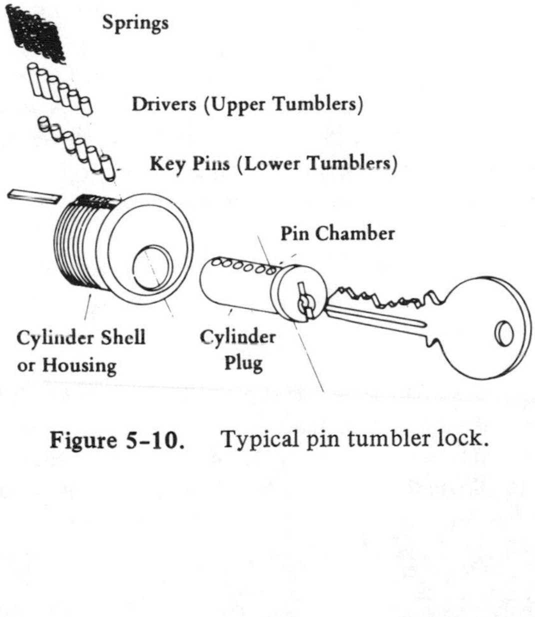

Figure 5-10. Typical pin tumbler lock.

mis-mount the locking hardware so that the deadbolt does not engage. Thus, the spring latch bolt lock offers little security. Short-throw deadbolt locks (five-eights-inch long or less) while resistant to the shim attack, also can be popped out of the strike by spreading.

Because of these considerations, to obtain even minimum security an exterior door should be protected by a lock which is equipped with a one-inch-throw deadbolt or interlocking deadbolt which is mounted directly in the door rather than in the door handle.

All of the many one-inch-throw deadbolt locks available on the market should be installed with at least one-fourth-inch bolts which extend completely through the door and engage sturdy metal plates on both sides of the lock. A lock which is fastened to the door with wood screws is easily compromised.

A good long-throw or vertical-throw deadbolt lock used with a reinforced strike, a solid door-frame-to-structure attachment, and good structural reinforcement in the wall itself will provide adequate protection for most home and business applications.

Glass located near any lock permits an intruder to break the glass, reach in, and unlock the lock from the inside. Here, a double cylinder lock may be used so that a key is required to operate the lock from either inside or outside. Double cylinder locks keep the intruder from removing heavy or bulky items through the door. If children, handicapped or elderly persons use such a door, the glass should be reinforced and an interconnected life safety lock should be used which can be opened in one motion by someone with no prior training or experience.

Windows and Glazing

Windows have always been a particularly difficult problem in building security. Their primary functions are to provide light and ventilation and to serve as a barrier to weather. Windows are not ordinarily intended to provide a substantial barrier to intrusion, and it is often difficult, expensive and unsightly to increase their security capability without destroying their primary functions.

Window Locks. One helpful assumption is that intruders are reluctant to break glass, because it creates a distinctive sound which invites investigation. Thus, simply locking windows can provide a degree of security. However, existing latches on most windows cannot resist a strong jimmying or prying attack and can be opened once the glass has been broken. Minimum locking protection requires a device that will resist prying and manipulation.

The only type of window which cannot be easily secured from the inside is the jalousie window. This type of window is always a poor security risk, and should be either replaced or covered with bars or grillwork.

Security Grills and Bars. If the risk that an intruder will break the glass is high, sturdy metal bars, wire grills or expanded mesh placed over vulnerable windows can usually provide the security needed. If this degree of security is required, it should be applied to all windows closer than 8 feet to the ground, or to any window higher than 8 feet which borders on a roof line or is otherwise accessible. Grills and bars should usually be attached to the inside of windows. In residential applications, if the window is to be used as an exit in the case of fire or other emergency, fastening devices should release instantly.

Glazing Material. Glass is by far the most common glazing material. It is found in both single and double strength single panes, in dual panes for insulating purposes, in a tempered form two to five times stronger than ordinary plane glass and in various laminated forms. Only the laminated forms provide any substantial protection against breakage by an intruder. Laminated glass is made by bonding alternate layers of transparent plastic and glass. If sufficiently thick it can provide a significant barrier to penetration. Laminated glass, however, can be defeated if sufficient time is available. Glass with wire imbedded in it was designed exclusively for fire protection and is not considered as security glazing.

The two most popular plastic glazing materials are acrylic and polycarbonate. Both come in various patterns and in transparent, translucent and opaque colors. Acrylic is clearer than polycarbonate, while polycarbonate possesses much greater strength against impact.

Acrylic material comes in a wide range of thicknesses, and is much more impact resistant than ordinary window glass (17 times more resistant in one-eighth-to-one-fourth-inch sheets). Also, acrylic does shatter and will burn of itself, although it will withstand a wide range of climate extremes for many years without deterioration.

Polycarbonate material, like acrylic, weighs 50 percent less than glass of equal thickness. However, polycarbonate has 300 times the impact resistance of glass and 20 to 30 times the impact strength of acrylic. It is less clear and also somewhat less weather resistant than glass or acrylic, but still can provide service for a period of years, and will not burn of itself nor shatter.

The cost of either acrylic or polycarbonate is about four times that of glass. However, in a situation where frequent glass breakage (due to vandalism or other factors) occurs, plastic glazing material can pay for its additional cost. For intrusion resistance purposes, polycarbonate is superior to acrylic. Properly installed polycarbonate glazing provides approximately the same degree of window security as do bars and grills (providing that adequate locking devices are used on the windows). However, proper installation is quite important with either plastic because, unlike glass, it is subject to significant shrinkage and expansion because of temperature and humidity. Also, polycarbonate has a significant degree of flexibility, such that a determined attacker may be able to force it out of the containing frame. A deeper frame is therefore needed for polycarbonate.

Other Access Openings

Permanently installed (or hinged and lockable) bars or expanded metal grill work can be used to secure such building access points as ventilation ducts, utility tunnels, skylights, and other small openings which are required for the passage of wires, pipes, air or light. Other specialized building surface openings include very large vehicular openings for garages and commercial and industrial structures. Unusually large openings such as this can be secured following the same general principles discussed above for door systems but may require very specialized kinds of hardware and materials because of their size, shape, or method of operation.

Internal Barriers

Within the structure itself, a variety of barrier arrangements may be set up to protect specific targets of possible criminal attack. Internal barriers must not only provide specific security against intruders for high-value target items, they must also provide security against possible criminal activities by those who may have legitimate reason to be inside the structure (for example, visitors, customers, clients or patients, employees, and the general public). Perimeter barrier systems and building surface barrier systems are of no value whatever in preventing attack by persons who are entitled to enter—and remain inside—the facility.

Internal barriers generally serve to control movement and limit access in such a way as to reduce the likelihood for criminal attack to an acceptable level, while not interfering with normal activity within the building. They consist of both low-security structures such as interior walls, privacy doors, display cases, counter, racks of merchandise, light steel mesh screening, glazing materials, even ropes and chains, and high-security structures such as safes and vaults.

Low-Security Barriers

To illustrate the concept and use of low-security barriers, let us consider a few simple examples.

The supermarket operation makes a wide variety of merchandise readily available to customers and protects itself against theft by customers by channelling their movements. The arrangement of merchandise racks, checkout counters and entry and exit points in a supermarket is a kind of a maze in which the customer usually has only one way to gain access to the merchandise and only one way to leave the store (the checkout counters). While some opportunity for shoplifting remains in this kind of system, the fact that a customer must leave through a checkout counter lane means that any merchandise other than small items which the customer may be able to conceal will be tallied by the cashier. Doors and walls will normally prevent the customer from entering stock rooms, meat cutting rooms and the like, as well as the area where cash is counted and kept. Thus, customers enjoy easy access to the merchandise, but their opportunity for unauthorized removal of merchandise is restricted.

Discount stores operate on much the same principal as the supermarket but must take additional measures because much of the high-value merchandise consists of small items which are relatively easy to conceal. Additional barriers are often used to help protect particular kinds of high-value merchandise, such as cameras, small electronic items, firearms and jewelry, which are often sold from a small island within the store.

A good example of barriers used to restrict employees can be seen in the parts department of any large automobile repair shop. Here, counters, doors, walls, steel mesh screening and other physical barriers are used to restrict employee and customer access to the parts stockroom. Under normal conditions, the only way to obtain a part is to request it from the stockroom clerk.

Simple barriers are ordinarily used in any kind of warehouse operation to prevent customers from unauthorized access to the main storage area. Within the main storage area, special rooms, or simply wire mesh cages may be used to provide barriers against easy employee access to high-value goods.

Even though a relationship of trust presumably exists between the residents of a home and visitors and guests in the home, few people would think of leaving small high-value items such as cash, jewelry, cameras, guns, and so on lying around within easy reach. Instead, guns may be kept in a gun cabinet. Cameras are kept in a closet, in a cabinet, or in a drawer. Cash is kept out of sight, even if the barrier is nothing more than the traditional sugar bowl in a kitchen cabinet. Important family papers, cash and other small items may even be kept in a small locked cabinet or file drawer. Closed doors are used to signal areas of the house where the visitor is expected not to enter without permission.

It should be emphasized that low-security measures such as those described above are of very little value against determined attack but may be quite effective as barriers against impulsive and opportunistic attack. Their effectiveness can be enhanced by a total system of human and electronic surveillance, intrusion detection, and procedural security.

High-Security Barriers

Although high-security barriers will also serve the purpose of opportunity reduction, their primary intent is to defeat the determined attack against high-value targets, whether carried out by an unauthorized intruder or carried out by someone who has legitimate access to the premises. They include safes, vaults, money chests, strong rooms and so forth.

Robbery-Resistive Barriers

Many safes and money chests are primarily designed to protect high-value items where a custodian is present and there is no substantial physical attack. The essence of the theft or robbery types of attack is surprise and swiftness, and the attacker usually has no time to make a determined forced entry. Robbery-resistive containers need only be sturdy enough to prevent a quick prying or hammering attack and need to be heavy enough or attached so securely that they cannot be easily carried off. The under-the-counter money box, for example, however sturdy, is not robbery resistive. A money depository or steel safe which is anchored in concrete is robbery resistive.

Burglary-Resistive Barriers

Burglary resistant containers (such as safes and vaults) are designed to resist attacks by torches, tools, or explosives at some level of intensity for some period of time. They are usually made of very heavy steel, reinforced concrete or a combination of these materials and are used where a determined intruder might have a considerable period of time for a tool-aided attack.

Fire-Resistive Barriers

Fire protection is mentioned here because attack-resistive construction and fire-resistive construction are not necessarily the same thing. For example, a burglary-resistant cash safe made of very thick steel will probably not be fire-resistive, because heat is readily transferred through the steel, and the contents of the safe might be destroyed even though the safe remained intact. On the other hand, a fire-resistive safe is constructed primarily of insulating materials and is vulnerable to a tool-aided attack. One solution to this problem is to use two different types of containers; fire-resistive record containers, and a safe for valuable property items. Perhaps the best solution of all is to install a large fire-resistive container and to place within it a smaller burglary-resistive container. Also, U-L rated fire doors and fire walls can be formidable barriers.

Building Security Codes

Unfortunately, good security design has not been a high priority for those who design and construct buildings in this country. A new trend is beginning to emerge, however, as crime prevention practitioners and building officials around the country turn their attention to the development of building security codes.

The intent of building codes in general is to provide for public control over the construction, use and occupancy of buildings in such a way that reasonable standards for fire safety, life safety and occupational safety (among other things) can be enforced by government.

The addition of security components to local building codes has been seen by crime prevention practitioners as a way to set in motion an excellent opportunity-reduction process for the future. However, there are some key cautions which must be observed if the development of building security codes is to be productive:

- Security code standards should be based on performance specifications; that is, the required ability of a physical system to withstand attack.
- Standards should be uniform from one community to another, so that builders, architects and the manufacturers of security hardware and materials can themselves build, design and provide standard products.

The International Conference of Building Officials (ICBO), Building Officials and Code Administrators (BOCA) and Southern Building Code (SBC) have developed model security codes which states and communities can adapt to their own unique circumstances. These model codes are based on performance specifications and have the capability, if adopted widely, of providing the needed national uniformity. Other national, regional and state code development organizations are working along the same lines.

All crime prevention practitioners should be concerned with the development of building security codes for their communities, but no practitioner should attempt to develop a local code until he has first obtained the results of appropriate uniform code development efforts at the state, regional and national levels and determined their applicability to his jurisdiction.[1]

ELECTRONIC SECURITY SYSTEMS

As has been repeatedly pointed out, there is no barrier that cannot be defeated. And many of the barrier systems typically used to protect person and property are rather easily defeated, given some degree of determination, skill, and unobserved time on the part of the attacker. Physical barriers may be an effective deterrent but, more importantly, should always serve to delay the attacker until some response can occur.

The function of surveillance and intrusion detection systems is to provide some means for observing or detecting the criminal attacker during the delay period so that appropriate action may be taken against him. The action taken can be anything from arresting the attacker to taking his picture with a camera.

Surveillance and intrusion detection systems produce two important effects. On the one hand, they can be instrumental in the apprehension of criminals. On the other, they can provide a strong deterrent. If the criminal is aware that he will be observed and detected during the attack and believes that this will lead to a high possibility for identification or arrest, he may feel that the risk is too high and decide not to attack, unless he also feels that he can carry out the attack before a response occurs.

All barrier systems are passive in the sense that whatever their capacity to deter or delay an intruder, they cease to be effective as security systems once they are breached.

Surveillance and intrusion detection systems, where properly designed and appropriate, can provide a much greater degree of security than that permitted by the barrier systems themselves. But, the physical barrier system and the surveillance and intrusion detection system (including the response component) must be designed in harmony if the total security system is to have a deterrent effect.

Because of the need for great care in the design and installation of electronic security systems, clients should deal only with well-established electronic security companies which have good records of successful installations.

Electronic security systems consist of:

- Surveillance systems and
- Intrusion detection systems.

Surveillance Systems

The purpose of surveillance systems is to provide a direct visual means of observing possible criminal activities within a defined space. There are really only two ways to accomplish this: with a human observer or a film or television camera.

The Human Observer

The use of watchmen, lookouts, and guards is as old as humanity. As applied to the surveillance of a defined area, there are three types of human observation:

- Social observation;
- Patrol observation; and
- Location specific observation.

Social Observation

The simple presence of people (driving, shopping, walking, looking out their windows, etc.) can have a strong deterrent effect. In the presence of social observation, the opportunistic criminal may be discouraged, and the determined attacker must at least disguise his behavior and conduct his attack and escape so quickly that no one has time to act, intimidate the observers, or determine that they are not interested in reporting him. However, social observation cannot be considered a reliable surveillance tactic, since rarely are people present in a given target area all the time. Furthermore, the likelihood that such observation will be reported is affected by many factors which are not under the control of the person needing surveillance.

Patrol Observation

A variety of patrol strategies are used by police and private security personnel to create some probability of observing criminal activities while they are in progress. There has been considerable debate as to whether patrol strategies have any degree of preventive value, but it does seem clear that specialized patrol tactics may help – neighborhood citizen patrols, tenant patrols in housing projects, and tactical police patrols placed according to the results of crime pattern analysis, for example.

Location-Specific Surveillance

It is possible to hire private security personnel who are trained not only to systematically observe key aspects of a physical security system but also to report, or even to take action, in the event of intrusion. However, use of on-site observers is expensive, even if only done under short-term conditions (for example, the police stakeout). Furthermore, if the area of interest is at all complex, many people may be required to perform surveillance adequately.

Surveillance Cameras

The use of film cameras and television cameras for surveillance purposes is superior to any form of direct human observation in at least three important respects: cost, reliability, and documentation. Although a camera, its associated equipment, annual maintenance and film might cost several thousand dollars a year, it can provide full-time coverage of a given field of view at a very small fraction of the cost of providing the same coverage using human observers. Also, a camera, providing that it remains in working order, is not subject to the kinds of observer error that the human being is. Given sufficient light and quality design, a camera will faithfully record the field of view in the same objective way day in and day out. Finally, film or video tape documentation can be used to create a permanent record of any activity that goes on within the camera's field of view. Such records can be extremely useful in accurate identification of suspects, providing evidence for prosecution, and in verifying the true nature of any activities that went on within the field of view. These are enormous advantages in a total security system.

Film Cameras

Still or motion picture film cameras are only intended to provide a record of events that take place within their field of view. They can be operated either sequentially or by demand. A sequence camera is programmed to expose film at some pre-set rate. A demand-operated camera is activated by a person who wishes to record a particular event, or by an intrusion detection device. For example, a cashier might punch a concealed activating button during a holdup. A very high risk is associated with any situation in which an attacker knows he will be photographed. His only real recourse in such a situation is to disable the camera, destroy the film, prevent the camera from being activated, or screen himself from it. If he can do none of these things, the chances of his deciding to attack are fairly small. As Thad Webber points out[2] . . . *after camera systems were installed at all Chase Manhattan Bank Branches . . . holdup attacks—both professional and amateur—dropped to nearly zero*. In this case, the surveillance cameras, triggered by holdup alarms, were added to the existing security systems because analysis revealed that the holdup alarm systems then in use . . . *seldom brought police in time to apprehend bank robbers and prevent losses*. The effect of the surveillance cameras was to eliminate the delay time between alarm signal and response to that signal. As another example, camera systems are often used by stores to simultaneously photograph checks and their makers, thus helping to reduce check fraud.

It should not be thought that such devices are infallible. However, any measures to defeat the camera add difficulty to the task of completing the attack, and may require extraordinary planning on the part of the criminal. Experience has shown that as long as there are less formidable targets available, criminals will shy away from premises protected by film cameras.

Television Cameras

The television camera can be used in the same way as a film camera through videotape recording. There are advantages and disadvantages. For example, videotape pictures may not be as sharp as film images, but the image recovery is instantaneous, and this can be of great benefit in rapid criminal investigation and apprehension. In addition, equipment and maintenance costs are likely to be significantly higher than for an equivalent degree of film coverage, but the supply costs are less, because tapes can be used over and over again.

The primary advantage of the television camera is that it permits monitoring from a single site of activities at several sites. For example, the discount store manager can watch many different parts of the store from his office, and shoppers (and shoplifters) can even watch themselves via remote monitors. There are many possible applications of remote monitoring, but the key feature is human surveillance by indirect means. The person monitoring a direct observation system may use a video tape recorder to permanently record any desired activity, but the main purpose of the surveillance is to provide immediate response to any suspicious activity observed. Thus, remote television monitoring is a cost-effective way to replace on-site human observers.

Lighting

One application of lighting to surveillance is simply the need to provide sufficient lighting to permit photography. Here, the challenge is to design the camera systems and the lighting systems so that they complement each other.

A far broader application of lighting to surveillance is to enhance the effectiveness of the human observer.

Street Lighting

When streets and other areas used by pedestrians are well lighted, criminals are more easily seen and identified. Knowing this, potential attackers may hesitate to commit their crimes in well lighted areas. Adequate street lighting also encourages honest citizens to move about without fear, thus decreasing the possibility of attack to the extent that social surveillance permits.

There are several reasons why street lighting as currently installed may not be appropriate to the specific purpose of crime prevention. Often, street lights are placed so as to illuminate the roadway itself, without casting much light on sidewalks, yards, building surfaces, etc. Thus, it may be difficult to observe suspicious activities on either side of the roadway, and pedestrian traffic may be reduced. Lighting in residential areas may be designed primarily to promote the appearance of the neighborhood and the convenience of individual residents. For example, street lighting may, in historic areas, simulate old fashioned gas lights—a practice which undoubtedly makes the area more attractive, but provides relatively little illumination. Or, subdivision lighting may be non-uniform. In one case, controversy among residents—some of whom wanted street lighting and some of whom did not—resulted in a decision by the traffic department to place lights adjacent to those homes that desired street lighting, and to place no lights near those homes that did not desire lighting. Such design creates a situation in which surveillance is spotty at best, and people are discouraged from walking on the sidewalks at night.

Existing lighting, however placed, may simply be insufficient for proper visibility. Illumination for the purposes of reducing crime and the fear of crime may therefore require substantial redesign of existing street lighting systems and installation of new lights. The high cost of re-lighting programs makes it necessary to carefully examine the question of whether more lighting leads to less crime before proceeding with new installations.

People are definitely more fearful of crime during the dark hours than they are in the daylight.[3] But, are increased levels of fear during the nightime hours justified? Or does darkness simply bring on unreasonable fear? A study conducted in Minneapolis showed that the citywide rate of street robbery for a recent year was 33 percent higher during the dark hours than in daylight. Specifically, 70 percent of all assaults occurred at night, as did 66 percent of thefts from automobiles, 61 percent of automobile thefts, and 73 percent of rapes. In selected neighborhoods, 78 percent of all street assaults and 92 percent of reported rapes occurred during darkness.[4]

Re-lighting programs have been implemented in many cities in hopes of reducing crimes associated with darkness. Studies of these programs have not produced conclusive evidence that street lighting alone resulted in reduced crime rates. The reason seems to be that many other factors can influence crime rates.

For example, increases in police patrol activities may have accompanied the re-lighting. Other types of crime prevention programs may have been conducted simultaneously. And, the re-lighting program may have simply helped displace criminal activity to other areas, resulting in no net decrease of crime in the community as a whole. Or, lighting may induce complacency in people to the degree that other kinds of security measures may be reduced, and as a result there may even be a net increase in crime.

On the other hand, there is wide agreement that appropriate lighting is an important ingredient in reducing criminal opportunity. As a general rule however, re-lighting programs which are specifically intended to reduce crime should probably be restricted to areas where a major portion of crime does occur at night or where crime fear levels are high (whether justified or not). In any case, lighting should be installed as part of a comprehensive crime prevention program to realize maximum benefits from this costly investment.

Currently, there are six light sources which can be used in street lighting programs: incandescent lamps, fluorescent lamps, mercury vapor lamps, low-pressure sodium vapor lamps, high-pressure sodium vapor lamps and metal halide lamps. Generally speaking, incandescent light sources are uneconomical and inefficient compared to others. For example, a given quantity of electrical energy can produce up to 20 times more total light in a low-pressure sodium vapor lamp than in an incandescent lamp, and vapor discharge lamps can last up to 30 times as long as an incandescent lamp.

Providing uniform light requires attention to such things as the height of the luminaire (the lamp and its refractor and reflector), its particular directional light-emitting characteristics, the spacing of luminaires, the presence or absence of structures and vegetation which can shade vital areas, the reflecting capability of the surface material, other lighting which may be available, and other factors. Also, minimum lighting standards vary widely depending on the setting. For example, the amount of light per square foot usually suggested for a commercial area is 20 times that suggested for a residential alley.

In summary, the advantages of darkness to the criminal include the following:

- It is less likely that police patrols, neighbors or passersby will observe criminal activity;
- Darkness and shadows provide good cover for watching a target and for escape;
- Fear of being on the streets at night minimizes the number of potential witnesses;
- Darkness increases the ease with which a criminal can use surprise to gain control of his victim.

To remove the advantages of darkness to the criminal, the following questions need to be answered:

- Where should scarce lighting resources be allocated?
- How much light is needed?
- What is the best way to provide light?
- What is the cost to provide adequate lighting?
- What impact would increased lighting have on energy conservation?
- How can crime prevention lighting be funded?

Lighting can be a significant aid in surveillance and thus has an important role in crime prevention. However, it must be applied properly if it is to be effective (particularly if cost is a key factor), and it should not be viewed as a crime prevention strategy which is appropriate for all crime at all times and all places. Lighting programs should always be used in conjunction with other crime prevention strategies, and with general community improvement strategies.

Exterior Lighting for Specific Facilities

Street lighting itself, while very helpful, may not provide a sufficient surveillance capability for individual facilities. For example, at least two sides of every structure are usually shielded from street lighting. The presence of fences, surrounding buildings, irregularities in the building wall design, shrubbery, parked vehicles, and numerous other kinds of obstructions can also negate the surveillance value of street lighting. Thus, premises security lighting is a very important component in specific security system design. It can be used either in a diffused way (flood lighting) or with a specific focus (spot lighting) as appropriate to the circumstances.

Any area adjacent to a building which remains dark and obscure at night is a potential candidate for security lighting. Special consideration should be given to doors, windows and other access points, and to any area which provides a good place of concealment, whether or not adjacent to an access point.

With respect to an individual structure, a distinction needs to be made between surveillance lighting which is designed to improve surveillance from the inside-out, and that which improves visibility from the outside-in. For example, one can install flood lights on the side of a building which permit anyone inside to see the exterior area very well at night. However, those same flood lights could effectively blind a policeman or other person on the outside who wishes to see what may be going on at or near the building wall. The issue here, like the issue in the broader category of street lighting, is that building security lighting should always result from proper planning and design. Improperly designed and installed lighting may not only be ineffective, it may even create additional security problems.

Intrusion Detection Systems

Intrusion detection systems are an extension of the surveillance concept. Such systems permit activities in a given area to be detected and reported in absence of any direct form of human observation. They also permit the indirect monitoring to be conducted by exception; that is, the constant monitoring needed in direct observation is replaced by an alerting system which only demands attention when an undesirable act has occurred.

Intrusion detection systems consist of three basic components: the sensor, the control, and the annunciator. NCPI uses the goose to illustrate these three functions. (Animals have long served man's need for intrusion detection systems; the goose, in particular, was the living intrusion detection "system" of choice in many societies.)

As Figure 5-11 shows, the sensor component is like the goose's eye. Its function is to detect some condition or event. A sensor has no way to determine whether the sensed event is authorized or not, merely that it has occurred.

The control, like the goose's brain, nervous system, and circulatory system, provides the power for the intrusion detection system, receives information from sensors, evaluates that information and transmits commands for action. For example, the goose's eye may see someone approaching and transmit that information to the brain. However, the brain decides that the approaching person is his owner and takes no further action except perhaps to waddle toward the person in search of food. On the other hand, if the approaching person is interpreted as a stranger by the brain, instructions for action will go to the squawking system rather than the walking system. The annunciator is that part of the intrusion

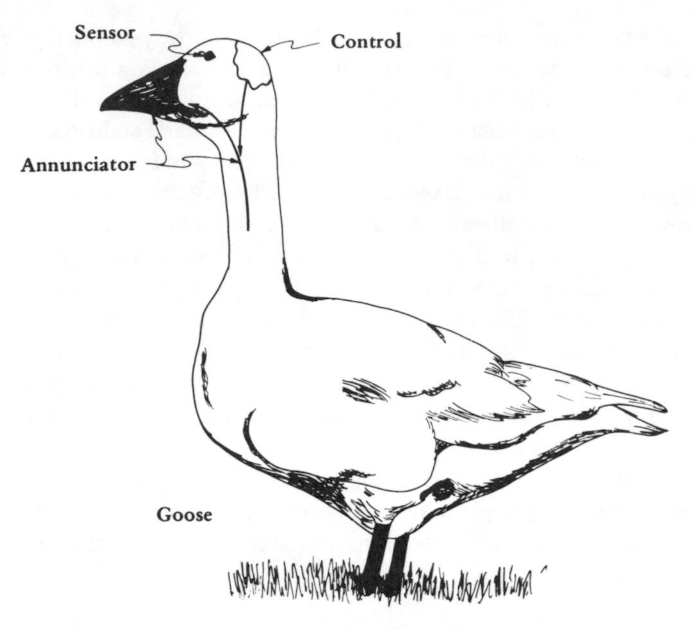

Figure 5-11. Nature's intrusion detection system.

detection system which alerts someone to the fact that a sensor has detected an event. The squawk of the goose alerts the farmer that someone or something is on the premises.

The fundamental purpose of the intrusion detection system is to generate an appropriate response to events which the system senses, evaluates, and reports. Without the response, the intrusion detection system is of no value. Figure 5-12 shows the flow of information in a total intrusion detection system. The completeness and balance of this information cycle should be the basis for evaluating the effectiveness of all intrusion detection systems. It is easy to see from this diagram that an interruption in the flow of information through the system at any point will render it useless. Thus, the security of the intrusion detection system itself is just as vital as the security of the target protected. If the intrusion detection system can be defeated, it is of no use whatever.

Sensors (See Figure 5-13)

Sensor devices can be grouped roughly by analogy to the human senses of touch, taste or smell, hearing, and sight.

"Touch" Sensors

"Touch" sensors include electromechanical (and a few electronic) devices that respond to movement (for example, a magnetic or plunger contact which senses the opening and closing of a door or window), applied pressure (for example, a

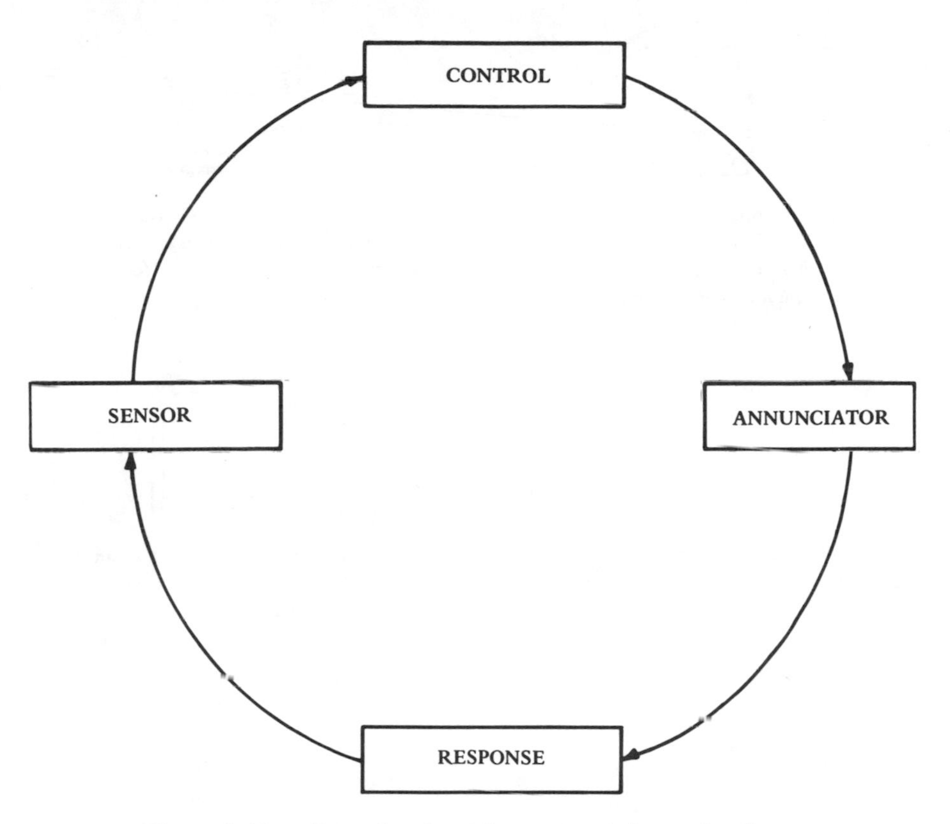

Figure 5-12. Intrusion detection system information flow.

pressure mat inside a door which is activated when someone steps on it), and heat (a thermocouple on the inside wall of a safe which senses the heat of a torch). There are also sensors which respond to a breaking action (for example, thin magnetic foil on window glass which is easily torn if the window is broken) and sensors which detect vibrations (for example, sensors mounted on a wall which can be activated by the impact of a sledgehammer on the wall).

"Taste/Smell" Sensors

"Taste/smell" sensors detect changes in the chemical makeup of the air and are widely used in fire alarm systems, as well as to detect burning attacks against safes and other hardened targets.

"Hearing" Sensors

"Hearing" sensors detect changes in airborne sound. Ultrasonic devices, for example, transmit sound waves throughout an area and detect the pattern reflected back. Such a sensor might be "tuned" to remain inactive as long as it receives only

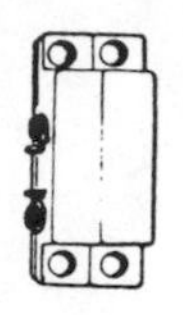

Magnetic contacts are attached to doors, windows, etc. so that when the door is opened the contacts are separated.

Pressure mats are usually placed under carpets and react to pressure from footsteps.

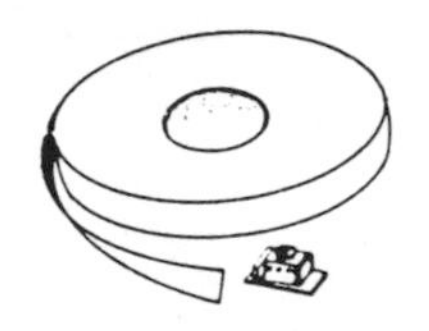

Foil is attached to glass or other surfaces and breaks when the surface is broken.

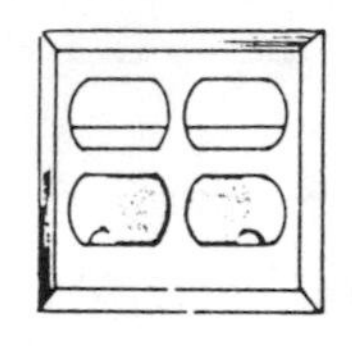

Photoelectric beams cast an invisible infrared light beam across doorways, etc. and react when the beam is interrupted.

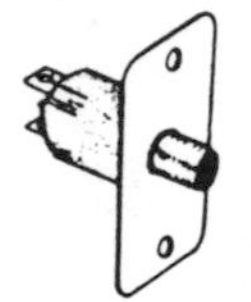

Plunger contacts operate in the same way as the light switch on a refrigerator door.

Motion detectors transmit and receive patterns of ultrasonic or microwave radiation. The pattern is changed when a person enters it, causing the detector to react.

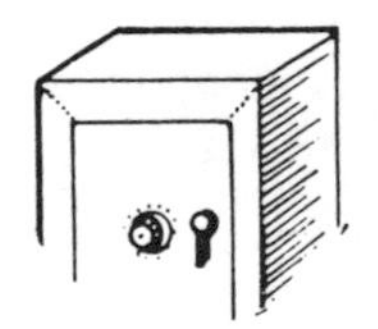

Electric and Magnetic field devices create stable fields close to specific targets such as safes and react when a person or object enters the field.

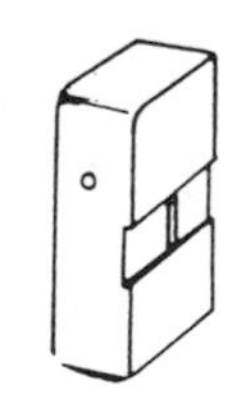

Vibration detectors are attached to surfaces and react to vibrations created by attempts to break through the surface.

Figure 5-13. Typical sensors.

reflected sound waves for the normal pattern of walls and objects within the room. However, should someone enter the room, the reflection pattern will change, causing the sensor to be activated. Also included in this category are devices which only receive sound. For example, a microphone can be set up to detect sounds made within a given space.

Sight Sensors

"*Sight*" sensors are activated by electromagnetic radiation. Photoelectric sensors detect changes in light patterns (for example, when a beam of light across a doorway is interrupted by a person walking through the door, a photoelectric sensor will be activated). Microwave sensors function like the ultrasonic detectors described above except that microwave radiation, rather than ultrasonic radiation, is transmitted and received. Electric field, magnetic field, and thermal energy sensing devices detect changes in energy fields which occur when a person enters a protected space, an object is moved, and so on (for example, such devices can be used to establish low-level electric fields in the immediate vicinity of safes and are activated by the slight change in the field which occurs when a human body approaches or touches the safe).

Sensor Application (See Figure 5–14)

In general, there are four ways in which sensors are applied. These are:

- Point protection;
- Trap protection;
- Space protection; and
- Perimeter protection.

Point Protection

Point protection sensor devices are used to protect specific high-value targets such as money, jewelry or guns. Such sensors can detect movement of the target itself or a human body approaching or touching the target, as well as heat or vibration caused by efforts to penetrate a hardened container.

Trap Protection

Trap protection is a special application of any sensor device in a manner or location that would not normally be expected by an intruder (for example, a pressure mat under a rug).

Space Protection

Space protection sensing devices detect the presence of an intruder in an enclosed space. The ultrasonic and microwave sensors described above are good examples of this type of application.

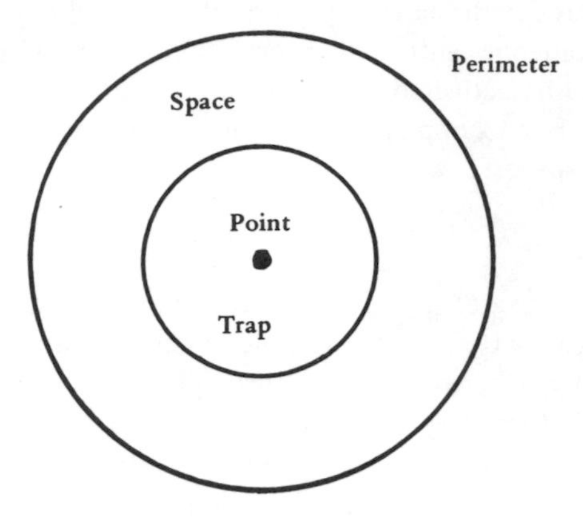

Figure 5-14. Sensor applications.

Perimeter Protection

Perimeter protection devices are used in conjunction with the perimeter barrier or boundary marker systems that enclose the secured premises. For example, magnetic contacts detect the movement of doors, windows, and gates; vibration sensors and thin wire grids detect attempts to break through walls; metallic foil senses the breaking of a window; and vibration sensors, noise detectors and electric field sensors detect attempts to climb or break through a fence.

The choice and location of sensors requires careful thought because inappropriate design can create substantial inconvenience in the conduct of routine activities and create loopholes in the security system. Thad Webber describes a situation in which a hasty decision was made to use ultrasonic sensors to protect the inside of a large warehouse. Plans for the installation of detectors were made before merchandise was moved into the warehouse and before office walls were erected. The piled merchandise and the walls obstructed the functioning of the ultrasonic sensors such that an intruder could penetrate many parts of the building without risk of detection.

Control

The control portion of the intrusion detection system nearly always contains the following components:

- **Power sources** provide the energy to operate intrusion detection systems through primary (non-rechargeable) batteries, public utility electricity, or secondary (rechargeable) batteries. The most reliable source is a combination of public utility and secondary batteries.
- **Protective circuits** provide the means of conveying information from all sensors in the system to the common control point via wire, radio waves, existing

electrical circuits, or combinations. This component is like the network of nerves that run from the human senses to the human brain. The protective circuit can be one of the more vulnerable elements in an intrusion detection system.

- **Energizing techniques** provide the means for testing the system, and for programming the system to report the activation of sensory devices. For example, many of the sensors in a commercial building are shut off during the business day. They are tested and energized at the time of closing by key-operated control switches, time delays, and remote signals. A major problem associated with this component is the potential for false alarms which may be created through improper design, installation or use of the energizing component.
- **Signal transmission** permits information from the sensor and protective circuits to be processed, coded, and transmitted. It may include combinations of relays, switches, telephone dialers, special transmitters, multiplexing equipment, and other signaling devices. The purpose of this component is to provide a signal which is secure from tampering and will transmit the correct information through the annunciator to the human respondent.
- **Annunciation circuitry** conveys information from the control to the annunciator through wire, telephone lines, radio waves, line carriers, coaxial cable and other methods.

Annunciation

The annunciation component must provide for reception of signals from the control device and the initiation of an appropriate response. Since the receiving device is essentially controlled by the control component, the design of the annunciation component is largely concerned with its ability to initiate response. There are four common kinds of annunciation: the local alarm, the proprietary alarm, the central station alarm, and the police department alarm.

- **Local alarms** consist of annunciators such as bells, sirens, and flashing lights and are used either inside or outside the secured building to scare off an intruder and to alert responsible people in the vicinity. Local alarms are relatively inexpensive and may be sufficient in some cases. But, there may not be people in the vicinity to be alerted and, if alerted, may not respond appropriately.
- **Proprietary alarms** annunciate at a remote monitoring station maintained by the owner of the protected structure. This type of annunciation is quite adaptable to large institutions such as universities, medical centers, apartment complexes and public housing projects. The guard force which monitors the annunciation devices and responds to alarms would normally have access to the interior of all structures and be knowledgeable as to the layout of those structures.
- **Central station alarm service** is provided by alarm monitoring companies which offer services to individual subscribers. Subscribers, who might be store owners, office building managers, home owners, plant supervisors and so on pay the central station company to accept and install annunciation devices connected

with their facilities. The central station can notify police, guard forces, the subscriber, insurance agents and others if it receives an alarm signal. The central station company can also maintain records of openings and closings, provide respondents with key access to the building from which the alarm came, and other services.

- **Police department alarm service** is provided directly within the police station where police can be dispatched immediately in response to alarm signals. Service available under this arrangement is limited to the police response itself, and other arrangements must be made to provide access into the facility for investigation and to check the intrusion detection system. Because of the rapid increase in the number of alarm subscribers, police departments are becoming reluctant to provide this service unless a town is too small to support a commercial central alarm operation.
- **Other types of alarms** may be located almost anywhere—at a telephone answering service or the homes or businesses of trusted friends.

The selection of annunciator type and location depends largely on the type of response needed or desired in the event of an alarm. As cost is also a significant factor, one should usually aim to select the annunciator location which provides the lowest feasible cost consistent with the security needs of a subscriber.

Response

The type of response that an alarm generates is also an important part of the intrusion detection system. Unless the response is appropriate to the circumstances at hand, the investment in an intrusion detection system will not be cost effective.

Criteria in designing the appropriate response capability are as follows:

- The respondent should be armed;
- The time between alarm and arrival of respondent should be as short as possible;
- The respondent should be trained in weapons use, apprehension procedures and alarm system operations;
- The respondent should have a reliable means of access to the premises and a knowledge of its layout and contents; and
- Procedures should be in effect to protect persons (including the respondent) who may be on the premises.

These response services may be provided in a variety of ways and by one or more agencies. For example, a commercial alarm company may receive the alarm and dispatch its own employees. Or, the alarm company may simply report to the police department, which in turn dispatches patrol, and the owner himself may be notified.

Designing the System

The major considerations in designing an intrusion detection system are as follows:

- Types of targets to be protected;
- Existing barrier systems and security procedures;
- Needed, desired or available speed of response and degree of skill or training required or available from respondent;
- Need for access to keys for entry into premises;
- Familiarity of respondents with the premises themselves;
- Needed levels of security in alarm monitoring facilities;
- Need for records for openings and closings of the premises;
- Desirability and feasibility of using alarms as a psychological deterrent to the criminal;
- Need for safety precautions for innocent bystanders, employees and police; and
- Cost limitations.

With these considerations in mind, the practitioner can analyze the relative merits of local, proprietary, centralized, police or other alarm locations in terms of needed security and cost. He then proceeds to design the sensor system. He works from perimeter sensors to space sensors to trap sensors to point sensors, designing sensor layouts that provide a level of security equivalent to that provided by the annunciation design previously selected. Finally, the practitioner designs the control element, considering power source, protective circuits, energizing techniques, signal transmission and annunciation circuitry. The control system should be designed so as to be compatible with the annunciation component and the sensor component, maintaining the same level of security which has already been designed into the rest of the system.

False Alarms

Alarm effectiveness should be measured in terms of the ability of the system to deter criminals and assist in their apprehension. False alarms can seriously compromise alarm effectiveness and are currently the major problem associated with intrusion detection systems. This problem has two dimensions:

- Quantity of false alarms, if high, can create heavy, unproductive workloads for police and private security respondents; and
- Ratio of false alarms, if high, to total alarms can create respondent apathy, regardless of the quantity.

The major cause of false alarms is subscriber error. Other causes include equipment failure, improper installation and telephone line problems.

The primary response to false alarm problems should be coordinated efforts aimed at:

- Reducing false alarms due to subscriber error, substandard equipment and improper installation;
- Controlling the use and application of alarm systems which affect the police communications center;

- Eliminating questionable alarm dealers;
- Providing feedback on alarm effectiveness to alarm system dealers and users and crime prevention practitioners;
- Encouraging the use of reliable systems designed according to sound principles of crime risk management.

Effective coalitions of crime prevention practitioners and reputable alarm companies have resolved false alarm problems without legislation. Where a need for legislation became apparent, such coalitions have stimulated effective laws and ordinances. When law enforcement agencies have caused laws and ordinances to be passed in absence of coalitions, the results have been to reduce the effective use of alarms as crime prevention tools.

SECURITY PROCEDURES

Although there is a wide tendency to regard physical security barriers and electronic security devices as the most important elements in a security program, the fact is that procedural security is the most important single element in a good crime risk management system. We can generally categorize security procedures as follows:

- Personal safety;
- Asset control; and
- Security system protection.

Personal Safety

The first concern of the crime prevention practitioner should be to protect the client and those for whom he is responsible from bodily harm, psychological intimidation and fear.

General Life Safety

No part of the security system should create additional hazards for facility occupants. For example, barrier devices should not interfere with the ability of building occupants to leave quickly in the event of fire or other emergency. Procedural training may be necessary so that family members, employees, customers and others on the premises can quickly defeat the security system if it becomes necessary to escape.

Safety From Intruder Assault

Burglars, robbers and thieves primarily seek to remove cash or property. Nevertheless, many such intruders are capable of harming people with little provocation.

In general, facility occupants should be trained to avoid confrontation with the criminal and, instead, report the incident as soon as consistent with self protection. For a family member, this might mean leaving the house if a burglary is discovered in progress, and going to the nearest telephone to call the police. For a store employee, pressing a silent alarm button, going to a distant phone or alerting security forces or management within the facility might be the approach. In any case, procedures should be developed for such situations and all persons trained in their use.

Should confrontation with the attacker be unavoidable, as in a holdup, personal safety procedures such as the following should be used:

- Take no action that would jeopardize personal safety (Don't attempt to be a hero.);
- Treat displayed firearms as if they were loaded;
- Activate alarms only if possible to do so without detection;
- Attempt to alert others, if possible;
- Follow the robber's directions exactly, but don't volunteer to do anything; and
- If possible without being obvious, study and memorize any features of the attacker which will help identify him.

Specific procedures along these lines should be developed by each client, and all personnel (but particularly those most vulnerable, such as cashiers) trained in their application.

Sexual Assault

Confrontation with a potential rapist is a particular problem for women. The best guidance, of course, is to avoid potentially dangerous situations. This translates into a general set of guidelines:

- Never admit a strange man to the home if alone;
- Lock all doors and windows when alone at home or in the car;
- Keep shades and curtains drawn;
- Leave exterior lights on at night;
- Walk with others, not alone;
- Never hitchhike or accept a ride from a stranger;
- Stay away from dark places;
- Be careful in choice of social companions;
- Never go alone into dark or isolated areas in a place of work; and
- When in doubt, always avoid—don't be brave.

If the confrontation occurs anyway, the woman may have to choose among a number of alternative tactics—some of which may be effective, and some which may be dangerous. Procedural advice here should be carefully dispensed by the practitioner, who must be mindful both of the person he is advising and the situations to which the advice might apply. The following tactics are presented for illustration only:

- Flight—The woman can try to run away if a place of safety is at hand. Otherwise, flight may merely enrage the attacker.
- Scream for help—A viable alternative if a source of help is available. Shouting "fire" may attract more attention than other types of appeals. Screaming may frighten the attacker away even if it does not attract attention. Or, it may enrage him.
- Behave assertively—A growing school of thought suggests that, in the initial stages of the encounter, the rapist may be testing the victim's potential behavior. If she appears intimidated by his words and approach, he will continue. If she appears calm and unafraid, he may desist.
- Fighting—Physically attacking the assailant can be very dangerous. If the woman is sure that she can immobilize the attacker long enough to escape to safety, a kick to the groin or instep or a blow to the eyes or nose may be effective. If the attempt fails, however, the enraged attacker may hurt the woman badly.
- Use of weapons—Firearms, tear gas and other weapons might be considered, subject to the danger that the attacker may use them against the woman if she is unable to use them effectively herself.
- Manipulation—A variety of manipulative tactics have been suggested, primarily of the seductive type. The theory here is that if the woman pretends to be sexually attracted to her assailant, she may disarm him long enough to escape when he is off-guard. The danger is that if the escape is not made good, the assailant may become enraged by the ruse.
- Submission—If all else fails, the woman may be well advised to submit, on the grounds that she may thereby spare herself harm beyond the sexual assault itself.

Other Assaults

Most of the avoidance and confrontation procedures spelled out above also apply to assault, robbery, mugging, molestation, and other situations which can also involve men, older people, and children.

Asset Control

A wide variety of procedures is available for use in protection of cash and property. The following material is presented primarily with respect to commercial clients, but the principles apply to other settings as well.

Internal Security

The primary source of asset loss due to crime for most business operations is workplace theft (also referred to as internal theft, fraud, embezzlement and shrinkage).

Procedural controls which guide, restrict or force accountability for employee activities can accomplish the objective of reducing this source of asset loss, often at little cost or difficulty. But, **the manager must first realize that he is sustaining, or could sustain, loss due to employee theft.**

The question of management attitude is all-important in the reduction of employee theft. The crime prevention practitioner should be prepared to invest significant effort in gaining the attention of management. In general, this is best done by appealing to the profit motive or other primary objective of the organization.

If we define profit as advances made toward the attainment of established goals, it is then possible to discuss protection of assets for business, government, institutions, religious organizations, charitable organizations, political groups, service clubs and many other forms of activity together.[5]

Once management's attention has been gained, the practitioner can work through a logical series of procedural safeguards.

Perceptual Security

The concept of perceptual security has many applications, but in general aims to increase the **perceived** strength of security in some areas so that management's limited resources can be concentrated in other areas.

Whatever the exact mix of security procedures developed for a given organization, it will be impossible for management to enforce all controls to the same level of rigor. One excellent way to handle this management function is to institute a program of irregular, random audits and spot-checks of all protection of assets procedures. If the spot-check program is truly random in nature, no one can know when to anticipate audit of a given operation. The uncertainty thus created amounts to a psychological control of illegal activity.

Purchasing Procedures

The purchasing office or purchasing agent is in a position to victimize an organization unmercifully unless proper controls are established in the following major areas:

- **Centralize the purchasing function** if at all possible. This makes it much easier to control and may also permit larger purchases at lower unit cost.
- **Control purchase orders** by pre-numbering them in sequence (for better accountability) and ensuring ample distribution of copies (central file, accounts payable, receiving, for example).
- **Separate purchasing, receiving and accounting** to reduce opportunities for fraudulent purchases.
- **Avoid conflict of interest situations** in which key employees hold interests in supplying companies.
- **Require supporting documentation** for each purchase or expense invoice, and cancel such documentation upon receipt by perforating or otherwise defacing it so that it cannot be used again.
- **Use prenumbered checks** so that all expenditures may be tracked in sequence.

Receiving Procedures

The receiving function offers many opportunities for theft of property or embezzlement of money, unless procedures such as the following are established:

- **Secure the area** where all merchandise is received.
- **Count or weigh all material** received and compare the results with the shipping documents before verifying receipt.
- **File claim forms immediately** for damaged merchandise.
- **Use prenumbered receiving control forms** to record units received in any shipment. A copy should be attached to each other document related to the shipment.
- **Control access to receiving area** and prohibit employees from leaving premises through receiving door or parking nearby, and prohibit drivers of delivery vehicles from entering the secure receiving area.
- **Assign two people to verify** each shipment received. Change at least one of them frequently.

Storage Area Procedures

Loosely controlled warehouse, stockroom or other merchandise and supply storage areas offer dishonest employees a fine chance to steal. Such opportunities can be reduced by the following procedures:

- **Secure access to storage area** so that only authorized persons may enter.
- **Arrange stock** in a neat and organized manner.
- **Inventory stock** on hand through perpetual inventory system (first-in, first-out) supplemented with frequent physical audits.
- **Restrict access to separate enclosures** containing high-value items.
- **Employ responsible persons** to supervise the storage area.
- **Maintain records** of stock in-and-out movements.

Shipping Procedures

The authorization of merchandise shipment and delivery and the actual shipping process are key risk areas. The following procedures can reduce criminal opportunity:

- **Maintain good documentation** from the first moment shipping is authorized. Itemized invoices permit both control of stock and proper billing.
- **Separate selecting and packing functions.** Use of one employee to assemble an order and another to check and pack it helps minimize both errors and theft opportunities.
- **Use factory-sealed cartons**, when possible.
- **Check merchandise as it is loaded on the truck**, when possible.
- **Protect vehicles and contents from theft in transit.**
- **Control movements and access to cargo** for vehicles in transit.

Cash Control

The procedures by which cash is handled should include the following, at a minimum:

- **Require that the cash register drawer be closed after every transaction.**
- **Provide each customer with a receipt of the transaction.**
- **Conduct surprise cash counts at registers.**
- **Require verification of over-rings and under-rings.**
- **Maintain separate systems for cash-handling and bookkeeping**, as shown in Figure 5-15.

Employee Relations

In addition to the generally beneficial effect of a firm attitude toward employee theft on the part of management and a series of good procedural controls over goods and cash, procedures aimed directly at employees can be useful.

- **Screen new employees** thoroughly, while being mindful of civil rights regulations.
- **Provide surety bonding** for all key employees.

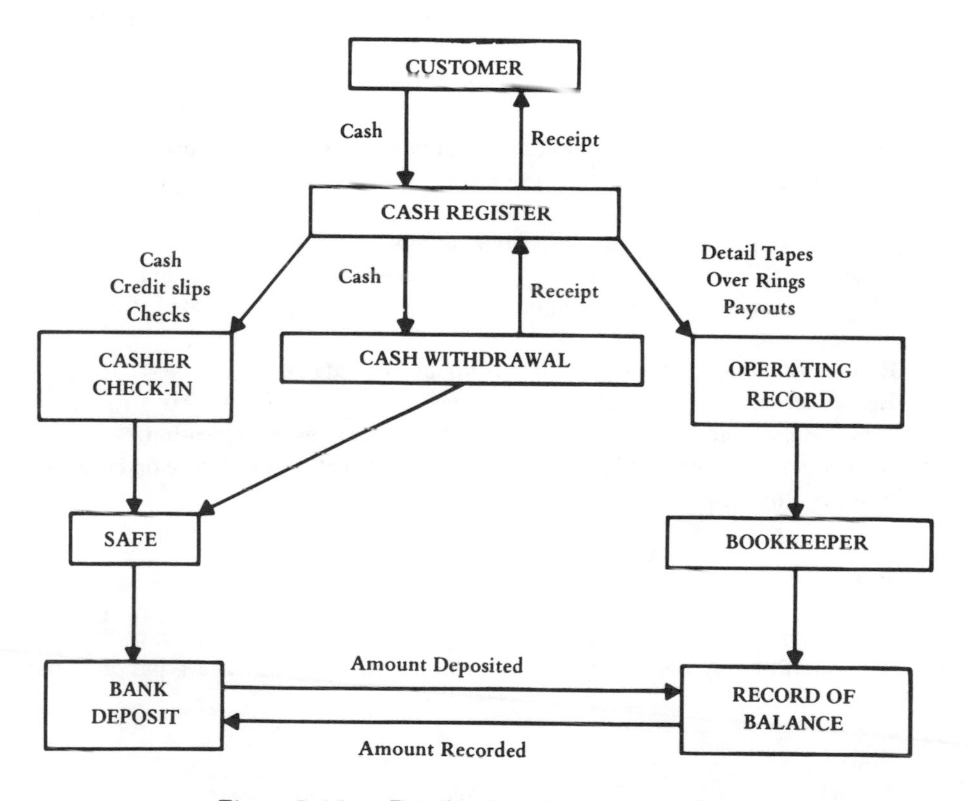

Figure 5-15. Retail cash and cash records flow.

- **Pay all employees by check**, and maintain separation of the check preparation-payment function and the cancelled payroll check reconciliation function.
- **Watch for tell-tale employee behavior**, such as gambling, excessive drinking, signs of family problems and other behavior which may signal increased desire to steal. Be prepared to help the employee take positive corrective action.
- **Encourage employees to report problems and grievances** by being truly concerned for, and responsive to, their needs. Theft-for-spite can be minimized through a "human needs" orientation on the part of management.

Computer Theft or Embezzlement

The increasing use of computer systems to maintain records and conduct financial transactions provide a wealth of opportunity for theft. This specialized field is beyond the scope of this book. The primary concern here is that management be made aware of the tremendous potential for loss inherent in dishonest use of computer systems and the need to obtain expert guidance in securing the computer.

The kinds of computerized programs which can be manipulated by computer-embezzlers include: payroll, accounts payable and receivable, inventory records, cash accounts, customer accounts, scrap and salvage records, and travel and entertainment records.

In general, prevention procedures include the following:

- **Document all changes to computer programs before they are made**, through a central supervisory function.
- **Restrict access to the computer center.**
- **Separate responsibility for computer access** according to sound rules for separation of functions such as paying, receiving, accounting, and payroll. Also, the computer programming function should be separated from the operating function.
- **Require that continuous records be maintained of data use.**
- **Record all errors, restarts and running times.**
- **Maintain duplicate copies of important data files in a separate location.**
- **Simulate a wide variety of possible embezzlement methods and develop countermeasures for each.**

External Security

In this section we shall briefly discuss the major procedural steps used in preventing crimes committed by persons outside the client's organization. The types of crime which we shall deal with are:

- Robbery;
- Fraud; and
- Shoplifting.

Robbery

Robbery is a crime of confrontation and intimidation. Although the target of the robber is cash and valuable property, personal injury or even death can be a by-product of the confrontation.

As was discussed under Personal Safety, procedural prevention of robbery seeks to protect life safety as well as reduce the potential for loss. Accordingly, all members of the client organization should first and foremost be trained in personal safety procedures. In addition, the following procedural steps may be considered:

- **Maintain only minimum cash reserves** in easily accessible places such as cash registers. Deposit cash in bank as often as possible and keep cash to be deposited in robbery-resistive containers.
- **Prominently post notices concerning cash precautions.** For example, "This safe can only be opened by armored car messenger," and "This service station keeps less than $25.00 on hand after 9:00 p.m."
- **Safeguard cash movement** processes by using armored cars to take cash to and from the bank, by hiring an escort service if employees carry the cash withdrawals and deposits, or by using random time schedules for cash deposits.
- **Arrange for maximum possible human surveillance** of key parts of the operation by providing adequate exterior and interior lighting, placing cash register near front windows, and by removing signs or merchandise from doors or windows which obscure visibility into the premise.
- **Instruct all members of the organization** in proper use of holdup alarms and procedures for identifying robbers, reporting to police, transfer of cash to robbery-resistive containers, and other preventive techniques used.

Fraud

The most typical kinds of external fraud are fraudulent checks and fraudulent use of credit cards.

Bad Checks. The main cause for loss from fraudulent checks is the lack of adequate check cashing procedures. Proper preventive procedures should include the following, at a minimum:

- **Train all personnel** involved in check cashing to examine each check carefully for completeness, accuracy and legibility.
- **Limit the amount** of money for which a check will be accepted or cashed.
- **Require corroborating (valid) identification** from the check casher.
- **Establish a central check approval person or station.**
- **Use positive identification techniques** such as microfilm cameras and fingerprinting methods.
- **Verify** addresses, telephone numbers and, when possible, bank accounts.

- **Subscribe to bad check list services** through trade associations, police organizations or Better Business Bureaus.
- **Beware of unusual check features** such as counter checks, post-dating, improper endorsements, apparent erasures or corrections, and differences between numerical and written amounts.

Fraudulent Credit Cards. Criminals enjoy easy access to credit cards bearing the names of other persons. Losses due to this type of fraud can be reduced by use of the following procedures:

- **Maintain current files of cancellation bulletins** from credit card companies. Require that such files be checked each time a credit card is offered in payment.
- **Call the credit card company for authorization** if the signature on the card does not match the signature of the purchases; the card appears mutilated or altered; the purchaser has no other identification; the amount of purchase is above an established limit; or there is any other reason to suspect the authenticity of the card.
- **Train all members of the organization** to follow established credit card procedures without exception.

Shoplifting

Shoplifting is on the increase in many parts of the country, and the primary source of loss may be ordinary customers rather than professional shoplifters. The following procedures can help reduce this type of crime:

- **Learn the characteristics of shoplifters and their typical attack methods.**
- **Train all sales personnel** to greet customers promptly, to observe them as closely as possible, to approach suspected shoplifters-in-progress with a cheerful, "May I help you?" or other non-threatening approaches, and to notify appropriate management personnel if it is believed that a person has already taken merchandise.
- **Display high-value merchandise in such a way that it cannot be easily taken without sales personnel help.**
- **Keep merchandise displays neat and orderly.**
- **Inspect merchandise to be checked out carefully** so that large items cannot be used to conceal smaller ones.
- **Tag all merchandise in such a way that the price cannot be altered or the tag transferred to another item.** Special tags may be used which activate electronic alarms at the door if the tag is not removed by the casher.
- **Be prepared to prosecute apprehended shoplifters and post conspicuous notices to this effect.**
- **Establish clear and legally sound procedures for detaining suspected shoplifters and safeguarding evidence.**

- **Provide each purchaser with a receipt** so that shoplifted items cannot later be exchanged for cash.

Security System Protection

The security system installed in facility is only as good as the procedures used to maintain and activate it. The major areas of procedural concern are:

- Key and lock combination control;
- System activation; and
- System testing and maintenance.

Key and Lock Combination Control

It is essential that keys (and combinations for combination locks) be safeguarded. In general, this requires that keys only be assigned to personnel that absolutely require them; use of master keys be kept to the absolute minimum; keys be changed upon resignation or termination of key-holding employees; combinations be entrusted to the minimum number of people; combinations not be written down and not developed from birthdates or other obvious sources.

System Activation

Clear procedures should be in effect for activating the security system. In general, this requires standard, disciplined opening and closing procedures and procedures for use of security systems which must remain in effect during business hours (for example, closing safes, using locks on interior doors, proper activation of holdup alarms and cameras).

System Testing and Maintenance

A security system is of no use if it is inoperative. Each client should develop and employ fail-safe procedures for ensuring that the security system is operating properly at all times and that standby measures are available to maintain security in the event the system is "down" for repair.

System Response

In the event that intrusion is detected or suspected, procedures should exist which allow response forces to enter the premises to investigate and which permit the system itself to be checked for false signals. In the event that the response finds the system to be inoperative, standby measures should exist to protect the facility until the system can be repaired.

Security Survey Guidelines

In closing this summary of security devices and procedures, we present sample security survey guidelines for the business establishment and the residence. These sample guidelines indicate the range (and approximate order) of items to be considered by the practitioner during the survey.

SAMPLE SECURITY SURVEY GUIDELINES—BUSINESS ESTABLISHMENT

I. **Possible Maximum Loss Through Criminal Attack (Assessment of Targets)**
   A. Personal safety
   B. Cash
   C. Merchandise
   D. Damage factors

II. **Direct Protection of Targets**
   A. Safe
      1. Rating
      2. Anchored
      3. Lighted
      4. Visible from street or mall
   B. Cash Registers
      1. Visible from street or mall
      2. Open at night
      3. Limited cash accumulation
      4. Locked when unattended
      5. Limited access
   C. Merchandise
      1. Controlled storage room
      2. Removed from windows
      3. Controlled displays
      4. Inventory accountability
      5. Identifiable tags or marking system
   D. Deposits
      1. Prepared in protected area
      2. Made daily
      3. Armored service
      4. Made by two or more employees
      5. Varied times and routes

III. **Employee Training**
   A. Shoplifting
   B. Robbery
   C. Checks and credit cards
   D. Internal controls (opening and closing procedures, cash handling, purchasing and receiving, etc.)

IV. **Building Surfaces**
   A. Front, left side, right side, rear
      1. Construction

2. Doors
3. Windows
4. Vents
5. Lighting

B. Roof
1. Doors
2. Skylights
3. Vents and ducts
4. Lighting

C. Floor
1. Construction
2. Cellar
3. Ongrade
4. Post and lift

D. Key control
1. Changes as necessary
2. Accountability

V. **Outside and Perimeter**
A. Trees and shrubs
B. Loading docks
C. Trash storage
D. Roof access
E. Fences and gates
F. Police access

VI. **Surveillance**
A. Lighting
B. Visibility
C. Cameras

VII. **Intrusion Detection**
A. Sensors
B. Control
C. Annunciation
D. Response

Source: Adapted from NCPI training handout.

SAMPLE SECURITY SURVEY GUIDELINES—RESIDENCE

I. **Possible and Probable Maximum Losses Through Criminal Attack (Assessment of Targets)**
A. Personal safety
B. Cash
C. High-value personal possessions
D. Damage factors

II. **Direct Protection of Targets**
A. Cash storage
B. Storage of jewelry, cameras, guns, silver, etc.

III. Family Member Training
- A. Telephone/door answering procedures
- B. Locking responsibilities
- C. Intruder-in-the-house procedures

IV. Building Surfaces
- A. Front, left side, right side, rear
  1. Construction
  2. Doors
  3. Windows
  4. Vents
  5. Lighting
- B. Roof
  1. Construction
  2. Doors
  3. Skylights
  4. Vents and ducts
  5. Lighting
- C. Floor
  1. Construction
  2. Cellar
  3. Ongrade
  4. Post and lift
- D. Key control
  1. Changed since occupancy
  2. Accountability

V. Outside and Perimeter
- A. Trees, shrubs, hedges
- B. Roof-garage-cellar access
- C. Fences and gates
- D. Visibility

VI. Surveillance
- A. Lighting
- B. Visibility

VII. Intrusion Detection
- A. Sensors
- B. Controls
- C. Annunciation
- D. Response

Source: Adapted from NCPI training handout.

CONCLUSION

In this chapter we have covered the range of security devices and procedures and their applications, but have by no means explored their depth. The intent has been to provide knowledge of an overview nature, rather than, in any sense, to provide the practitioners with a "how-to" guide.

We must emphasize that many activities of a risk-spreading nature are likely to be expensive and should only be considered after all possible risk avoidance and risk reduction measures have been taken. By the same token, the practitioner needs much more knowledge of the specifics of security devices and procedures than can be presented in this volume before he or she can make cost-effective recommendations.

6

Applying Environmental Design Concepts

In Chapters 4 and 5, we described the practitioner's role in helping the individual client reduce criminal opportunity within the confines of his own environment.

In this chapter and in the remaining chapters, we discuss the practitioner's roles in helping to reduce criminal opportunity within the community environment. By community environment, we mean those combinations of private spaces (homes, stores, schools, factories, warehouses, etc.) and public spaces (streets, sidewalks, parks, parking lots, etc.) that make up the block, neighborhood, subdivision, shopping center, industrial park, downtown area and other components of the town or city.

Crime prevention is by no means a highly refined technology. Yet, the principles and techniques of designing crime risk management systems for individual clients have gone through a several-decade development and refinement process and, although there is plenty of room for innovation and improvement, the reliability of these techniques and principles is fairly well established.

The application of crime risk management principles to the community environment, however, is new and, in many respects, still highly experimental. This means that, although a considerable body of conceptual knowledge is available to guide the practitioner, he must find innovative and creative ways to apply this conceptual knowledge. Crime prevention in the community environment is thus an exciting and open-ended field of activity in which the practitioner of today is creating the technology of the future.

TRANSITION FROM CLIENT TO COMMUNITY

As he moves from the individual to the community environment, the practitioner continues to be concerned with reducing the risks of personal injury and property loss due to crime, but there is a significant difference in his outlook.

In serving the individual client, he must maintain an essentially private viewpoint. That is, he is only interested in reducing the victimization potential of that client. In serving the community, he must apply a public interest viewpoint. That is, he is interested in reducing the risks of personal injury and property loss due to crime for everyone who occupies or uses the environment, not just those who choose to become his individual clients.

This transition from the client to the community environment is like moving from the tree to the forest. The individual is still important, but the object of the practitioner's efforts is to improve the security of the community as a whole.

In applying crime risk management principles to the community, the practitioner is dealing with crime risks related to the characteristics of the physical, or built environment and crime risks related to the behavior of those who create, use and occupy the physical environment. These two kinds of crime risk overlap to a large extent. For purposes of clarity, however, we discuss the practitioner's roles in influencing physical design and social behavior in two separate chapters. This chapter primarily describes the ways in which the practitioner may apply risk management principles to the physical environment. Chapter 7 describes methods for stimulating appropriate social behavior through citizen participation in community crime prevention programs.

LEVELS OF PHYSICAL DESIGN APPLICATION

There are three levels of crime prevention applications to physical design. The first, Crime Risk Reduction Through Physical Design, is concerned with alterations in the physical environment which can directly affect criminal activities. The second, Crime Risk Reduction by the Users of the Physical Environment, describes the ways in which physical design can be used to stimulate crime prevention behavior by those who use the physical environment. The third, Crime Prevention Through Environmental Design (CPTED), summarizes the current state-of-the-art in a rapidly growing field of study and experimentation which aims for nothing less than the development of comprehensive crime risk management systems (involving both physical design and social action strategies) on a community-wide scale.

CRIME RISK REDUCTION THROUGH PHYSICAL DESIGN

At this level, the practitioner is concerned with physical design techniques which can directly reduce opportunities for criminal activity. The major difference between applying these techniques to the individual client (as described in Chapters

4 and 5) and applying them to the community is that a single individual or group can no longer manage crime risk. Instead, the practitioner must deal with multiple "clients", and this requires that he lay heavy stress on the development of cooperative arrangements with and among individuals, groups and public agencies.

Crime Risk Reduction in the Existing Physical Environment

It would be ideal, we suppose, if the practitioner could conduct a mammoth security survey of each community in his jurisdiction, make appropriate (and interconnected) recommendations to each of the many private owners and public agencies that are responsible for the parts of each community, and then work to ensure compliance with those recommendations. Even in a small jurisdiction, however, such an approach would require an effort of Herculean proportions far beyond the ability of the practitioner and his organization, even if laws and local custom would allow him to take such sweeping action.

Client Groups

As a practical matter, the practitioner can only work directly on a security survey basis with those clients or client groups that request his services. However, he can identify priority communities and priority areas within communities based on his study of crime patterns and attempt to enlist the cooperation of property owners and agencies within those areas.

His approach here is to work with groups of owners toward developing a more secure collective physical environment, and to stimulate and coordinate the efforts of appropriate public agencies toward the same goal. He can, however, operate indirectly on a community-wide scale through groups of observer-reporters.

Observer-Reporters

Each municipality typically contains several occupational and professional groups whose members are in a position to observe physical crime risks in the course of their normal activities. Among such groups are:

- Building inspectors;
- Fire marshalls and other fire service personnel;
- Patrolmen and other law enforcement personnel; and
- Others who regularly visit buildings and public areas in the community.

The practitioner's first task is to enlist the cooperation of such groups and train individual members to observe common kinds of risks in the physical environment such as:

- Inadequate lighting conditions;
- Inadequate physical security provisions in individual structures;

- Places of concealment for attackers such as vacant structures, dense shrubbery, trash accumulations, isolated parking areas, bus stations, public rest rooms, alleys and so on;
- Situations which create potential access difficulties for police; and
- Local situations which present a variety of security risks such as construction sites, transportation depots, parking structures, shopping centers, housing projects, parks and playgrounds.

Once alerted by reports of specific risks, the practitioner may visit the scene of the report to make his own risk assessment. He then can approach the individuals, organizations or agencies responsible, discuss the risks observed, and suggest corrective measures. He may offer to perform comprehensive security surveys and otherwise help to reduce the observed risks. For example, he might offer to contact appropriate municipal agencies for help in reducing risks which are not under the control of the property owner or manager.

The practitioner should be sure to always inform the observer-reporter of the action taken in response to each risk report. This can both reinforce the observer-reporter's personal motivation and provide a convenient opportunity for further training. Not the least of the benefits of this approach is that it can lead to the development of substantial expertise in the observer-reporters. They can, in time, begin to initiate risk-reduction action themselves—thus further extending the practitioner's ability to apply risk management principles to the existing physical environment.

Property Owner Associations and Agencies

In another kind of approach to risk reduction in the existing physical environment, the practitioner can identify and work with organized groups which represent primary land users in the community, such as:

- Homeowners and renters;
- Apartment owners;
- Subdivision developers;
- Construction firms;
- Shopping center managers;
- Parking facility operators;
- Departments of parks and recreation;
- School boards;
- Housing authorities;
- Industrial park operators; and
- Departments of public works.

His objective should be to stimulate and train such groups to perform their own physical risk assessments as a normal operational routine and contact him for assistance as necessary.

Crime Risk Reduction in the Future Physical Environment

Through his public awareness campaigns and public education activities (see Chapter 7) the practitioner can create improved levels of public knowledge as to the ways in which crime risk reduction principles can be incorporated into new construction. Through specific efforts to inform and educate builders, architects, land developers, construction contractors and others primarily responsible for new construction, he can increase the probability that crime risk reduction techniques will be applied in new construction. However, his primary direct input to the future physical environment will come through his formal or informal participation in the jurisdiction's physical planning process.

The Mandate for Participation in Physical Planning

In recognition of the important relationship between physical planning and future crime reduction (as well as other aspects of the law enforcement mission), the National Advisory Commission on Criminal Justice Standards and Goals, in its *Report on Police,*[1] established the following standard for police-community physical planning.

> *Every police agency should participate with local planning agencies and organizations, public and private, in community physical planning that affects the rate or nature of crime or the fear of crime.*
>
> 1. *Every government entity should seek police participation with public and private agencies and organizations involved in community physical planning within the jurisdiction.*
> 2. *Every police agency should assist in planning with public and private organizations involved in police-related community physical planning. This assistance should at least include planning involving:*
>   a. *Industrial area development;*
>   b. *Business and commercial area development;*
>   c. *Residential area development, both low rise and high rise;*
>   d. *Governmental or health facility complex development;*
>   e. *Open area development, both park and other recreation;*
>   f. *Redevelopment projects such as urban renewal; and*
>   g. *Building requirements (target hardening), both residential and commercial.*

Participation in local planning is an essential part of the practice of crime prevention, because it provides the opportunity to reduce or remove crime risks associated with the physical environment before construction starts.

The Physical Planning Process

Municipal governments perform four primary physical planning functions:

- Comprehensive land use planning—looks at current land use patterns in the community and attempts to identify desirable patterns for future growth and change;

- Zoning—establishes and regulates the conditions under which land is used;
- Development plan approval—determines the precise configuration of any proposed land development or redevelopment; and
- Building code development and enforcement—sets specific standards for building construction, use and occupancy.

As a practical matter, the practitioner's first task is to determine exactly how these planning functions are handled in his jurisdiction. Most communities have an independent planning (or planning and zoning) commission consisting of leading citizens who are appointed according to provisions of local ordinances or state laws. In some cases, the planning staff is employed by the commission. In other cases, the planning staff is employed by a planning department within municipal government. In a few cases, there is a planning department but no independent commission, with the community advisory function handled through a series of *ad hoc* committees. In any case, land use planning, zoning and platting are handled by some combination of commission, committee and planning staff, with the mayor or municipal council serving as arbitrator of disputes over land use.

Usually, building code development and enforcement is handled by a separate building inspection department. Some communities have established a community development department which handles all physical planning functions.

Crime Prevention Contributions to Physical Planning

Having identified the physical planning structure in his community and its key officials, the practitioner can start developing ways to provide input to the planning process. Unless a formal procedure already exists for his involvement in the planning process, the practitioner should hold a series of introductory discussions with appropriate officials. In these sessions, he should explain the importance of crime prevention in physical planning and offer to provide technical assistance. He can then gradually develop a permanent role as an advisor to planners.

The contributions that a practitioner can make to the physical planning process are limited only by his technical skill and imagination. There are, however, two major areas in which he may concentrate his efforts.

Development Plan Review

The practitioner may offer, or be asked, to review proposed development plans for residential subdivisions, shopping centers, entertainment complexes, medical centers and other major proposed construction. He should look for potential crime risks associated with exterior environment features such as:

- Building setbacks;
- Fences, walls, hedges and other boundary markers;
- Trees and shrubbery;

- Streets, sidewalks and alleys;
- Lighting;
- Public areas and facilities; and
- Parking lots and structures.

He should also be concerned with crime risks in parts of individual structures, such as:

- Walls, roofs and floors;
- Doors, windows and other external access points;
- Stairways, hallways, restrooms, elevators, lobbies and other common areas;
- Lighting;
- Internal access points;
- Placement of utilities and ducting; and
- Common overheads.

Building Code Review

Although increasing numbers of municipalities have adopted or are developing security components in the local building code, the practitioner may find that building security provisions are inadequately set forth or enforced. In either case, his approach should be to work closely with local building officials and other interested parties to develop improved enforcement procedures or an improved code.

As is discussed in Chapter 5, he should stress the necessity for working with both the public and private sectors, and the need to harmonize local codes with state and national codes.

CRIME RISK REDUCTION BY USERS OF THE PHYSICAL ENVIRONMENT

Physical design can be used to stimulate social attitudes and behavior which can help reduce both the opportunities for crimes and the fear of crime through:

- Intensified use of streets, parks and land around structures;
- Increased visibility of intruders to legitimate occupants and users;
- Increased tendency for people to look out for each other and to act if a crime is observed;
- Increased ability to discriminate between people who belong in an area and those who are intruders; and
- Increased sense of shared interest in improving and maintaining the quality of the physical and social environment.

Informal Social Control

The presence of these kinds of social attitudes and behavior leads to informal social control of crime. Informal control is both distinct from and complementary with formal control (that is, the actions and reactions of the criminal justice system).

The effect of informal social control can be to influence members of a social group to conform with the group's norms for appropriate behavior, to influence users and occupants of an area to protect each other from intruders, and to create the probability that users and occupants will turn to formal controls when necesary by calling police and otherwise cooperating with the criminal justice system (giving testimony in court, for example).

The Influence of Physical Design

The relationship between physical design and informal social control of crime is a new idea only in the sense of its systematic application to the modern urban scene. Prior to the development of the modern city, most societies took some precautions to relate security in the physical environment to a responsibility for security actions by the inhabitants themselves.

In the rush of modern urban development, however, economic and political priorities seem to have far outweighed security priorities, with the result that many urban settings now seem deliberately designed to discourage informal social control. No colonial community would have done so. Even when stockades were no longer needed for defense against Indians. New England towns continued to be constructed so that the homes and stores formed a hollow square around a central Common where social activities could take place and where livestock could be kept in relative security. In this kind of environment, everyone knew everyone else's business, and while this meant less personal privacy than the modern city dweller may enjoy, it also meant a high degree of shared responsibility for controlling undesirable behavior and unwanted intrusion.

Only recently have students of modern urban society begun again to take serious note of the relationship between physical design and informal social control. The concept was first applied to modern cities by Jane Jacobs in 1961. In her book, *The Death and Life of Great American Cities,*[2] she theorized that multiple land uses along residential streets provided an interaction between the physical design and the users (pedestrians and residents) which promoted natural and informal surveillance and, therefore, increased the safety of the streets.

Lee Rainwater, in an evaluation of a public housing project in St. Louis (1966), discussed the effect of physical design on the attitudes of public housing residents, pointing out that inappropriate architectural design was directly related to anti-social behavior.[3]

Elizabeth Wood, writing in 1961 and 1967, suggested that current design patterns in public housing projects appeared to discourage informal social relationships and gatherings, thus preventing the development of social interactions through which residents could create informal social controls and self-policing.[4]

Schlomo Angel, in 1968, found that variations in the level of pedestrian and vehicular traffic could either encourage or discourage crimes.[5] Too few users provided enough potential victims, but not enough potential witnesses.

Gerald Leudtke and associates found, as the result of LEAA-funded studies in Detroit, that . . . *many of the features of urban form and structure . . . could tend to facilitate or decrease the probability of crime. Such physical features include the condition and maintenance of buildings, streets and alleys; evidence of recent construction; mixtures of land use; rates of pedestrian traffic and pedestrian accumulation within various land uses; location of structures on an urban grid pattern; and distance to adjacent structures. Other examples are types of parking facilities; visibility into structures from roads, sidewalks and adjoining buildings; concealment by trees, shrubs, parked automobiles, fences, signs and advertising; the visibility of entrance points; building setbacks; and, the number and arrangement of entrance points in a building.*[6]

In 1969, Oscar Newman and George Rand[7] developed a theory of territoriality (now referred to as *Defensible Space*) which held that proper physical design of housing encourages residents to extend their social control from their homes and apartments out into the surrounding common areas. In this way, they change what previously had been perceived as semi-public or public territory into private territory. Upgrading the common areas in this way results in increased social control and an interaction between physical environment and its users that reduces crime.

As Newman himself defines it, *Defensible Space is a surrogate term for the range of mechanisms—real and symbolic barriers, strongly defined areas of influence, improved opportunities for surveillance—that combine to bring an environment under the control of its residents. A defensible space is a living residential environment which can be employed by inhabitants for the enhancement of their lives, while providing security for their families, neighbors, and friends. The public areas of a multi-family residential environment devoid of defensible space can make the act of going from street to apartment equivalent to running the gauntlet. The fear and uncertainty generated by living in such an environment can slowly eat away and eventually destroy the security and sanctity of the apartment unit itself. On the other hand, by grouping dwelling units to reinforce association of mutual benefit, by delineating paths of movement, by defining areas of activity for particular users through their juxtaposition with internal living areas, and by providing for natural opportunities for visual surveillance, architects can create a clear understanding of the function of a space, who its users are and ought to be. This, in turn, can lead residents of all income levels to adopt extremely potent territorial attitudes and policing measures, which act as a strong deterrent to potential criminals.*[8]

A 1972 study by Reppetto,[9] in Boston indicated the need to expand the crime-prevention-through-physical-design process to include whole neighborhoods and to provide for comprehensive data collection efforts which would both define the nature of crime patterns and suggest appropriate countermeasures.

Reppetto also was able to show that closely-knit communities do tend to protect their members through informal social controls, a finding further emphasized by Conklin in *The Impact of Crime:*

A tightly knit community can minimize the problem of street crime. However, informal social control also poses a threat to the diversity of behavior that exists in a pluralistic society, even though it may curb violent crime. Still, street crime would decline if interaction among the residents of a community were more frequent, and if social bonds were stronger. A sense of responsibility for other citizens and for the community as a whole would increase individuals' willingness to report crime to the police and the likelihood of their intervention in a crime in progress. Greater willingness of community residents to report crime to the police might also obviate the need for civilian police patrols. More interaction in public places and more human traffic on the sidewalks would increase surveillance of the places where people now fear to go. More intense social ties would reinforce surveillance with a willingness to take action against offenders.[10]

C. Ray Jefferey, in his classic theoretical work *Crime Prevention Through Environmental Design* (1971),[11] written before Jefferey became aware of the works of Newman and others, proposed a three-fold strategy involving not only physical design but also increased citizen participation and the more effective use of police forces. He contended that the way to prevent crime is to design the total environment in such a manner that the opportunity for crime is reduced or eliminated.

Jefferey contends that both the physical and the social characteristics of an urban area affect crime patterns and that better physical planning is a key to unlocking the potential for improved physical security and the potential for development of informal social control. He also argues for high levels of precision in the analytical stages that precede physical planning for crime reduction.

One of the major methodological defects in ecological studies of crime rates has been use of large units and census tract data as a basis for analysis. The usual units are rural-urban, intracity, intercity, regional, and national differences . . . Such an approach is much too gross for finding the physical features associated with different types of crimes.

We must look at the physical environment in terms of each building, or each room of the building, or each floor of the building. Fine grain resolution is required in place of the usual large-scale photographs . . . Whenever crime rates are surveyed at a micro level of analysis, it is revealed that a small area of the city is responsible for a majority of the crimes. This fact is glossed over by gross statistical correlation analysis of census tract data which ignore house-by-house or block-by-block variations in crime rates. For purposes of crime prevention we need data which will tell us what aspects of the urban environment are responsible for crime, such as the concentration of homicide or robbery in a very small section of the city.[12]

Defensible Space

Oscar Newman and others have explored and further defined the defensible space concept in recent years through design studies and experiments involving existing and new public housing projects. The following summary of defensible space techniques will give the practitioner an initial understanding of this important application of physical design to the urban residential environment.

Design for defensible space involves attempts to strengthen two basic kinds of social behavior called **territoriality** and **natural surveillance**.

Territoriality

The classic example of territoriality is the "man's home is his castle" tradition of the American single-family home and its surroundings. In this tradition, the family lays claim to its own territory and acts to protect it, and this image of home as castle reinforces itself . . . *by the very act of its position on an integral piece of land buffered from neighbors and the public street by intervening grounds.*[13]

As the urban setting has grown, the single family home has become, to developers, an economic liability. Family housing has moved into the row house, apartment complex, high-rise apartment structure and massive public housing project. Whatever the benefits of this transition, the idea of territoriality has been largely lost in the process. The result is that . . . *most families living in an apartment building experience the space outside their apartment unit as distinctly public; in effect, they relegate responsibility for all activity outside the immediate confines of their apartment to the public authorities.*[14]

As residents are forced by the physical design of their surroundings to abandon claim to any part of the outside world, the hallways, stairways, lobbies, grounds, parking lots and streets become a kind of no-man's land in which criminals can operate almost at will. Public and private law enforcement agencies (formal controls) attempt to take up the slack, but without the essential informal social control that a well-developed social sense of territoriality brings, law enforcement can do little to reduce crime.

Natural Surveillance

The increased presence of human observers which territoriality brings can lead to higher levels of natural surveillance in all areas of residential space. However, the simple presence of increased numbers of potential observers is not enough, because natural surveillance, to be effective, must include an action component. The probability that an observer will act to report an observed crime or intervene in it depends on:

- The degree to which the observer feels that his personal or property rights are violated by the observed act; or,

- The extent to which the observer is able to identify with the victim or property under attack; and
- The level of the observer's belief that his action can help, on the one hand, and not subject him to reprisals on the other.

Obviously, the probability for both observation and action is greatly improved by physical conditions which create the highest possible levels of visibility.

Design Guidelines

Defensible space offers a series of architectural guidelines which can be used in the design of new urban residential complexes to promote both the residential group's territorial claim to its surroundings and its ability to conduct natural surveillance.[15]

Site design can stress the clustering of small numbers of residential units around private hallways, courtyards and recreation areas. In these restricted zones, children can play, adults can relax, and strangers can easily be identified and questioned. Such private spaces can be created by internal and external building walls and access arrangements and by the use of perceptual barriers such as low fences, shrubbery and other boundary markers.

Site inter-relationships design can be used to create semi-private connecting and common spaces between and among the private family clusters. Walkways, vehicle access-ways, parking areas, recreational facilities, lobbies, laundry and shopping areas can be designed so that each cluster relates to them much as each resident of a cluster relates to his common private space. Physical design can thus be used to further extend the sense of territoriality and the possibility for informal social control.

Street design and the design of other public spaces can be engineered to make these spaces into semi-public extensions of the residential clusters and their connectors. Closing streets to through traffic, installing benches and play areas near the streets, providing adequate lighting, and placing perceptual barriers to indicate the semi-public nature of the area can help to define these spaces as part of the shared residential group territory.

Surveillance-specific design can be used in each of the above design areas to increase general visibility by providing adequate lighting, by reducing or eliminating physical barriers to visibility, and by the visibility-promoting location of key areas (for example, entrances, lobbies, elevator waiting areas, recreational and parking areas) so as to be directly visible from as many points of view as possible.

Modifying Existing Physical Design

Cost limitations prevent substantial reconstruction of most existing urban residential facilities. However, a number of relatively low-cost techniques can be used to modify existing facilities so as to promote territorality and natural surveillance. These include:

- Installing adequate security devices (locks, doors, windows) in each residential unit;
- Dividing common lawn areas (front or back) into private yards and patios through the use of shrubbery, low fences and other perceptual barriers;
- Improving the attractiveness and semi-privacy of pathways and other common outside areas by use of decorative paving and lighting; by installing benches and other seating arrangements at strategic intervals; by careful landscaping; and by tying play areas, parking and vehicle access ways to the overall design;
- Reducing the number of public access points and providing the remaining points with good lighting, visibility and security; and
- Establishing audio and video surveillance (monitored by residents or by security staff) in strategic internal areas.

It should be emphasized, in summary, that creating defensible space is not the same as creating a hardened security system (as might be found, for example, in a high-rise luxury apartment). In fact, it is almost the opposite. Defensible space operates on the premise that the living environment must be opened up and used by residents and others, not closed in. It is only in the open, used environment that people can be stimulated to establish the self-policing condition which is informal social control. In this open living environment, opportunities for crime may continue to exist, but the probability for criminal activity is reduced.

It should also be emphasized that the physical design component of defensible space should always be accompanied by efforts to develop and sustain active citizen participation and by strategies for improved interaction between citizens and law enforcement agencies.

CRIME PREVENTION THROUGH ENVIRONMENTAL DESIGN

Crime prevention through environmental design, or CPTED, is a rapidly growing field of study and experimentation that attempts to apply physical design, citizen participation and law enforcement strategies in a comprehensive, planned way to entire neighborhoods and even major urban districts, as well as to specific urban subsystems such as public schools and transportation systems.

Cautions

Before summarizing the CPTED approach, we would suggest that the practitioner view CPTED developments with a healthy skepticism, at least for the present. There are several reasons why a sense of caution is in order:

- Although the effectiveness of some of the specific techniques used in CPTED experiments can be verified, the overall effectiveness of the CPTED approach has yet to be conclusively demonstrated;

- There is some disagreement among crime prevention theorists as to the correctness of the assumptions on which current CPTED programs are based;
- The magnitude of the typical CPTED project may be well beyond the practitioner's current ability to plan, implement and manage; and
- The cost of a typical CPTED project can represent a major financial investment, and unless the investment can be justified on a research and demonstration basis, there is no guarantee that it will be cost effective.

Despite these cautions, it is useful for the practitioner to be aware of the principles and current applications of the CPTED concept so that he can watch its developments and make appropriate use of the knowledge that it may produce.

Recent Projects

The most well-known of the recent CPTED efforts was the CPTED research and demonstration project conducted by the Westinghouse Corporation under LEAA funding. Other research and, in some cases, demonstration projects were also sponsored by LEAA and HUD.

CPTED-Westinghouse

The CPTED-Westinghouse program, according to its Director, Edward Perce,[16] . . . *incorporates physical, social, law enforcement and management techniques to achieve its goal of reducing crime and the fear of crime.* Within the demonstration projects, this goal is to be achieved through . . . *access control, surveillance, activity support and motivation reinforcement.*

Access control involves . . . *setting up barriers to prevent unauthorized people from entering an area . . .*

Surveillance aims to . . . *keep intruders under observation by means of police patrols, electronic devices, or organized programs among residents and users of an area . . .*, as well as to improve street lighting, and eliminate visual barriers . . .

Activity support . . . *involves increasing human use of an area by making it more attractive . . . (and) . . . does not consist of physical changes alone but can also include activities that foster a spirit of community among residents . . .*

Motivation reinforcement aims . . . *to encourage residents and users of an area to have and enact positive attitudes about their living and working environment and to discourage potential offenders by increasing the risk of apprehension and by reducing the payoff of crime . . .*

These global objectives were to be carried out through four related types of strategies:[17]

- Territorial Defense;
- Personal Defense;
- Law Enforcement; and,
- Confidence Restoration.

Territorial Defense Strategies

Territorial Defense Strategies emphasize prevention of property-related crimes such as breaking and entering, auto theft and household larceny. Within this group there are five related strategy areas: land use planning; building grounds security; building perimeter security; building interior security; and construction standards.

Land use planning strategies involve planning activities aimed at avoiding land use mixtures that have a negative impact on neighborhood security, through zoning ordinances and development plan reviews.

Building grounds security strategies provide the first line of defense against unauthorized entry of sites and offer social control mechanisms to prevent dangerous and destructive behavior of visitors. The emphasis is on the access control and surveillance aspects of architectural design. The target environment might be a residential street, the side of a housing complex, or alleyways behind or between business establishments.

Building perimeter security strategies provide a second line of defense for protecting site occupants and property by preventing unauthorized entries of buildings. They involve physical barriers, surveillance and intrusion detection systems, and social control mechanisms.

Building interior security strategies provide the third line of defense for protecting site occupants and property by preventing unauthorized access to interior spaces and valuables through physical barriers, surveillance and intrusion detection systems, and social control mechanisms.

Construction standards strategies involve building security codes which require construction techniques and materials that tend to reduce crime and safety hazards. These strategies deal both with code adoption and code enforcement.

Personal Defense Strategies

The second basic strategic approach focused on the prevention of violent or street crimes such as robbery, assault and rape and the reduction of fear associated with these crimes. Specific strategies included: safe-streets-for-people, transportation, cash-off-the-streets, and citizen intervention.

Safe-streets-for-people strategies involve planning principles derived primarily from the CPTED concepts of surveillance and activity support. Surveillance operates to discourage potential offenders because of the apparent risk of being seen and can be improved through various design modifications of physical elements of the street environment (e.g., lighting, fencing, landscaping). Pedestrian traffic areas can be channelled to increase their use and, hence, the number of observers through such measures as creating malls, eliminating on-street parking, and providing centralized parking areas.

Transportation strategies are aimed at reducing exposure to crime by improving public transportation. For example, transit waiting stations (bus, trolley) can be located near areas of safe activity and good surveillance, or the distance between stations can be reduced, thus improving accessibility to specific residences, business establishments, and other traffic generating points.

Cash-off-the-streets strategies reduce incentives for crime by urging people not to carry unnecessary cash and to provide commercial services that minimize the need to carry cash.

Citizen intervention, unlike the three previous activities, consists of strategies aimed at organizing and mobilizing residents to adopt proprietary interests and assume responsibility for the maintenance of security.

Law Enforcement Strategies

The third general approach involved police functions that support community-based prevention activities. There are two activities: police patrol and citizen/police support.

Police patrol strategies focus on ways in which police deployment procedures can improve their efficiency and effectiveness in responding to calls and apprehending offenders.

Citizen/police support strategies consist of police operational support activities that improve citizen/police relations and encourage citizens to cooperate with the police in preventing and reporting incidents.

Confidence Restoration Strategies

This fourth general strategy for commercial and residential environments involved activities that are aimed primarily at mobilizing neighborhood interest and support to implement needed CPTED changes. Without such interest and support, it is unlikely that programs of sufficient magnitude to be successful will be possible, particularly in many high-crime-rate neighborhoods where people have lost hope. There are two specific strategy areas: investor confidence; and neighborhood identities.

Investor confidence strategies promote economic investment and, therefore, social and economic vitality.

Neighborhood identity strategies build community pride and foster social cohesion.

Most of these specific strategies are discussed in this and other chapters (some under different names). As a whole, this list of strategies is well-organized and provides a good framework with which to view the possible interaction of a variety of crime prevention efforts.

Demonstrations

To see how these strategies were applied, let us look briefly at two of the recent CPTED-Westinghouse demonstration projects.

Portland, Oregon had a project involving a commercial corridor 50 blocks long and four blocks wide. When the project began . . . *The corridor faced deterioration, increasing crime, and a general decline in conditions during the late 1960s and early 1970s. Violent crimes had become disproportionately high, based on the area's share of the city's population. In a 1973 survey, Union Avenue business people perceived the crime level, more than any other factor, to be the largest impediment to the successful operation of their businesses. In fact, almost one-fourth of them reported a desire to move in the next year or two.*[18]

The objectives established for the project are listed below:

- Reduce opportunities for crime and reduce fear of crime by making streets and open areas more easily observable and by increasing activity in the neighborhood;
- Provide ways in which neighborhood residents, business people, and police can work together more effectively to reduce opportunities and incentives for crime;
- Increase neighborhood identity, investor confidence, and social cohesion;
- Provide building security surveys and public information programs to help business people and residents protect themselves from crime,
- Make the area more accessible by improving transportation services;
- Remove crime incentives by providing alternatives to carrying cash on the streets;
- Improve the effectiveness and efficiency of police patrol operations; and
- Encourage citizens to report crimes.

The steps taken to achieve these objectives included:

- Outdoor lighting, dial-free emergency phones, sidewalk and landscaping improvements;
- Block watch, safe homes, and neighborhood cleanups;
- A campaign to discourage people from carrying cash;
- A major improvement project for Union Avenue itself;
- Special bus shelters;
- Improved streetlighting;
- Bus service for the elderly and handicapped; and
- Residential and business security surveys.

Early reports of results were mixed—project officials said that the results were encouraging, but unofficial local reports indicated that there were problems. In any case, the final project evaluation report released during 1981 concluded that the CPTED project was successful in altering citizen perceptions and in positively improving the economic vitality of the area.

Broward County, Florida had a demonstration project involving four high schools. This project sought to:

- Protect person and property through increased natural surveillance, access restrictions and attempted to . . . *foster a sense of belonging to and responsibility for the school environment;*[19]
- Improve educational policy through scheduling of activities to promote surveillance and attempted to identify and help students who have problems in the school environment; and
- Restore confidence by encouraging community activities involving school facilities, by improving the physical quality and image of the facilities, and by enhancing school pride.

Reports indicated that many of the techniques used are practical and at least somewhat effective.

CPTED-Hartford, Connecticut[20]

This planning and demonstration program, funded directly by LEAA, HUD, DoL and the City of Hartford, was aimed at a residential area so near as to be almost part of a downtown commercial district.

Hartford was the first CPTED project involving an entire neighborhood. Based on a thorough analysis of crime patterns and physical, social and economic characteristics, planners were able to determine that:

- Burglary, robbery and purse-snatching were occurring on residential streets rather than main routes;
- Residents were afraid to use public streets and had little contact with each other;
- Fear was disproportionately high;
- Commuter traffic on residential streets was further disrupting the neighborhood;
- Most offenders were "imported" from other areas; and
- Police had done "all they could" about crime.

Among the approaches used to overcome these problems were:

- Closing, narrowing or one-waying streets to change traffic patterns;
- Creating new community groups and strengthening an old one;
- Improving community-police communications through a Police Advisory Committee; and
- Assignment of permanent police patrol teams to the area.

It is significant to note that the changes suggested by planners were substantially revised by residents themselves before implementation. The city of Hartford, in fact, was careful to make its share of funding contingent on the approval of plans by the residents.

The project evaluation brought out several key factors for use in similar future projects:

- Residents must understand the problems and approve the solutions;
- Police and other elements of local government must be deeply involved in the planning process; and
- Solutions can only be designed in terms of the unique situation in a given community.

A follow-up evaluation study indicated that the physical changes had less effect on the success of the program than the procedural and social changes that were prompted by the project. Police patrols were altered and resident activities changed as a result of the design changes. Of course, the physical changes provided the impetus for the other activities.

The Future of CPTED

The most consistent finding in evaluations of CPTED and related projects has been that the users of space must be involved in design decisions. Their involvement insures that the designs are realistic and that the users will comply with the behavioral objectives of the plans. Numerous applications of CPTED concepts have been tried successfully on a spot basis, which has tended to support the idea that the more simplistic approaches are the most viable. That is, it seems reasonable to assume that the crime prevention practitioner may confidently use CPTED strategies in very specific, controlled environmental settings.

There are many hundreds of examples of CPTED strategies in practice today. It is unfortunate that most of the successful applications have not been publicized well, since they are usually part of ongoing field activities that do not come to the attention of evaluators or government agencies. However, it has been noted that most applications center on some mixture or interaction between the three basic CPTED processes of natural surveillance, natural access control and territoriality. The most basic common thread is the primary emphasis on naturalness—simply doing things, that you already have to do, a little better.

The most productive uses of CPTED, in the foreseeable future, will center on the following simplistic strategies:

- Provide clear border definition of controlled space.
- Provide clearly marked transitional zones which indicate movement from public to semi-public to private space.
- Relocate gathering areas to locations with natural surveillance and access control, or to locations away from the view of would-be offenders.
- Place safe activities in unsafe locations to bring along the natural surveillance of these activities (to increase the perception of safety for normal users and risk for offenders).

- Place unsafe activities in safe spots to overcome the vulnerability of these activities with the natural surveillance and access control of the safe area.
- Redesignate the use of space to provide natural barriers to conflicting activities.
- Improve scheduling of space to allow for effective use, appropriate "critical intensity," and the temporal definition of accepted behaviors.
- Redesign or revamp space to increase the perception or reality of natural surveillance.
- Overcome distance and isolation through improved communication and design efficiencies.

The future of CPTED rests with the persons who shape public and private policy. Crime prevention practitioners will have to communicate CPTED concepts in terms that relate to the overall priorities of their organizations or communities. Productivity, profitability and quality of life are concerns that affect policy makers—not security or crime prevention for its sake. Accordingly, chief executives, builders, architects, planners, engineers and developers will have to embrace CPTED design objectives. Elected officials and legislative bodies will have to be held accountable for assuring that CPTED has been considered in capital improvement and development plans. Property owners and residents of neighborhoods and commercial areas will need the opportunity to question planning, zoning and traffic signalization decisions. Finally, strategic plans that encompass twenty-year community development periods will require an assessment of crime prevention needs and programs.

CONCLUSION

The application of environmental design concepts by the crime prevention practitioner can be as cost effective as the design of crime risk management systems for individual clients. Such application must be based, however, on sound analysis of particular crime patterns and the physical and social conditions which are related to those patterns. It should stress innovative solutions that are appropriate to the particular circumstances, that are cost effective and that will not create more problems than they solve. It should stress working with "things as they are" rather than with "things as they ought to be."

The practitioner needs, above all, to become well acquainted with the people and organizations responsible for physical development and redevelopment in his or her community. The best opportunities for applying crime prevention through environmental design occur when buildings, street layouts, streetlighting programs, new subdivisions, shopping centers and housing projects are still in the planning stages, and crime prevention principles can be incorporated before construction starts.

In keeping with the theory that the quality of the physical environment impacts human behavior, we think that crime prevention and community development go hand-in-hand. Physical design that enhances the environment from a balanced economic-social-political standpoint can also discourage criminal activity, and the concept of crime prevention through environmental design can be used in any situation – high-density urban areas, small cities and towns, and even rural areas. The essential role of the practitioner is to see the "whole picture" and to see to it that physical design, citizen participation and police activities fit together.

In terms of physical design itself, the major task of the crime prevention practitioner is to analyze existing and planned physical design, determine how it relates to existing or potential crime patterns, and recommend physical design countermeasures to the proper person or organization.

Another major task for the crime prevention practitioner is to help develop the citizen participation strategies needed to complement physical design changes or to overcome deficiencies in physical design. This task is the subject of the next chapter.

7 Developing Citizen Participation

In the community-wide crime prevention program, citizen participation and law enforcement action strategies work together in altering social and physical environments so as to reduce criminal opportunity.

Chapter 6 discussed physical design strategies. In this chapter, we turn to an overview of citizen participation strategies and the role of the crime prevention practitioner in designing and implementing those strategies.

We have already defined the crime prevention practitioner as an enabler, rather than a doer. We have pointed out that the practitioner enables by working with and through the citizen-doers, and have suggested a few of the many roles that private and public organizations and particular areas of skill and interest can play. Now we turn to the ways in which citizens and police can work together in developing productive crime prevention programs.

CITIZEN-POLICE COOPERATION

Police-citizen cooperation to prevent crime is probably as old as mankind. Societies have always designated individual members as watchmen or guards, whose primary function was to alert the rest of the group to problems requiring emergency action. The idea of police as a public force organized to protect the community from its deviant members has arisen only in fairly recent times. Even so, as we have seen, the fundamental purpose of initial police units was to work with an active citizenry to prevent crime from occurring. In our own country, however, police have become increasingly identified as enforcers of the law rather than as public service workers. If one is in favor of laws that the police attempt to enforce, one can look with appreciation at police activities. If one feels, on the other hand, more like a victim than a beneficiary of those laws, the policeman can hardly be looked on as an ally. The development of this kind of police-citizen schism in our country probably reached its height in the urban riots of the late 1960s. Out of this experience came widespread recognition of a gap between police and some segments of the public, which led to the development of police-community relations efforts whose sole purpose was to find ways of building better communication patterns between citizens and police. And whether or not the police-community relations approach worked, it did represent a very important return to the old idea that gaps between interests of police and the interest of citizens are extremely undesirable.

Crime prevention, contrary to the thinking of some, is neither a facet of or an outgrowth of police community relations. Presenting a favorable image of police to the community is not the primary objective of crime prevention. On the other hand, crime prevention properly practiced by police does tend to improve police-community relations. But this is an incidental effect of crime prevention rather than a primary objective and arises only from citizen appreciation for a valuable service rendered.

The motivated citizen works **with** rather than **for** the crime prevention officer, who is much more a resource availabe to the citizen than the reverse. Within lawful limits, citizen crime prevention activities are in no way directed by police. However, they may be supported and coordinated by police, and in cases where citizen activities border on police functions (organized citizen patrols, for example), police supervision may be needed to avoid violations of the law. Effective community crime prevention programming results from the proper combination of police and citizen activities. The one cannot be subservient to the other—instead, both must collaborate as partners. **Thus, where citizen participation strategies are correctly developed, there is no need for conflict over the issue of program control.**

Citizen groups and criminal justice groups have legitimate roles to play in comprehensive crime prevention which support and complement each other. No interest should dominate the program, on the one hand, but each interest should control and manage its own activities, on the other. For example, it is no more appropriate for a police agency to dictate the kind of approach a community group should develop than it is for a community group to dictate how a police administrator should allocate police forces.

The crime prevention practitioner (much more likely to be a sworn police officer than a civilian, but in either case almost surely either employed by or sanctioned by a government agency) is the essential middleman, controlling nothing except his or her own direct program resources, but enabling all community resources and interests to work together in harmony.

The practitioner operates as a manager rather than as an authority figure, seeing to it that all essential community interests share in the crime prevention program planning process, that goals and strategies arrived at through planning are carried out to the best ability of the groups involved and the resources available, and that the results of the program are correctly identified, interpreted and shared so that strategies and goals can be refined as necessary.

THE PREPARATION PHASE

By the time the practitioner is ready to start reaching out to the public, he or she should have developed a very clear and detailed understanding of crime patterns in the jurisdiction and should have formulated general strategies for dealing with those patterns. This initial planning process by the practitioner will be discussed in Chapter 8.

There are several reasons why no outreach effort to the public should be made until the preliminary planning is done:

1. Unless the practitioner has done the necessary homework, there can be no clear picture as to what the public is expected to do. The only recourse in such a situation is to put out generic information on home and business security, and to promote generalized projects such as Operation Identification. While these generic approaches are not without merit, they are only one part of comprehensive crime prevention strategies.
2. Without planning, the practitioner may not have the ability to meet demands for service that will arise from the public—including requests for very specific strategic guidance by citizen groups.
3. Unless planning includes adequate preparation of the members of the local law enforcement agency, representatives of local government, and other key individuals, members of the public who ask these individuals for further guidance may be rebuffed or told that "It's just another public relations effort." Such response can be deadly for a crime prevention program.

Thus, the citizen participation process should not be started until the practitioner is ready to deliver solid, serious information and back it up with service and support. This is more than academic advice. Numerous local crime prevention programs have collapsed, or, at the very least, been set back substantially, because the practitioners insisted on starting public information campaigns before they were ready to deliver workable guidance and support to citizens.

The Crime Prevention Organization

An essential part of the preparation phase is the development of an adequate jurisdiction-wide crime prevention planning and management organization, as will be discussed in Chapter 8.

The crime prevention organization can help stimulate continuing, purposeful, and systematic activities generated by individuals, citizen groups and the neighborhood and public agencies at the community level. It can help direct this activity toward objectives that are consistent with the philosophy and practice of crime prevention and compatible with the program goals established through the citizen input mechanism.

Participation by Decision-Makers

An important element in the practitioner's preparation is to find ways to involve the key decision-makers in the community. Early participation by public officials and leaders in the private and voluntary sectors both sanctions and strengthens the program. The practitioner can use the listing of potential roles presented in Chapter 3 as a guide for this phase of his preparation.

Factors in Communicating with Citizens

As part of the preparation phase, the practitioner should make sure that the projects he wishes citizens to participate in are clearly defined and communicated. Vagueness and imprecision in project definition can easily lead to less than desirable levels of citizen participation. When citizens fail to react as a practitioner might wish, he may be tempted to cry citizen apathy. And while it is true that some individuals and groups may be apathetic to the idea of crime prevention, it is also true that the phrase *citizen apathy* can be used as an excuse for the practitioner's failure to communicate clearly with citizens. The point is that good communication with citizens is essential to the success of citizen participation strategies.

If citizens are to participate in crime prevention programs (or any other public endeavor, for that matter), they must be provided with adequate **knowledge**, **justification** and **opportunity**, and their **fear and distrust** must be neutralized, if possible.

Knowledge

As our society becomes increasingly sophisticated and educated, citizens become more aware of their right to full information from those who seek their money, time or energy. Although our crime prevention cause is worthy, we must realize that no individual or group should support crime prevention without knowing its purpose, workings, worth, and the probability that it will deliver the benefits we claim for it.

The crime prevention practitioner must, therefore, be able to tell people exactly what they can do, how they can do it, how much it will cost (in dollars or time), what is likely to happen (or not happen) as a result, and what resources are available to help them. People must also be able to determine that what is asked of them is the right thing to do compared to other actions they might take against crime problems. And, they need to know that crime prevention action will not needlessly expose them to new risks.

Justification

Groups and individuals also have every right to demand that the practitioner tell them why they should become involved with crime prevention. Participation may involve cost (in money or effort) and risk (real or perceived), both of which must be balanced against the benefit to be obtained. If people say "Why bother?" or "I'm afraid to do that." or, "It won't work.", it is a sure sign the practitioner has failed to justify the proposed participation to them. And, if the practitioner has not done a good job in developing knowledge and justification, the citizen who says "Why bother?" may be quite sensible. One way to get around this problem is to involve potential participants in the planning process. This, of course, is the secret of success of any kind of community organization activity and should be stressed in developing citizen participation in crime prevention. And it is a good way to activate those who are predisposed to be receptive to crime prevention—previous victims and aware neighborhood leaders, for example.

To repeat, individual or group participation in crime prevention can only flow from a very clear understanding of why participation is needed and what will be the personal and community benefits. The facts must be presented, and, in turn, the practitioner must listen to the citizens' interpretation of those facts, and the activity must be jointly planned based on the resulting mutual understanding.

Opportunity

The participation activity and the resources necessary to conduct it should be available to anyone wishing to participate, without significant disturbance to their normal pattern of activity. Every person has pressing concerns and demands on time. Each of us is more likely to do something if it is made easy for us, and the crime prevention practitioner must recognize that chances for participation are greatly increased if ample opportunity is provided.

Fear and Distrust

It would be naive not to expect a significant portion of the public to reject, at first, any opportunity to participate in crime prevention programs, particularly in low-income urban areas where fear of reprisal and distrust of law enforcement or the criminal justice system may be high. Such situations will call for very careful approaches by the practitioner, particularly if he or she is the law enforcement officer. The challenge here is to find imaginative ways to communicate knowledge and justification through people who are trusted by the group at hand.

CITIZEN PARTICIPATION STRATEGIES

Citizen participation strategies are categorized as follows:

- Citizen awareness and knowledge strategies;
- Group project strategies; and
- Informal social control strategies.

There is considerable overlap among these strategy types, yet each has a distinct purpose as described below. They really form a continuum from relatively superficial citizen contacts to the most intensive community organization leading to neighborhood solidarity and enduring social control.

Awareness and Knowledge Strategies

Awareness and knowledge strategies are basically aimed at informing the public as to what crime prevention is, how it works, what citizens can do, why they should act, and what services and resources are available to help them.

Awareness

The awareness component consists of newspaper articles, television and radio public service spots and interviews, billboards, posters, shopping center exhibits, brochure mailings and other general audience approaches.

The information should be simple and repetitive. The campaign should, if possible, be continued on a perpetual basis, or at least be repeated at regular intervals. Increasing numbers of states have established statewide crime prevention media campaigns, and these can be very helpful to the local practitioner. However, they should supplement, not replace, the continuing local public awareness program.

The cooperation of the news media, advertising agencies and other members of the local communications industry is essential to the success of a public awareness campaign. The practitioner should take pains to explain the program to communications people and request their help. In turn, he should learn from them how and in what format to prepare news releases, promotional copy, visuals, print materials and so forth. A close working relationship is of the utmost importance.

It should be noted here that the practitioner will hardly ever be working in a vacuum of awareness. Increasing numbers of national associations, for example, provide crime prevention educational materials to their local constituents and urge local affiliate organizations to develop local crime prevention education programs. Local people already touched by crime prevention in this or other ways will usually be only too glad to respond to the "awareness call" sounded by the practitioner.

Knowledge

The awareness campaign, though important, only opens the door to citizen participation. The next step is to add knowledge to awareness.

The public awareness campaign will result in widespread recognition of crime prevention and the purposes and methods of the local program. It will trigger requests for information, security surveys, speaking engagements and other direct assistance. And, the practitioner can expect some direct action to result—usually, simple actions like Operation Identification registrations and purchase of deadbolt door locks. The people who make contact with the practitioner in response to an awareness campaign will be a small fraction of the population, but they are likely to be people who can lead in further development of citizen participation.

The practitioner must be prepared to respond quickly and skillfully to all public requests for assistance, because this is how he or she establishes a track record for high-quality client service. Such service delivery may mean working overtime; citizen groups seldom meet during the normal business day. Nevertheless, the dedicated practitioner will be prepared to sacrifice his or her own convenience, because the ultimate success of citizen participation strategies depends on a high-quality response by the practitioner at this stage.

The primary focus of the practitioner at this citizen knowledge-developing stage will be to further educate those who have expressed preliminary interest and to further attract those who, by virtue of position within the community, need to be involved.

Secondly, the practitioner must be prepared to help those who are ready and willing to start taking action. For the individual, this means providing crime risk management guidance and security surveys. For the citizen group or civic group it means providing accurate information on subjects of interest to members. A businessmen's group, for example, might be primarily interested in commercial burglary or robbery prevention and asset protection. A neighborhood group might be interested in preventing street crime. Women's and senior citizen groups may be interested in reducing crime risk from assault, purse-snatching, fraud and so on. Each special group will have a special need.

The practitioner, in meeting these knowledge needs, sets the stage for additional knowledge delivery services, because "satisfied customers" create other clients. If one women's group hears an interesting talk on rape prevention, the word will spread and other groups will want to follow suit. This natural process builds demand for additional services.

Thus, the practitioner builds his wider clientele through delivery of quality services and "word of mouth" promotion of those services. This domino effect of his knowledge-building strategy is both to be desired and to be expected. The practitioner should not hesitate to use volunteers to share and extend the workload. Interested persons can and should be trained to help in the knowledge-spreading process. Citizen-volunteer spokesmen, although their total knowledge of crime prevention is more limited than that of the practitioner, are sometimes more effective in educating colleagues and social peers than the practitioner.

It is also essential at this stage that the practitioner reach out to provide knowledge to a variety of community officials, starting with members of law enforcement agencies and extending to elected and appointed officials throughout government. These are the people who will later provide the political, economic and direct service support of the comprehensive crime prevention program, and they must become involved at the knowledge stage if they are to support the program in the action stages.

Group Project Strategies

As the practitioner carries out the awareness and knowledge strategy components, an increasing number and variety of groups will be motivated to start crime prevention projects. The practitioner must be prepared to guide such groups into projects which are both useful to the comprehensive crime prevention program and suitable to the interests and characteristics of the group.

To properly carry out group project strategies calls for a great deal of skill, understanding and creativity on the part of the practitioner. There can be no such thing as a "standard" group project. And, it must be kept in mind that only a part of the practitioner's purpose in helping groups to establish projects is the achievement of the specific result associated with the project. At least as important is the need to ensure that the group will have a rewarding experience so that its members will continue to want to work with crime prevention.

Some groups will be mostly interested in the security of their own members. Other groups will be oriented toward broad community service. Of the latter type, some will be interested in short-term ventures, and others will only consider long-term involvements. Some will be able to marshall substantial resources for a project. Still others, whatever their interests, will only be capable of performing simple tasks requiring little effort. But, **every group can do something that is useful and rewarding.**

For example, one practitioner was approached by a small group of retired people whose members had little energy but who were willing to spend a few hours a day, on occasion, doing something useful, as long as it didn't require hard work. It happened that a high school in their part of town had a high truancy rate, and the practitioner suspected, but could not prove, that the high incidence of daylight burglaries in the area around the school was related to the high truancy rate. His suggestion to the group was that they assign members on a rotating basis to go to the school for a couple of hours each morning, receive attendance reports from homeroom teachers, and call the parents of any student not in class to inform them that their child was absent that day. The school principal was in favor, and the work itself was undemanding.

After a month or so of this very simple effort, the principal was able to report a substantial decrease in truancy, and the practitioner was able to report a similar decrease in daylight burglaries near the school. This is an excellent example of a creative match between a group interest and an activity of potential benefit. It also exemplifies the desirability of setting up group projects which are inherently beneficial regardless of the crime prevention-specific outcome.

Here are some other examples:

- A Women's Club might assist in conducting victimization surveys, and this effort might lead to the decision to form a women's league against crime.
- A local Chamber of Commerce might sponsor a series of training sessions on commercial and institutional loss prevention;

- An Exchange Club might raise funds needed to construct and maintain a portable crime prevention exhibit;
- A senior citizens group might set up a "buddy shopping service" to help older people travel safely between home and store;
- A PTA might sponsor a series of special crime prevention training sessions for school children;
- A neighborhood group might develop a "safe house for children" project or a Neighborhood Watch project;
- A builder's association might sponsor training sessions in construction site security or the use and application of mechanical security devices and materials;
- A labor union might sponsor home security training sessions for members;
- A Lions Club might sponsor a summer crime prevention fair for children;
- A recreation vehicle sales group might donate a second-hand mobile van or trailer for use as a mobile crime prevention exhibit;
- A consumer advocacy group might sponsor the development of a publicity campaign directed at door-to-door swindles;
- A minority advocacy group might develop a "soul patrol" project in which youthful leaders provide roving community watch services;
- A citizen's band radio club might develop a mobile radio watch project among members;
- A public housing project tenants organization might develop a tenant patrol program;
- A youth organization might develop a door-to-door home security campaign;
- A postal workers or sanitation workers organization might develop a surveillance and reporting project;
- A League of Women Voters group might assist in developing needed information on community perception of crime problems;
- The gas, or water, or telephone company might train its meter-readers and maintenance workers to observe and report security risks;
- A woman's group might sponsor rape prevention seminars and a rape-crisis counseling service;
- A civic group might sponsor a community-wide bicycle registration project;
- A church group might sponsor a home-contact project for elderly people;
- A bank, supermarket or drugstore chain might purchase property engravers and make them available to customers;
- A group of civil engineers or architects might sponsor a physical design crime risk survey program;
- Any volunteer group might provide clerical assistance to the crime prevention organization, trained assistants to help in conducting security surveys, or other "labor-intensive" support of the program;
- A local firm could sponsor weekly or monthly telecasts featuring descriptions of key current types of crime and suggestions for countermeasures; and
- Any organization can assist in the development, production and distribution of educational materials as well as provide citizen input to the crime prevention planning process.

These possibilities are by no means exhaustive—the actual range of group project possibilities is limited only by the imagination of the practitioner and his ability to match the interests of a group with an appropriate project.

In a situation where many groups are doing many things, however, the practitioner must be able to provide adequate guidance and coordination. Unless this important management function is provided by the practitioner, the group project efforts can become chaotic and even conflicting. The wise practitioner will fully utilize steering committees, advisory councils and other project management mechanisms to spread the management workload. Through this type of group project activity, the practitioner is not only able to involve existing community organizations in conducting most of the tasks needed in the comprehensive crime prevention program, he or she is also able to set the stage for the third major citizen participation strategy component.

Informal Social Control Strategies

We have briefly discussed informal social control as a key aspect of crime prevention strategies. In the long run, informal social control is the primary means by which crime will be prevented. In other words, the goal of the practitioner's efforts should be the permanent adoption of effective crime prevention attitudes and behavior by the social groups that make up the community. The comprehensive crime prevention program should always build toward this end, recognizing that all other strategies (that is, environmental design, law enforcement action, and individual client risk management) contribute to, stimulate, support or supplement daily life activities in which people maintain good standards of crime prevention behavior and assume responsibility for preventing victimization of their neighbors and associates.

As Conklin points out: *Informal Social Control in a community operates through a web of social relationships that develops over time. Relatively trivial interpersonal contacts gradually generate a network of trust and interdependence. This process is strengthened by the influence of public characters such as shopkeepers and newspaper salesmen who are in frequent though limited contact with many residents in the community. They spread news among the people and help bind the community together . . . (and) . . . help maintain a sense of community that informally controls deviant behavior in the area. However, if neighbors do not know each other and if no web of social relationships exists, people will not be able to guard each other from harm. Without minimal contacts among residents, people will not even know who is a neighbor and who is a stranger in the area.*[1]

On the negative side, as Conklin points out: *If people react to crime with fear and distrust, they may withdraw from social contacts in public places. As a result, there will be fewer people on the streets and residents of the area will be less likely to watch the streets. This weakens social control and leaves public areas to criminals. They will not be seen committing crimes or will not be reported if they are seen.*[2]

The importance of informal social controls in determining the extent of criminal behavior is well illustrated by Conklin's description of a study of two neighborhoods in Cambridge, Massachusetts, one with a high rate of juvenile delinquency and one with a low rate. Social characteristics in the two neighborhoods were much alike. But in the high delinquency area, there was higher variation in religion and ethnic background. Neighbors knew fewer neighbors by name, had fewer interests in common, and disliked their community more. Persons in the high-delinquency neighborhood were no more accepting of delinquency, but were less likely to take action if they were not the direct victims. The residents of the low-rate area were more likely to take action if they saw a delinquent act in progress. *When people ignore such acts, there develops an atmosphere where delinquency can grow more easily. The lack of social integration appears to have certain direct effects in a lowered level of social control of delinquent and predelinquent activities.*[3]

On the other hand, where social cohesion is low, *One of the most beneficial spin-off effects of citizen involvement in crime prevention is the increased neighbor interaction it fosters—restoring concepts of mutual assistance, civic responsibility and accountability that are so important to building a "sense of community" and to collective involvement in many broad-scale programs for community development and neighborhood revitalization.*[4]

There appears to be a powerful linkage between effective crime prevention and enhanced community life. From the crime prevention practitioner's perspective, the citizen participation strategy of developing informal social controls works in two ways.

Moderate to High Neighborhood Cohesiveness

In neighborhoods where relatively high levels of social interaction and informal social control already exist, the practitioner's task is to assist the established social group and informal leaders in developing refined security tactics. The practitioner may be able to identify such neighborhoods from his crime pattern analysis as their existing crime rates are likely to be much lower than average. He may also be able to identify such neighborhoods on the basis of the level of social organization that they display. However, he should not be misled by mere appearance and should carefully observe such neighborhoods to determine how cohesive they really are.

The practitioner will have little difficulty in becoming acquainted with neighborhood leaders—in fact, they may have already responded to **awareness, knowledge** and **group project** promotions. If not, they will probably welcome the practitioner's approach, and be very interested in forming a Neighborhood Watch program or other organized participation in crime prevention.

A good example of this type of setting is the BUILD organization of Buffalo, New York. BUILD was established in 1967, and serves a mostly Black and poor constituency through a federation of over 260 local groups. Its purposes are broad—community service, economic development, local school control, elderly housing projects, organizing of low-income tenants, and improved law enforcement and criminal justice operations, to name a few.

From this organized base, it became possible to establish solid crime prevention efforts, including:

- Periodic flyers on criminal victimization which solicit community cooperation in police investigations;
- An anti-prostitution campaign;
- Tenant anti-crime organizations;
- A proposed store-front "Crime Prevention Alert Center" system which would provide, for each 6-8 square block area, . . . *an operating base for ad hoc escort services for the elderly, volunteer and paid security patrols, hot-lines for witnesses and victims of crime, periodic assessment of security needs . . . publication of highly localized crime prevention newsletters and alerts on crime trends and preventive measures, monthly neighborhood hearings on crime and crime prevention, proposal development and identification of funding resources to support anti-crime initiatives.*[5]

Neighborhoods Lacking Cohesiveness

Where neighborhoods lack cohesion and social interaction, the practitioner may well find crime rates which are moderate to high compared with other areas, and is unlikely to find an existing social structure which can be used as the immediate basis for an organized crime prevention effort. However, the practitioner will be able to identify some people who are leaders and opinion molders, if he or she uses a careful approach. Such an approach may require that the practitioner consult with police who patrol that neighborhood, with social service workers, with political leadership from that area, with local ministers and others who are familiar with the way things work. If the practitioner has been successful in developing group projects and programs, some of his or her current crime prevention "constituency" may be able to help.

In any case, the practitioner's objective should be to introduce the idea of crime prevention to the neighborhood through people who know, understand and are trusted by the occupants of the neighborhood. This is particularly true if the practitioner is a police officer and the neighborhood is distrustful of police. It is important to realize that the initiative needs to be taken by the local leaders themselves, for developing crime prevention programs in such neighborhoods is much more a task of community organization than of crime prevention itself.

An interesting model of the self-initiated multi-neighborhood organization approach is the formulation of the Block Association of West Philadelphia, described by Alicia Christian as follows:

For the multi-racial community surrounding Philadelphia's University of Pennsylvania, the 1971 Christmas season is memorable, not for its holiday joy, but for a rash of burglaries, rapes and muggings. West Philadelphia's 1972 New Year celebration was marred by three rapes in two weeks. Mrs. Ellie Wegener, one of the principal organizers of the Block Association of West Philadelphia (BAWP), noted the general feeling of fear, anger and outrage that prevailed in the community: "... the fear of crime was producing a barricade mentality: people were buying more locks and becoming prisoners inside their own homes. People all around us blamed the court systems, the government, anyone who was convenient to blame! They did not consider the possibility that they themselves could play a role in this new crisis."

Mrs. Wegener and her minister husband invited neighbors to a meeting at their home. The group decided that the block club structure (with block and regular meetings) would be ideal for building a sense of community strength and unity around crime prevention and allow each block to define its own priorities. Within four months of the initial meeting, neighbors on thirteen blocks were attending regular monthly meetings. Guest speakers such as policemen, narcotics agents, and other professionals in law enforcement and criminal justice were invited to provide suggestion on how residents might protect themselves.

BAWP's organizing model involved two block leaders, one from each side of a street. Association units were formed by alliances of up to 25 blocks in an area. BAWP had no formal board structure, although two people were initially elected to coordinate the program. Monthly meetings were generally informal. The Association issued a monthly newsletter and sponsored such events as block parties, barbecues, summer play-in-the-street affairs, and day camp projects....

BAWP's community walks and the widespread resident use of freon horns were a part of its program for deterring street crime. Groups of two or three volunteers regularly walked the neighborhood, watching for suspicious activities. If crimes were observed, they simply called the police and activated their horns to alert other neighbors. Walkers, who keep logs of events, also distributed BAWP literature, visited aged residents, watched abandoned homes and homes of vacationers.

All residents in a block were approached to join the club. The secretary kept an updated listing of members (names, addresses, telephone numbers). In addition, records were kept as to who was assigned and who actually appeared for block patrols. Emphasis was placed on cooperation among blocks and maintaining close communication with police.

BAWP established positive, supportive relationships with the Philadelphia police department, many of whose members praised its operation. BAWP participants noted that the program has contributed to neighborhood stability and that some real estate values, after a period of marked decline, have risen 50 percent since its inception. BAWP has also succeeded in building a spirit of community solidarity within racially diverse neighborhoods....

In 1973, the Association received $27,000 in Pennsylvania LEAA block grant funds to train organizers. By 1974, a separate training organization had evolved from BAWP and became the Citizens Alliance for a Safer Philadelphia (CLASP). In 1975, the CLASP Neighborhood Safety Training Program became statewide receiving $135,000 from the Governor's Justice Commission to institute its training/action model in several towns and cities throughout the state.[6]

A MODEL APPROACH TO NEIGHBORHOOD ORGANIZATION

As adapted from the August 1977 issue of *NCPI Hotline,*[7] the following provides a good general summary of an ideal approach to neighborhood organization:

1. **Develop and organize community background data** such as crime and loss patterns, police patrol districts, census tracts, natural geographic boundaries, and other socio-economic and demographic patterns. The purpose of the background data is to provide a reasonably complete picture of crime patterns and related socio-economic conditions, and to help determine how varied and cohesive the neighborhood population is.[8]
2. **Use collected data to select target areas.** High priority areas should be identified along with control areas so that the true impact of the project may be assessed. A control area is a comparable neighborhood that does not participate.
3. **Establish criteria for levels, kinds and distribution of participation.** The practitioner should make determinations prior to attempting to organize a neighborhood as to what a workable participatory model for that neighborhood should look like. For example, what percentage of residents should be involved? How should their residences be distributed (e.g., every other house? alternating facing houses? how many per floor or wing of an apartment building? etc.): Should residents remain anonymous for surveillance and reporting purposes? Should potential participants be screened to eliminate potential suspects? What residents should take organizing lead? Should police present low profile at first? What kinds of project activities are likely to be best received at first? What levels of acceptance (or suspicion) are likely? And so on.
4. **Approach neighborhood leader.**[9] People who have been identified as having significant influence in the area should be approached first. After they have been informed as to the possible nature of a project and its potential value to the area, they may be asked to invite friends and other potential group members to participate in preliminary, exploratory meetings. It is important to remember that local leaders serve many important functions such as information dissemination, recruitment, and stimulation of group interest. They also can provide the practitioner with valuable feedback on the progress and interest in their areas.[10]
5. **Provide education and training.** Group members and related police personnel should become acquainted with their respective roles in the crime prevention efforts. The goal is to build the basic mechanism necessary for citizens and police to work together. Initial citizen education and training would probably include crime reporting procedures, guidance on what to report, and basic security and personal safety tips. As interest is generated and people begin to increase interaction with police, the police must encourage the actions of the group members and provide guidance for future contacts. It is imperative that not only the beat officer, but other police personnel, such as the patrol commander and radio dispatcher, be aware of the group and lend their cooperation.

6. **Provide feedback to police and citizens.** If a citizen's call results in a good arrest, he should be notified and recognized (this can occur through monthly bulletins or meetings). If the call resulted in an officer being dispatched in a situation where police response was inappropriate, he should also be notified and courteously advised on what should and should not be reported to the police. Citizens should also provide feedback to the police department on police response. Was it timely, courteous, accurate?
7. **Formulate crime-specific tactics.** When project performance reaches a level that reflects a capacity for the project to function as an efficient, unified, and directed entity, it is time to look back to the crime data files to determine the most serious crime problems facing project areas and devise crime specific tactics to address the problems. Times, places, and methods of criminal attack must be considered to identify what specific things a citizen can do to reduce the chances of criminal victimization. For example, if it is determined that most burglaries in the project area are of single-unit dwellings with little or no force required, then the project should first attempt to educate its members regarding residential security hardware and procedures. If these tactics displace burglaries, on-going crime analysis will provide the knowledge to develop redirected tactics.
8. **Implement crime-specific tactics** throughout the organization as they are developed. This may be accomplished in several ways, such as the practitioner or local patrol police attending the periodic group meetings to provide specific training, or training sessions for group leaders, who, in turn, train the groups and supervise the process of implementation. Crime-specific tactics should be implemented comprehensively throughout the project to achieve maximum effectiveness and avoid displacement.
9. **Assess performance of the organization.** Performance assessment should be provided by formal and informal feedback throughout the organizational period. At some point, however, the determination must be made that the project is sufficiently organized, educated, and trained to become essentially self-sustaining and regenerative with logistical support from the police.
10. **Evaluate impact on crime in the project area.** The project goal of reducing crime can only be reliably and validly assessed relative to crime specific tactics. Also, it is important that the tactics be quickly assessed so that they can be revised as necessary. When refined tactics have been implemented, the practitioner can legitimately establish that specific actions by citizens are affecting the rate of crime in the neighborhood.
11. **Encourage group to take on other needed changes.** Once the mechanism for community action has been established and proven effective, it can take on various community improvement projects. Widening the scope of activities of the organization can help sustain the crime prevention effort by offering participants a diversity of activities to meet their interests. Many of these projects will probably overlap, reinforcing each other, and increasing total chances of success.

Development of informal control can only be successful to the extent that citizen groups acquire the internal momentum and purposefulness necessary for sustained activity. A neighborhood group, for example, that reduces burglary through a quick burst of activity and then disbands has accomplished a short-term objective, but will fail in the future to maintain a burglary reduction without an on-going development and review process. The extent to which crime will be reduced **and the reduction maintained** is no greater than the extent to which the neighborhood assumes permanent collective responsibility for suppressing harmful behavior within the area.

The approaches described here can also be applied to a variety of community settings—the shopping complex, the public housing project, the high-rise apartment complex, the mixed residential-commercial area, or any other portion of a community. The major ingredient required in establishing a geographic area of any kind as a target for participatory projects is the actual or potential presence of some kind or level of cohesiveness around which the people who live or work in the area can build a common interest.

Finally, it must be clearly understood that the organizing of participatory projects within groups of citizens is always a delicate matter, requiring skills of sensitivity and understanding from the organizer, as well as varying levels of technical expertise. Above all, the crime prevention practitioner must be prepared to be the flexible catalyst for change, rather than its identified leader.

CONCLUSION

The development of citizen participation in a community-wide crime prevention program must proceed from the concept of the practitioner and the citizen as partners. After all, the community is being asked to assume collective responsibility for crime reduction rather than to serve as a kind of subordinate extension of the law enforcement agency.

Proper planning and good communication are of the utmost importance in developing citizen participation, particularly at the outset. Coordination becomes especially important as the program develops, for the many groups and interests which can become part of the participatory program need to operate in harmony.

An early priority for the practitioner should be to develop the participation of key individual groups and agencies in the community. Unless such groups (both at the jurisdiction-wide and at the neighborhood levels) are behind the program and actively participating in it, the program may never fully jell.

Finally, the practitioner must be prepared to move with the ever-changing interests and social characteristics of the community. Priorities may change for individual groups, neighborhoods and the community as a whole, and the practitioner must constantly analyze these shifts, reinforce flagging interest, and if necessary, abandon groups whose interest has faded so as to concentrate on groups whose interest is stable or rising. Above all, he must seek and maintain the widest possible circle of alliances in the public, private and voluntary sectors, because it is from these allies that the strength and continuity of the program will flow.

8 Planning the Community Program

We have indicated how important planning skills are throughout this volume to the crime prevention practitioner. In this chapter we will discuss the key elements of crime prevention program planning, and show how, most of all, the success of a comprehensive crime prevention program is dependent upon the quality of the planning that goes into it.

A plan is quite literally the foundation for any program. It is crucial that the practitioner understand planning, not as an exercise to be endured, but rather as **the single most important ingredient in determining whether he or she will succeed in preventing crime.** The kind of planning that consists of putting together words merely to satisfy some bureaucratic requirement is not only useless, it is harmful. Such an approach practically guarantees that we will never understand what we are trying to do, let alone achieve success. The only thing it does is produce documents to decorate a bookshelf or stuff a filing cabinet.

Proper program planning is hard, painstaking work. Most of us find it easier to simply start doing something—to act rather than to plan. Yet, if we wanted a new house, would we simply give a carpenter nails, lumber, and hammer and a saw and tell him to build something?

The practitioner who has understood the basis for designing crime risk management systems, selecting security devices and procedures, applying environmental design concepts and developing citizen participation, now must understand the basis for planning the program through which those skills will be applied. In this chapter we focus on the three main issues of crime prevention program planning:

- Designing the organization;
- Defining the crime problems and priorities; and
- Developing program objectives.

DESIGNING THE ORGANIZATION

The organization established to plan, manage, and coordinate the crime prevention program is the core of that program, and it is crucial that this organization have the capabilities necessary to get the job done. The following issues must be considered in designing the organization:

Design Issues

Permanence

Just as there is a continuing need within the community structure for a police or sheriff's department, a public health department, and a fire department, so there is a continuing need for a crime prevention organization. It takes time for the best crime prevention program to change community patterns so as to reduce criminal opportunity, and those changed patterns must then be maintained and continually reinforced. In addition, crime patterns will always change, and new opportunity reduction patterns will always be required. The practitioner must look for organizational designs which have a good probability for permanence.

Resources

Comprehensive crime prevention program organizations are not expensive to support compared with many other types of community programs, because the bulk of the resources in a well-planned program flow from community efforts and the supporting activities of public agencies. Also, the budget of the crime prevention organization itself may be small compared to the total quantity of resources involved in the program. Nevertheless, establishing and maintaining a community-wide program does require significant resources, and these must be obtained (and retained on a continuing basis) in competition with the needs of other community programs. Thus, it is important that the organization be designed so as to attract ongoing support.

Acceptance

The practitioner may encounter acceptance problems in developing the crime prevention program. One of the most difficult groups to convince of the merits of crime prevention may be the local law enforcement agency. Other elements in local government should also be considered as potential sources of difficulty. Private interests may present acceptance problems, as may citizen groups and others.

While these acceptance problems can usually be solved over time, it is important to design the organization in such a way as to neutralize as many acceptance problems as possible. This usually means involving the potential sources of acceptance problems in the organization design process.

Ripple-Effect

Plans for the crime prevention organization design should take into account the types of activities that can be effectively conducted by individuals and groups outside of the crime prevention organization itself, and the best means by which these "ripples" can be started and sustained. In addition to reducing the direct costs of the program, good ripple-effect planning has the obvious benefit of helping to overcome resource and acceptance problems. Thus, the practitioner's aim must be to share program responsibility as early and as widely as possible.

Coordination

In any locality, there are likely to be a number of activities already underway related to crime prevention. Schools; neighborhood groups; organizations of youth, older people and women, established service and voluntary clubs; tenant organizations; and others may have developed crime prevention projects. There may be a crime prevention unit (CPU) in the police department which provides services, but has not developed a comprehensive program. Any such existing effort has potential for further program development. On the other hand, failure to bring together all crime prevention activities during the organization design phase can lead to misunderstandings, competition and refusals to cooperate as the comprehensive program develops.

Innovation

Experience has shown that where individuals and groups are given the opportunity to be creative, innovative crime prevention approaches can emerge. All of the standard projects now used by practitioners developed out of an innovative response to a particular problem situation. Thus, the organization should be designed to encourage experimentation and innovation on the part of those who work with it or within it.

Results

The organization should be designed for results. All organizational elements and their activities should be aimed at producing specific positive impacts on crime. There is a great difference between the community program that exists simply to exist, and the program that exists to produce results. The former may never quite get its act together, and the latter is clear on the basic philosophy that impact is the goal, rather than activity by itself.

With these basic considerations in mind, the practitioner can begin to develop the program's organizational structure.

Formal Sanction

The planning process must define and establish a crime prevention organization which can effectively carry out the crime prevention program. Whatever the exact makeup of the organization, its responsibilities, structure and relationships, staffing and other resource needs should be defined and provided for through some legally-binding municipal sanction.

Sanction can be provided through departmental order if the crime prevention organization is entirely located within the police department, sheriff's department or department of public safety. It can also be provided by executive order of the municipality's chief executive or by city council ordinance, whether or not the crime prevention organization is located entirely within a law enforcement or public safety agency.

Perhaps the ideal form of sanction is a combination of the ordinance, executive order and departmental order, each binding the appropriate level of community government to a defined set of roles and responsibilities.

The need for formal sanction applies even if the crime prevention organization is to be established as an independent, not-for-profit corporation, as the arm of some existing not-for-profit entity, or in some other non-governmental form. The need still exists for local government to recognize the organization and affirm its responsibilities and purposes. In addition, local government must approve and affirm the support from law enforcement and other government agencies that the independent organization will need.

The importance of formal sanction lies in its ability to clearly define what the municipality expects from either the government-based or non-government-based crime prevention organization, what resources and other support it is willing to provide, and what form of broad-based community input will be acceptable. And while crime prevention programs may be started without formal sanction, it must sooner or later be obtained, because sanction not only authorizes the program, it also sets forth the kind of commitment that the municipality is willing to make to the program. Sanction is a powerful mechanism. Its absence can weaken a program and dilute its energies, and its presence in proper form can provide a major boost for program effectiveness and survival.

Organizational Structure

The organizational structure must set forth, in clear and specific terms, the crime prevention program's:

- Governance, management responsibilities and reporting relationships;
- Internal staffing patterns and arrangements for external manpower support;
- Arrangements for funding, office space, equipment and other resources; and
- Mechanisms for community input and coordination.

We do not hold that any organizational model is inherently better than any other, as long as the four basic functions are provided for. In some cases, the organization may be entirely contained within the local law enforcement agency, with the citizen input mechanism provided for by an advisory council or citizens' task force. In other cases, the citizen input mechanism may be the actual governing body (for example, the mayor's commission on crime prevention), with staff responsibilities assigned to the law enforcement agency. Or, the governing body may be the city council itself, with operating responsibilities delegated to staff agencies, citizens boards of trustees, and the like. If more than one jurisdiction is involved—for example, a county-wide crime prevention program involving several cities and unincorporated areas—the governing body may be the sheriff's office or the board of county commissioners, with an advisory council consisting of the mayor and chief law enforcement officer of each incorporated jurisdiction within the county. Each jurisdiction, in turn, might have its own advisory body.

The suitability of one organizational form over another depends entirely on the local situation. In one case, the police chief might be such a staunch advocate of crime prevention that it is appropriate for the community as a whole to delegate the entire responsibility for managing the crime prevention effort to the police department. In another case, circumstances might dictate that there be separate staff units, one within the police department and another in a civilian organization, both coordinated by a central council of some sort. It is even possible, in situations where no public agency is interested enough to act, for a group of leading citizens to set up a private non-profit organization.

What is important is that the organizational structure chosen is set forth precisely and rationally, and that it is supported by evidence of commitment from all key parties to fulfill the responsibilities that the organizational structure calls for. This latter point is often overlooked. Because informal support arrangements and oral agreements have a way of breaking down over time, the organization's planners should obtain contracts, letters or memos of agreement and other appropriate documentation of arrangements for support made with anyone external to the organization itself.

Law Enforcement Role

As we have said throughout this book, law enforcement agencies must play a pivotal role in the community-wide crime prevention program. This role can be established within the program's organizational structure in a variety of ways, ranging from locating the organization within the law enforcement agency itself to establishing specific supporting relationships between the organization and the law enforcement agency's crime prevention unit. In any case, it is essential that provisions be made not only to draw upon the law enforcement agency for specific support but also to set a process in motion through which crime prevention can gradually become an important priority in the total community law enforcement program.

Citizen Input Mechanism

The need for an appropriate advisory group is so important as to deserve special mention. Whatever the form chosen for this mechanism in the organizational structure, it should include representatives of all significant community interests—public, private, voluntary and citizen-based. The listing of "Other Roles" in Chapter 3 reflects the kinds of interests that should be represented.

The advisory group should be called upon to make genuine contributions to the planning and, later, to the operational phases of the crime prevention program. The task of working with a group of diverse citizens can be time consuming, but the practitioner must look at this activity as being crucial to both the short-range and long-range success of the program. It may simplify the logistics of working with such a group to split it into two groups—a relatively small council or executive committee which can work with the practitioner on a day-to-day basis and a much larger task force or committee which can assemble periodically to review the work of the council or executive committee.

DEFINING THE CRIME PROBLEMS AND PRIORITIES

There are two distinct phases in this stage of the planning process. The first, crime analysis, provides for problem definition. The second, priority setting, involves a decision-making process based on problem definition.

Crime Analysis

The practitioner has two separate tasks to perform in relation to crime analysis. The first is simply to develop a sufficient crime analysis base for the planning of the program. The second, and perhaps more crucial, is to develop a permanent crime analysis function within or available to the crime prevention organization.

If the local law enforcement agency already has a satisfactory crime analysis capability, the crime prevention practitioner will simply arrange to have access to it, through interdepartmental arrangements if the crime prevention organization is a crime prevention unit or bureau within the police department, or by interagency arrangements if the crime prevention organization is based outside the law enforcement agency.

If insufficient crime analysis capability exists, the practitioner will have to build it. This is more likely to be the case than not for . . . *To date there has been little systematic analysis of the dynamics of crime. Most of the current statistical knowledge about the dynamics of crime comes from the FBI uniform crime reports. While these reports have value when presenting a national picture of crime, they do not detail the geographic distribution of crime nor its operation at the neighborhood level.*

A description of crime city-wide cannot substitute for further analysis at the neighborhood level in preparing localized crime prevention programs . . . Different neighborhoods have different crime problems. Only through the use of citizen and police knowledge coupled with localized statistics can the problems in a neighborhood be articulated and appropriate strategies be developed.

A combination of factors must be studied—victim characteristics, the community and physical setting, suspect characteristics and the suspect modus operandi. *With this information it is possible to more clearly define the crime problem. The availability of this information will facilitate the determination of strategies most appropriate for preventing and controlling crime.*[1]

The practitioner who is forced to build his own crime analysis capability may find it necessary to obtain some voluntary or paid professional help in designing a data collection and analysis system that is within his ability to operate. His crime analysis system need not be highly sophisticated, but it must permit him to easily examine specific types of crime in relationship to the conditions under which they occur. The types of data he needs and the kinds of planning information which his analysis should produce are described below.[2]

Data Sources

The primary data sources for crime analysis are as follows:

- Offense reports,
- Citizen interviews,
- Offender interviews,
- Housing and population data from the Census,
- City directories,
- City planning department materials,
- Informal interviews with public officials and community representatives, and
- Direct observation.

Offense Reports

Offense reports prepared by police officers at the scene of a reported crime can be prolific sources of information, if conscientiously filled out. Statistical analyses of groups of offense reports can paint a very detailed picture of prevailing crime patterns, by type, by location, by time of the day or day of the week, by attack methods, and even, to the degree known, by type of suspect. In addition, total and average loss information can be developed from offense reports. The crime analysis function should routinely screen and develop detailed breakdowns of the data contained on offense reports.

Citizen Interviews

Offense report information may be incomplete because it can only deal with reported crimes, which may be much less numerous than actual crimes and because police officers may have difficulty obtaining all information called for by the offense report form. It also does not reveal citizen perceptions of crime and citizen fear of crime. For these reasons, citizen interviews, also referred to as victimization surveys, are an important supplementary source of data. Citizen interviews attempt to measure the actual crime victimization experienced by interviewees, the levels and kinds of personal and family concerns about crime, and the degree and nature of security precautions already in use. These measures are then compared to personal, household and geographic characteristics of those interviewed. Citizen interviews can be conducted on a random sample basis city-wide, in selected crime problem areas as revealed by the study of offense reports, or both.

Offender Interviews

Interviews with selected prison inmates and other ex-offenders may be a good source of information on typical offender likes and dislikes with respect to different types of targets, security devices, escape routes, and parts of town, as well as preferred attack methods and the ways in which the local criminals assess their own risk. Such information will probably not be an accurate cross-section of the views of the total criminal population, and may be suspect on the grounds of self-servingness. Nevertheless, offender interviews can provide a good cross-check on the validity of information from offense reports and other sources.

Demographic Information

Census data, city directory information, city maps, and other urgan planning information can help the crime analysis unit establish the characteristics of the targets-at-risk. This can be done both on a city-wide scale (for example, the numbers of single family housing units, convenience stores, supermarkets, jewelry stores, liquor stores etc.) and on a neighborhood scale (for example, housing by income level, occupation, family status, and other measures). Knoweldge of targets-at-risk is essential if one is to properly understand crime patterns and the impact of crime.

Interviews with Officials and Community Representatives

Informal interviews with public officials such as police officers, other criminal justice professionals, representatives of other government agencies, and community representatives such as ministers, and leaders of various civic, service, voluntary and neighborhood groups can extend, enlighten, and perhaps most importantly explain the relevance of most of the statistical information gathered through other means.

Direct Observation

Another valuable aid in the process of understanding community crime patterns is direct observation of selected areas in the community. Much information on potential criminal opportunity can be gained by simply driving or walking through subdivisions, shopping areas, other residential neighborhoods, parks, and other settings and observing key characteristics of individual targets and areas as a whole. Such "windshield surveys" take relatively little time but add an invaluable dimension to the informational perspective of the crime analysis process. The practitioner can enlist police patrolmen, housing inspectors, fire marshalls and others (see Chapter 6) to help in this direct observation process.

Information Provided by Crime Analysis

Let us briefly consider some of the kinds of information useful in crime problem definition.

Cost of Crime

Cost is an important dimension which is often absent from crime prevention planning at the community level. The practitioner first must be able to understand the direct cost of crime (value of property stolen and cost of lost work time or medical treatment resulting from crime-related injury). Property loss cost can be estimated from offense report data. Costs and losses due to injury, fear, intimidation and other personal crime effects are more difficult, but can be estimated to some degree through citizen interviews. In addition, the cost of operating criminal justice system activities in the community can be determined through examination of the municipal budget, and the cost of risk management measures, such as security devices, security personnel and insurance can be estimated from interviews.

These and other types of direct crime cost information can be used to develop the dollar cost dimensions of general and specific crime problems and the potential value of prevention efforts. For example, it might be interesting to know the average value of preventing a liquor store robbery or a home burglary. It might also be interesting to know what the cost/value relationships of a particular preventive result might be. For example, what would be the value of a five percent reduction in commercial burglary? How much might it cost to achieve that benefit?

There are other, less obvious, costs that are also important to understand. One of the most significant of these is the possible cost of neighborhood decline due to crime and fear of crime. If fear of victimization causes people to move out of high crime areas, and demand for housing and store space in those areas consequently decreases, property values and public tax revenues from those areas will also decrease. At the same time, declining neighborhoods tend to require increased municipal services. For example, a Minneapolis study showed that in the area most highly vicitimized by residential burglars, the average value of an owner-occupied home was $3,300 less than the city-wide average. And in the most highly vandalized area, the average value of a owner-occupied housing unit was about $2,100 less than the city-wide average. The study also revealed that *... these two specific crimes ... generate a total estimated tax revenue loss of about seventeen million dollars. Given this figure, a reduction in the residential burglary rate and vandalism rates by just ten percent would correspond to an increase in the property tax revenue of about 1.7 million dollars.*[3]

This kind of information obviously permits an additional cost/benefit dimension to be added to the crime prevention planning process by making it even more obvious that effective crime prevention strategies can tend to pay for themselves.

Citizen Concern About Crime

There are usually substantial differences in the way people perceive crime depending on their personal, social and economic circumstances. Consequently, it should be expected that there will be substantial variations in community opinion concerning the importance of various crime problems. For example, a population group that is highly concerned about robbery might tend not to cooperate with a proposed crime prevention strategy which emphasized burglary prevention. In addition, groups of people who have either much higher or much lower levels of concern about crime than is warranted by actual crime patterns may need special educational efforts or modified crime prevention strategies.

The issue of crime fear is a sensitive one and must be handled carefully in the crime prevention program planning process. It is not advisable, for example, to use scare tactics as a method for motivating citizen participation in crime prevention strategy. On the other hand, where there is significant crime fear, even if statistically unwarranted, there may be a motivational factor which can be used in promoting crime prevention strategies.

A particular aspect of citizen concern is usually the fear of injury associated with crime. Through crime analysis, the practitioner may find that the risk of personal injury varies greatly with the type of crime and with victim behavior during the criminal attack. Such information can be useful in formulating strategies for reducing irrational fear.

Crime Rate by Opportunity

The population's risk of a particular crime can be measured with the least distortion by comparing crime incidence with number of opportunities for that crime within an area. Only the crime rate by opportunity is easily converted into the probability that a given target will be attacked during a given period of time. If the practitioner calculates crime rates on the basis of available targets, rather than on a population basis or simply in terms of numbers of crimes, he or she has a very useful way to display and understand crime patterns. Such an approach, for example, permits clear distinctions to be made among high, moderate, and low crime areas.

In addition, one can determine opportunity rates by particular target subtypes. For example, instead of residential burglary as a single category, one might look separately at single-family homes, two-to-four-family homes, and apartment units and burglaries involving garages and residential storage areas. Each represents a significant variation in target type and perhaps attack method. As this kind of analysis is carried out in finer and finer detail, patterns which can be dealt with by crime prevention strategies will begin to emerge.

Time of Occurrence

It is useful to determine the distribution of crimes by target type, by hour of the day, day of the week, and month of the year. Unfortunately, much of the time-related information available is of limited value. If the victim is not present during the crime, for example, the time may be recorded as range of hours and days during which the crime probably occurred. On the other hand, the time of occurrence for crimes such as robbery and assault can be more precisely identified. Understanding the hourly, daily, weekly and monthly fluctuations in target-specific crimes may be of great help in developing specific preventive strategies.

Attack Methods

The methods by which crimes are committed are very important to understand if one is to plan effective strategies. For example, if we learn that a high percentage of residential burglaries involved unforced entry, we may conclude that a significant percentage of residential burglaries could be prevented simply by the use of appropriate locking devices. Or, if we find that the rate of unforced entries into apartments is much higher than that for single family dwellings, we might conclude that a primary problem in apartments is lack of key control or failure to change locks between tenants. Or, we might find that most commercial burglaries involve entrance at the side or back, which permits us to stress security for such entrances accordingly.

Attack methods need our most serious scrutiny during the planning process, for unless we understand the ways in which crimes are committed, we cannot possibly develop effective opportunity reduction strategies.

Suspect Characteristics

Depending on the type of crime, information on suspects may either not be available or not be reliable. Nevertheless, where possible, tentative estimates of suspect characteristics may be useful in adding a further dimension to the practitioner's understanding of crime patterns. Knowledge of age, sex or race may help in establishing cause and effect relationships (as, for example, in the case of the high school referred to in Chapter 7, where daylight burglaries in the vicinity could be correlated with school truancy rates because of the age of the few suspects for whom information was available). If place of residence is known for a few suspects, it may be possible to develop some tentative conclusions on suspect mobility. In Minneapolis, for example, analysts found that 82 percent of known residential burglary suspects lived within one-half mile of their target. On the other hand, the analysts found that burglaries in a few residential areas were primarily committed by persons living in other areas some distance away. This kind of knowledge can be of great use in plotting prevention strategies on a neighborhood-by-neighborhood basis.[4]

The value of crime analysis to the practitioner is that it makes possible a very detailed understanding of the relationships between specific crime patterns and specific local environments, as well as more general patterns and relationships on a city-wide scale. Thus, crime analysis, like the physician's diagnosis, becomes the essential basis for development of problem-solving strategies. The practitioner who uses general approaches without first conducting an adequate crime analysis is like a doctor who would automatically prescribe penicillin to everyone who walks into his office. Such an approach may be of some random benefit, but will be ineffective or even harmful in some cases.

Priority Setting

The crime analysis will probably reveal a wide variety of significant crime problems, and the practitioner will be faced with the need to make choices involving types of crime, types of targets, and parts of the community. Crime prevention programs, particularly in the early phases of program development, cannot possibly deal with all crime problems simultaneously. Thus, the practitioner will be faced with the need to make choices as to how, where and why to focus his or her efforts.

Priority-setting can be both a major challenge and a major need. As we have seen, the crime prevention approach must be strategic in nature if it is to accomplish anything. The practitioner must resist the temptation to do a little something about every problem, because the shotgun approach is usually both wasteful and inconclusive. On the other hand, the practitioner may be exposed to substantial political or administrative pressure to prove the value of crime prevention or deal with a wide variety of troublesome crimes or both. The way to avoid this kind of problem is to involve a range of people in the decision-making process.

The organizational mechanism for broad-based citizen input described earlier should become deeply involved in priority-setting. This advisory council, citizens' task force, mayor's commission or other body must have the opportunity to thoroughly review the practitioner's general recommendations for action. Then, the advisory body can make its own priority recommendations to the practitioner. Such recommendations can be further refined by the practitioner, re-reviewed by the advisors, and the process recycled as necessary to achieve a set of priorities which is both feasible from a crime analysis viewpoint and desirable from a community viewpoint. It should be stressed that while crime analysis will produce objective recommendations, value judgments by community groups and public officials must also be taken into account.

Key administrators (the police chief, the mayor, criminal justice planning bodies and so forth) should also review and provide input to the priority setting process, because it is through these administrators that program resources will flow. The result will be a ranking of targets for the practitioner's efforts. For example:

- School vandalism;
- Rape;
- Residential burglary in X subdivision;
- Bicycle theft;
- Street robbery and assault in Y commercial area; and
- Commercial burglary in the Z warehouse district.

It may be that the target crime problems and the order of priority for their solution are not entirely consistent with the actual seriousness and quantitative impact of those problems. Instead, the priorities will be aligned according to the perceived importance of the problems. For example, bicycle theft may not have much economic impact compared to burglary and robbery, but it is an annoying type of crime affecting many people. Rape, though perhaps low in incidence compared to other types of crimes may be considered by the community as a much more serious problem than some of the more numerous types of crime.

The practitioner must accept such apparent inconsistencies, and not merely because it is politically expedient to do so. In the end, community cooperation is the essence of crime prevention. The practitioner who responds enthusiastically to the priority recommendations of community representatives helps encourage the active community participation so essential to the long-range success of crime prevention programs.

On the other hand, there is nothing to prevent the practitioner from developing a few priorities of his or her own. Where important crime issues exist that are lost in the community consensus of priority, the practitioner may be able to obtain approval to experiment with approaches which can be converted to major thrusts later as the experiments bear fruit and the community is persuaded to adjust its priority viewpoints.

DEVELOPING PROGRAM OBJECTIVES

Having developed the crime analysis base and determined the priorities for action, the practitioner must develop and implement the strategies by which the desired results are to be achieved. This conclusive part of the planning process, referred to as **strategic planning**, involves making action decisions systematically and with the greatest possible awareness of their potential results. Strategic planning attempts to answer the following question: "Given the problems we face, the resources available to do the job, and all of the things we might do to solve the problems, what actions have the greatest likelihood of producing the results we desire?"

It is important to distinguish this approach from the much more common kind of planning which asks, "Given the problems we face and all of the things we might do about them, for what actions can we find the necessary resources?"

This latter approach is like the doctor who says, "There are several drugs that might help my patient. Which of them do I have as free samples in my drawer?" We would, of course, prefer that he asked himself, "Which drug will do the most good?" Thus, the crime prevention practitioner's task in strategic planning is to develop that strategy for action which will do the most good for the problem at hand.

Setting Objectives

The primary task of strategy development is to set objectives. By objectives, we do not mean statements of general direction and purpose or hoped for results. Instead we mean specific, concrete statements of results to be achieved. For example, "To reduce vandalism" is not a statement of objective, but, "To reduce the dollar cost of vandalism at high school X by 50 percent within one year" is an objective.

Objectives are not abstractions. They are the action commitments through which results are to be achieved. They are also the standards against which achievement is to be measured. They focus and direct the crime prevention program and serve as its fundamental strategy. Thus, they must be capable of translation into specific tactics and must enable resources and efforts to be concentrated. They must winnow out the trivial actions and focus on the key actions needed to achieve program results. They must therefore be selective.

Objectives must lead directly to work. Work itself is always specific, has clear, unambiguous results, a deadline, a performance standard and a specific assignment of accountability. (By definition, work excludes all of those activities which, while energy consuming, have no specific purpose or result. This is no mere play on words. Unless the practitioner's efforts are work, as defined above, they will lead nowhere.)

In a nutshell, objectives provide direction and make action commitments. They do not determine the future, but **they are the essential means by which energy and resources are mobilized for the making of the future.** Thus, they must state a specific target for work, a specific result to be obtained through work, and a specific deadline for accomplishment of the result.

The importance of proper objective-setting simply cannot be overstressed. Objectives determine the program—for good or ill. If the objectives are arbitrary or vague, the program will be arbitrary or vague. If the objectives call for minimal accomplishment, the program may produce minimal results. If the objectives call for unrealistically high results, the program will be an exercise in frustration. If the set of objectives is incomplete, the program will stumble. If individual objectives are in conflict with each other, the program will become chaotic. If no objectives are set, the program will simply spin its wheels.

Direct Objectives

Many local crime prevention programs have failed to live up to their potential promise because of deficiencies in crime-specific objective setting. For example, in a southwestern city of about 100,000 population, the police department crime prevention unit established the following as one specific objective for the second year of their program: **To stabilize the incidence of residential burglary throughout the city.** The following table summarizes their work in connection with this objective and the specific results attained:

Planned activity	Measured activity	Measured impact
Establish and sustain 40 new neighborhood groups	57 established, CPU staff meets about once a month with each group	None of 600 participant households burglarized (daily burglary reports)
Conduct 250 residential security surveys	538 surveys conducted	Burglary 0.9% in surveyed homes, vs. 1.6% city-wide: surveyed victims apparently did not follow recommendations: local sales of "improved" security hardware doubled
Enroll 700 new Operation ID participants	1056 new participants	Burglary 0.4% compared to 1.6% and some attempts aborted because of marked property
Conduct 200 public presentations	136 conducted	80% of participants subsequently requested specific CP service
Disseminate public information	Radio/TV announcements newspaper articles talk shows carton stuffers Welcome Wagon	Some services requested as a result, staff concluded that "it helps"
Establish patrol focus in high crime residential areas	Provided weekly crime activity report to Patrol Div.	Report "useful"
	Maintained pin map (burglary) in Patrol Squad Room	Pin map "marginal"
Draft a security code for adoption by city	Not drafted but key actors "educated"	"Education" process working OK, first draft expected next year.

From the information presented in this table, it appears that the work was generally successful. The practitioners established almost 50 percent more neighborhood groups than they had planned, and they delivered over twice the planned number of security surveys. The areas where the planned activity was not completely achieved (public presentations, drafting of security code) show reasonable progress. The "measured impact" of most of the activities is encouraging or at least revealing.

One can easily imagine, therefore, the sense of dismay when the Uniform Crime Reports at the end of the year revealed a 61 percent increase in residential burglary compared to the previous year.

Why such a disappointing result? One can't say for sure, but there are some obvious contributing factors.

- It is easy to imagine that the public awareness campaign could have resulted in an increased tendency for citizens to report residential burglary—thus creating, to some degree, a statistical increase in crime rather than a real one.
- The direct service activities of the CPU (neighborhood groups, security surveys, Operation ID enrollment, public presentations) from which citizen action could be expected, touched only a small fraction of the city's residential units, many of whose occupants may already have been more security-conscious than the average.

In essence, the stated objective of stabilizing residential burglary city-wide was a severe overreaching of the CPU's capability during that year. On the other hand, the planned activities themselves more nearly approached reasonable statements of objective. The practitioners might have stated a series of objectives for the year related to residential burglary as follows:

- To stabilize the incidence of residential burglary in 40 selected neighborhoods through establishment of Neighborhood Watch groups;
- To reduce the incidence of residential burglary compared to the city-wide average for 250 selected homes through security surveys and for 700 homes through Operation ID enrollment;
- To generate requests for crime prevention services through public presentations;
- To increase the reporting of residential burglary through a city-wide public awareness campaign; and
- To obtain agreement from key public and private officials to work together on the drafting of a building security code.

Such objectives obviously set the stage for useful work. They are direct, limited and specific.

The crime prevention unit in another southwestern city during the same time period set for itself the following objective (among others); **To stabilize the rate of increase of residential burglary in Patrol District X.**

Having selected a limited target area, a limited target crime and a modest quantitative result, the practitioners saturated that patrol district with daily, door-to-door appeals to residents to accept security surveys and with invitations to form neighborhood groups. The following table summarizes their work:

Planned activity	Measured activity	Measured impact
Conduct security surveys on a saturation basis	522 surveys in District X (burglary victims surveyed first, then adjacent homes	56% reduction in residential burglary compared to previous year
Establish neighborhood group through a saturation process	74 neighborhood group meetings held, averaging 22 people each for total of 1,600	

Given the way in which the stated objective was transformed into specific work, it is not surprising that a significant reduction was achieved. However, the objective would have been even more appropriate had it been stated as follows: **Achieve a major decrease in residential burglary in Patrol District X through saturation programming involving security surveys and neighborhood group establishment.** This was apparently the true objective in the minds of the practitioners anyway; the stated objective may have been worded cautiously to avoid a public overpromise.

In these examples, we have described one situation in which the objective as stated was almost totally unrelated to the specific work conducted. And although the work itself was useful, the comparison between the work and its results in terms of the objective was painfully inadequate. In the other situation, the stated objective was overvague and, in retrospect, overconservative, but it did directly relate to the work that was conducted and the results that were achieved. This is an all-important distinction that the practitioner should not fail to observe in setting results-oriented objectives.

Indirect Objectives

So far, we have only discussed objectives that aim to directly reduce specific crimes. There are also indirect kinds of objectives that are just as important to the overall program as the direct objectives.

Promotional objectives set forth strategies for specific and general improvement in public knowledge and understanding of crime prevention programs and for building the foundation for subsequent direct action. **To obtain agreement from public and private officials to work together on the drafting of a building security code** is a promotional objective, as is **to generate requests for crime prevention services through public presentations.** There should be an objective stated for each area of promotional interest, and such objectives should in no way be confused or associated with crime-specific objectives.

Resource objectives deal with the human, financial and physical resources needed to carry out all other objectives. Though often taken for granted, or submerged in budgeting processes, resource objectives need to be the subject of conscious and deliberate thought and objective setting. Otherwise, the program will remain at the mercy of whatever resources may come its way or (all too often) may find itself entirely without resources.

Reporting objectives acknowledge and deal with the fact that any crime prevention program only exists as long as relevant elements in the community believe that it does a necessary, useful and productive job. Reporting objectives relate directly to program survival. It is crucially important, therefore, that the practitioner develop specific objectives for reporting progress to the individuals and organizations to whom the program is (even informally) accountable. This can even include the public as a whole—objectives for regular reports to the public through the newspapers, for example.

Productivity objectives deal with the way in which resources are used and their contribution to the total program effort. Of primary value to program management, productivity objectives attempt to define, for example, the way in which security surveys will be conducted and the average amount of time involved, methods and time allocations for work with neighborhood groups, and so on. While many people rightly object to working "by the numbers", appropriate productivity objectives help everyone in the crime prevention organization understand what is expected of themselves, and what to expect from each other. Moreover, these objectives are the primary source of performance guidance to the program manager.

Innovation objectives, finally, provide an excellent basis for moving toward greater program productivity and effectiveness. By clearly identifying those areas in which current service delivery methods can be improved, where new services and approaches are needed, where (perhaps) current services may be eliminated, and where program management processes may be improved, innovation objectives permit a clear working focus on desired program change. Thus, more than any other single kind of objective, they contribute to continued increase in program effectiveness and explicitly demand a creative approach to the total program effort by all members of the organization.

CONCLUSION

We have briefly described in this chapter the major elements involved in planning the community-wide crime prevention program. As is true for the other matters discussed in this introductory volume, we do not expect that the practitioner has learned, in detail, how to plan as the result of reading this chapter. We do expect the practitioner to understand the essential role of planning and to appreciate the key thought processes that go into planning. These thought processes will be explored further as we discuss program management and impact evaluation in the next two chapters, for there really can be no arbitrary separation of planning, management and evaluation functions. Planning sets objectives, management carries them out, and evaluation determines the actual results which then become new input to the planning function . . . and so the cycle continues as long as the program exists.

9 Managing the Community Program

The value of a crime prevention program needs to be apparent in terms of actual performance. Without proper management, it is impossible to deliver valuable performance.

This chapter briefly describes the key elements in proper crime prevention program management.

Management consists of the principles, practices and techniques used in achieving the objectives of the organization and is the process through which an organization operates. It plans, organizes and controls organizational activities so that the crime prevention program's objectives may be accomplished. The degree to which a crime prevention organization uses its resources **efficiently** to **effectively** attain its objectives is the degree to which it may be said to have good management.

Management is a systematic activity which must be focussed on performance and results. Cost control is needed too, but above all else, the practitioner-manager must emphasize results. He or she must learn to manage the crime prevention program for performance; unless high quality management is a first priority of organizational activities, no crime prevention program can possibly achieve its potential for helping people.

The tools of the crime prevention practitioner-manager are:

- Manpower resources;
- Financial and other resources;

- Performance and cost control measures;
- Impact measures;
- Work assignments; and
- Reporting mechanisms.

With these tools, the manager can begin and continue the task of achieving the objectives set forth in the planning stage.

MANPOWER RESOURCES

There have been a number of attempts to determine the minimum staff size for a crime prevention program. The state of Texas, for example, set forth the requirement that a police department-based crime prevention unit should have two full-time sworn officers or one percent of the authorized strength, whichever is greater.[1] In fact, the number of staff personnel in the crime prevention program should be determined by the workload requirements inherent in the program's objectives. Staff people should be employed or assigned full-time to the crime prevention program, and their working hours should be established as appropriate for the specific tasks of crime prevention as opposed to the general tasks of any agency.

Staff Training

The manager should arrange for the crime prevention program staff to be trained at the earliest possible time, preferably before the program gets underway. Many states now offer one-week basic training programs, some states provide two-week intermediate training, and the National Crime Prevention Institute provides a two-week basic course and a three-week comprehensive course. The three-week NCPI training program is the ideal, but as a practical matter, the program may not need or be able to afford such training for each staff member. However, each person should be trained for at least one week, and preferably two. The manager and any supervisory staff should have three weeks of training, as should any staff persons who must operate independent of direct supervision (as in a police precinct, for example, or in one of the several communities which make up a county-wide program). NCPI's new twelve-week training course will provide the most comprehensive advanced security, loss reduction and crime prevention training for the public and private sectors. This program will be geared to the person who must assume a high level of management or service responsibility.

Sources of staff manpower can be varied. However, each staff person should have background and experience which is related to the practice of crime prevention. Experienced police officers, for example, can become excellent crime prevention practitioners. Persons with experience in community organization, private security, building inspection, fire prevention, human services delivery, urban planning and crime analysis also can adapt readily to crime prevention practice.

Supplementary Manpower

Supplementary manpower can be a large factor in the crime prevention program's work. All members of local law enforcement agencies should become capable of applying crime prevention practices to a degree consistent with their daily work (for example, patrol). Other public employees, such as firemen, may be able to make significant crime prevention contributions. Chapters 3, 6 and 7 provide additional examples of potential sources of supplementary manpower. The manager's task with regard to supplementary manpower is primarily that of providing training. The more people who can be trained—even briefly—the more supplementary manpower is potentially available.

FINANCIAL AND OTHER RESOURCES

Normally, financial resources must be obtained before staff can be employed or assigned. However, in many cases, core staff can be reallocated from other duties at no cost to the program. While this expedient is useful in getting the program started, permanent staffing patterns should be based on financial resources which are under the control of the manager. Thus, the manager must develop and maintain a flow of funds sufficient to take care of all program needs. This means that the manager-practitioner must become skilled in budgeting.

Budgeting

The budget is the work program of the crime prevention organization expressed in dollar terms. Its purpose is twofold: (1) from the viewpoint of the program manager, the budget's purpose is to obtain funds necessary for program operation; and (2) from the viewpoint of the supervisory organization (police department, city council, mayor's office, citizen organization, state or federal grant monitor), the budget's purpose is to limit and control the program's expenditures. Budgets all into two general categories: line-item budgets and program budgets.

Line-item budgets break down planned expenditures according to category of expenditure: salaries, operating expenses, equipment purchase and so forth. **Program budgets** break down expenditures by program objectives. Of the two, the program budget offers much more potential for management control, since it ties expenditures directly to the work of the program. Line item budgets are only useful in a gross management sense (for example, have we spent all of our travel money yet?) and, to be helpful to the manager, must be reconstructed in terms of the objectives.

In order to deal effectively with the public budgeting process, the practitioner-manager must learn how that process works through all levels above the crime prevention program. This process-learning includes:

- Budget preparation formats;
- Timing of budget submission;
- Location of budget submission;
- Key personnel in the budget review and approval process and their viewpoints; and
- Sources of decision-making support.

In addition, the manager must learn to make realistic, defendable and justifiable budget requests.

Other Funding Sources

There are many potential non-government sources of funds at the local level. Service organizations, for example, often have small amounts of money which are available for projects of community benefit. Local service and business organizations can also stage or sponsor fund drives on behalf of crime prevention programs, or campaigns to generate other kinds of resources (for example, free printing of brochures, donated physical resources such as office furniture and equipment, portable display panels, and even mobile vans to house displays). Foundations at the local level can be sources of support (refer to *The Foundation Directory*[2] for information on foundations in your area). Insurance companies and Chambers of Commerce also have the potential capability to provide resources.

The key to unlocking all of these other resources is to first determine the local groups that might be of assistance, identify their types of interest and activity, develop specific project ideas that seem to fit with those interests and activities, and then approach organizational leaders to discuss the possibilities.

Whatever methods the manager uses to develop initial funding, it should be understood that maintaining an adequate fund flow and increasing that flow for program expansion purposes is a constant challenge for the manager. This is why it is so important to have resource objectives. Such objectives stimulate the manager to keep a lively interest in potential sources of funds and to develop methods for securing those funds well in advance of need. This is particularly important if state or federal grant funds are a significant factor in the initial funding pattern. Grant funds sooner or later run out, and the manager who has not taken the pains to develop alternative funding sources may find that his or her program runs out, too.

PERFORMANCE AND COST CONTROL MEASURES

The manager must constantly make decisions regarding the flow of work. Is enough effort being applied to a given objective to achieve the result in a timely fashion?

Is the quality of work high enough? Is too much effort being invested? All managers make seat-of-the-pants decisions in these areas. The good manager develops performance measures to guide his decision-making.

The manager makes specific work assignments which result in work being accomplished. Performance and results are then measured, permitting the manager to make better decisions regarding the next round of work assignments. If the methods used to measure performance and results are appropriate, the manager's decisions will get better and better as time goes on. On the other hand, if no measurement is attempted, each round of decision-making is of the same "by guess and by gosh" nature as the preceding round.

It is safe to say that the single most important activity for the manager, once appropriate objectives have been set and funds and staff obtained, is the development and use of good performance measures. With them, he can constantly improve the efficiency and effectiveness of program operations and even correct for bad decisions of the past before they prove harmful. Without good performance measures, the manager is at the mercy of whatever feedback he may randomly receive.

Thus, the practitioner-manager needs clear and common measures covering all areas of program work. The measures need not (and should not) be rigidly quantitative, nor need they be exact. But they must be clear, simple and rational. They must be relevant—in order to direct attention and efforts where they belong. They must work reliably, and their potential for error must be known and understood. They must be self-explanatory—that is, understandable without the need for complex interpretation or philosophic discussion. They need to focus on results, and they need to cover both quantifiable and nonquantifiable events. They must be received in a timely fashion by whoever needs them. They must be economical—providing the minimum amount of information needed. They must be operational—made to serve an action purpose in an action environment. Finally, they must be simple to use; complicated measurement methods do not work, because they confuse people, and they direct attention away from that which needs measuring and toward the measurement methodologies themselves.

Activity Counts and Activity Cost

This is the simplest kind of crime prevention program performance measure. It consists of listing the number of speeches made, number of security surveys conducted, number of brochures given out and so on. Such measures have limited value in that although they do indicate the gross volume of work performed, they cannot reveal how well the work was performed or what its results were. Activity counts are often illegitimately used as the primary or only measure of productivity. Such a "numbers game" is totally inconsistent with good management practice.

If, in addition to measuring the number of times a given activity is conducted, the manager also measures the total cost of that activity in man-hours or dollars, he or she can begin to understand how resources are being used.

Cost by Activity Unit

A further refinement in activity cost measurement, this type of measure focuses on the average cost of each unit of activity. For example, the manager might set up a simple time sheet to record estimated security survey time units as follows:

Residential Security Survey Time Sheet

Arrangements	Travel	Survey	Report Preparation	Total

Having logged the time expenditures in this activity for a suitable period of time, the manager can compute average costs, as shown in the table below. The times used in the sample time sheet to calculate average costs are arbitrary and used for example only. We do not know how much time an average security survey takes, and the point is that neither does the manager, unless he or she sets up measures to find out. In any case, what is the value of knowing that the average residential security survey cost is $35.00 (plus mileage and other incidental costs)? With this information, the manager can work to reduce average cost. For example, scheduling all surveys in the same geographic area for the same day might save travel time. Use of a standardized report format might save report preparation time. Perhaps more importantly, the manager is now in a position to begin to assess **result costs**, which will be further discussed in the following pages.

Cost per Average Residential Security Survey

Component	Average time	Unit cost*	Average cost
Arrangements	0.5 hour	$10.00	$ 5.00
Travel	0.5 hour	10.00	5.00
Survey	1.5 hours	10.00	15.00
Report preparation	1.0 hour	10.00	10.00
Total cost			**$35.00**

*Unit cost is the dollar value of a particular unit of effort, such as a man-day or man-hour of labor. In the case of labor, it is calculated as follows: total cost per man year (salary, fringes and any overhead as a percent of salary) **divided by** net number of working days (365 minus weekends, holidays, vacation and sick leave time and any non-program administrative time) **equals** unit cost per available man-day **divided by 8 equals** unit cost per man-hour.

For example, an annual cost of $17,600 divided by 220 days equals $80 per man day divided by 8 equals $10 man hour.

Acceptance Rates

Most crime prevention program activity is aimed, in one way or another, at persuading people to engage in some kind of new or modified opportunity reduction activity. Whether the practitioner is making crime risk management recommendations to a businessman, providing guidance to a Neighborhood Watch group, or working with an *ad hoc* group of architects, planners, building officials and developers to design a building security code, the desired result is some sort of action. We can define this desired action result as **acceptance**, and we can measure **acceptance rates.**

Let us consider, for example, the development of acceptance rates for the security survey. First, we need to have a numerical scale for the various kinds of acceptances we might expect. If we make five recommendations to a homeowner, the first priority recommendation might be worth five points, the second four points, the third three points, the fourth two points and the fifth one point and the total value of all recommendations would be 5 + 4 + 3 + 2 + 1 = 15.

Upon checking back with that homeowner 60 days later, we might find that recommendations one and three had been carried out, and the rest had not. The acceptance rate would be 5 plus 3 divided by 15 equals 0.53. We can compare acceptance rates for all homes we survey using the same method, no matter how many recommendations we make in each case. For example, if the acceptance rates for five surveyed homes are as follows: No. 1 – 0.53; No. 2 – 0.22; No. 3 – 0.75; No. 4 – 0; No. 5 – 0.91, our average acceptance rate for the five homes would be 0.53 plus 0.22 plus 0.75 plus 0 plus 0.91 equals 2.41 divided by 5 equals 0.4. In other words, our average acceptance rate is 40 percent.

Result Costs

We are now ready to calculate result costs, by comparing the cost of the average security survey to the acceptance rate.

Average survey cost = $35.00
Average acceptance rate = 0.4
Average result cost = $35.00 divided by 0.4 = $87.50

Thus, in our arbitrary example, we have learned that if our batting average for security survey acceptances is 40 percent, our average result cost for each home surveyed is $87.50. It is very clear from this comparison that whatever our average survey cost, its value as a result is very strongly affected by the acceptance rate. To visualize this more clearly, let us look at a range of result costs. Given that the average survey costs $35.00:

Acceptance rate	Result cost
10%	$350.00
20%	175.00
30%	116.67
40%	87.50
50%	70.00
60%	58.33
70%	50.00
80%	43.75
90%	38.89
100%	35.00

From this illustration we can see how costly the security survey process is if we are not obtaining at least a 40-50 percent acceptance rate. We can also see how important it is from a management viewpoint to measure both the costs of crime prevention activities and the acceptance levels that result from crime prevention activities.

Cost and Performance Standards

It is impossible, at present, to provide any universal guidelines for cost and performance standards in crime prevention. However, each practitioner-manager, through measurement and analysis processes such as briefly illustrated above, can begin to determine what the standards can be and should be for his or her particular program, and can work to improve those standards with time and experience.

IMPACT MEASURES

We must clearly distinguish between **performance** and **impact**. Performance, in all cases, relates to the direct results of the practitioner's efforts, which almost always can be defined in terms of some new or modified action on the part of a client, an organization, or members of an informal social group. Performance, as we have discussed it here, does not refer to the reduction of crime itself, unless such reduction results directly from the practitioner's own efforts, and such direct reduction by the practitioner will rarely occur.

Impact, on the other hand, refers to the extent to which new or modified opportunity reduction actions by people in the community reduce crime. Thus, there is a relationship between performance and impact, but impact must be measured separate from performance. Impact assessment is discussed by itself in Chapter 10.

WORK ASSIGNMENTS

As we have said, the achievement of the program objectives developed during the planning process depends on how well these objectives are translated into work. The job of scheduling work, assigning tasks to appropriate individuals and organizations and monitoring work progress will occupy a large portion of the manager's time, **whether or not the scheduling, assigning and monitoring task is done well.** It thus behooves the manager to approach this job in the most organized way possible.

Scheduling Work

In general, work should be scheduled in such a way that its desired results will occur by the date called for in the stated objective. This normally requires the manager to break down each objective into a series of specific tasks, each task with its own deadline for accomplishment, arranged in such a way that the total work flows as expeditiously as possible toward completion.

Assigning Work

Each specific task should be assigned to a specific person for accomplishment. The practice of specific assignment and accountability is extremely important, because this is the only method available to the manager to insure that the work is done. If the manager, instead, relies on general understandings of responsibilities for work, he or she will all too often discover too late that each staff person thought that the task was someone else's responsibility. In short, there must be an assigned crew chief for every significant work unit—someone who is responsible to the manager for its accomplishment, and to whom the manager can turn for progress reports and other information. This is especially important for work which is to be done by people or organizations outside the crime prevention organization. In the case of work undertaken by external groups and individuals, the only control the manager has is specific prior agreements on the work to be done and the time by which it is to be accomplished.

Monitoring Work Progress

The manager must state very explicitly the reporting requirements associated with each work unit. How often is the crew chief to report progress to the manager? What form shall the report take? Who else (and how and when) should be made aware of progress in that particular work unit? What performance and cost measures need to be associated with the work? When and how should measures be made? When and how should they be reported? These kinds of understandings, like the work assignments and schedules themselves, must be very precise. The manager must receive needed monitoring information in a timely manner, on the one hand, and should be spared unnecessary, untimely information, on the other. Precision in this area will not only provide the manager with appropriate decision-making information, it will also help insure that his or her time is not constantly occupied with work-related conversations which, however interesting, are irrelevant.

In the end, the manager's own time is the most precious of anyone connected with the program. All too many managers occupy themselves with conversations and crises to the extent that they fail to conduct their most important task, which is to serve as the source of constant direction for the progress of the work itself.

REPORTING MECHANISMS

The manager's job is to ensure effective and efficient accomplishment of the program's work. In turn, the manager is always responsible to others for the results of the program. Whether the manager's accountability relationships are simple (for example, he or she reports directly and only to the chief of police or sheriff) or complex (an advisory board, the chief, the mayor, the city council, the Chamber of Commerce, state and federal grant monitors, etc.) there should be clearly developed reporting mechanisms that properly fulfill the need for accountability. This area of the manager's responsibility is so important that specific objectives should be established for reporting (as was discussed in Chapter 8).

Reporting mechanisms may be of a chain-of-command, coordinative or informative nature. Chain-of-command reports are prepared for information and decision-making by those who directly supervise the program manager. Coordinative reports are made to those whose activities relate to the program, but who neither control nor are controlled by the program manager. Information reports are made to those who are or should be interested in the program's progress, but who neither supervise nor work directly with the program.

Through these reporting mechanisms, the manager seeks not only to maintain and expand the program itself but also to communicate its purposes and activities to all relevant groups and individuals so that the program may develop a firm foothold in the general context of community affairs. This matter of weaving the crime prevention program into the permanent fabric of community activities is the ultimate responsibility of the manager-practitioner.

CONCLUSION

Managing the crime prevention program consists of using resources effectively to accomplish specific work objectives which, in turn, lead to the achievement of a specific series of desired results. The mission of the crime prevention program is to cause or stimulate crime reduction activities in the community, and the task of the manager is to see that the program's mission is accomplished.

The manager must have a set of specific objectives to begin with. Then, he must be able to obtain resources, assign and monitor specific work tasks, develop and apply performance and cost control measures in order to determine the work's effectiveness, report the results of the work to appropriate individuals and groups and, finally, develop and apply impact measure to determine the results of the work.

If these management practices are not applied in a disciplined and consistent manner, the work of the crime prevention program can become confused and capricous, and the desired results may never be obtained.

10 Evaluating Impa

As a practical matter, there is a great deal of difference between evaluating the o
going crime prevention program and evaluating the experimental or demonstratio
crime prevention program. In the ongoing program, the primary purpose of impac
evaluation is to help the program manager make better decisions about futur
program developments. He may (and perhaps should) have access to a limite
amount of specialized help in designing his evaluation process, but the evaluatio
effort itself can be but a minor portion of the total program effort.

In the experimental or demonstration program, the primary purpose o
impact evaluation is to develop knowledge for use by researchers and by agencies
which might wish to duplicate the experiment. The evaluation component is likely
to be a large fraction of the total effort, involving rigorous scientific work by
specialized professionals.

This chapter deals only with impact evaluation in the ongoing program. Our
purpose is to show the manager-practitioner that the impact of any crime prevention program can be evaluated in a manner and degree sufficient to serve the needs
of the program decision-maker.

The basic requirement for accomplishing effective impact evaluation is not
the availability of specialized evaluation skills. These skills, while important, are
only tools. Rather, the key factor in impact evaluation is the practitioner's own
attitude. If the practitioner lacks this essential, critical attitude, the most complex,
costly, and professional evaluation program will be of little use.

Thus impact evaluation is, in essence, a critical point of view applied systematically to the crime prevention program.

THE PURPOSE OF EVALUATION

In the long run, evaluation may be the single most important task faced by the crime prevention program. Unless the program is capable of measuring its actual effect on crime patterns, the degree to which its plans and activities achieved results cannot be determined. Without this knowledge as to results, it is impossible to accurately plan for subsequent activities. Moreover, it may be difficult to convince the community that it is worthwhile to continue investing in and cooperating with the crime prevention program.

Specifically, evaluation can help the practitioner-manager to:

- Measure the degree of progress toward specific objectives and toward the general goal of reducing crime;
- Identify weak and strong points of program operations and suggest changes;
- Compare efficiency and effectiveness of existing program activities with other possible program activities;
- Challenge underlying program assumptions and improve the quality of program objectives;
- Suggest new procedures and approaches;
- Provide for timely recognition of negative program effects;
- Help establish priorities for resource allocation;
- Increase public support for successful approaches and reduce emphasis on unsuccessful approaches;
- Provide standards against which to measure achievement; and
- Develop a critical attitude among staff and advisory personnel and increase communication and coordination among them.

It is also important to understand some of the things that should not be considered as part of the purpose of evaluation. Edward Suchman[1] has compiled a list of the undesirable purposes for which evaluation is often used.

Eye-wash—an attempt to justify a program by evaluating only those parts of it that look good.

White-wash—an attempt to cover up program failure or errors by avoiding any objective appraisal and relying instead on unsolicited testimonials.

Submarine—an attempt to torpedo a program regardless of its worth in order to get rid of it.

Posturing—an attempt to use evaluation to impress others with the program's scientific approach and the professionalism of its staff.

Postponement—an attempt to delay action by pretending to seek the facts in hopes that a storm of protest will blow over by the time the study is completed.
Substitution—an attempt to cloud over or disguise failure in an essential part of the program by shifting attention to a less relevant but more defensible program part.

Such pseudo-evaluative tactics may have political uses, at times, but have no relationship whatever with the true purpose of impact evaluation. However, they may be confused with proper impact evaluation both in the mind of the practitioner and in the minds of those to whom evaluative information is presented.

It behooves the practitioner-manager to evaluate honestly, for his overriding concern should be the quality, strength and results of his program. Politics may be important to program survival in the short term, but in the long run, only program results count.

CAUSE AND EFFECT

Stripped of its professional jargon, the impact evaluation approach consists of systematically linking cause with effect. Thus, the evaluation process is basically no different than the process of developing an unbroken chain of evidence to link a suspect with a crime. In the case of the crime prevention program, the causes are opportunity reduction efforts by (or on behalf of) potential victims, and the effects are changes in crime patterns that result from those opportunity reduction activities.

It is not enough, however, to compare **general** causes and **general** effects. For example, if we determine from police offense reports that the opportunity rate of residential burglary in a given neighborhood is 100 per 1,000 homes, and if we develop a Neighborhood Watch program in that neighborhood along with security survey and other services, and a year later we determine, again from police offense reports, that the opportunity rate has dropped to 50 per 1,000 homes, can we conclude that our program has reduced residential burglary in that neighborhood by 50 percent? The answer, of course, is no, because we do not have conclusive cause-and-effect evidence, only circumstantial evidence, and our case in "evaluation court" can easily be destroyed by our inability to answer questions such as the following:

- What was the actual rate of residential burglary prior to and after your program (i.e., how reliable an indicator of the total burglary problem was your summary of reported burglary)?
- What was the actual rate of participation in the burglary prevention program (how many residences complied with security survey recommendations and what was the nature and quality of citizen reports during the program)?

- Can you prove that events unrelated to the program did not cause the apparent reduction (for example, increased police patrol, installation of streetlights, changes in neighborhood population, the economy, traffic patterns, the weather)?
- Did displacement occur (i.e., did burglars simply shift their operations to an adjacent neighborhood)?
- Did the decrease occur because of efforts by the residents themselves or simply because of the presence of crime prevention program staff in the neighborhood?

On the other hand, if reported burglary in the neighborhood increased by 50 percent, could we conclude that our program did not work? The answer, again, is no. We might have stimulated much higher levels of reporting, and thus created a statistical crime wave. Unrelated local, regional and national conditions might have been a factor. Police patrol might have decreased. Or, the average loss might have decreased substantially. Thus, the general, circumstantial approach to cause-and-effect linkage is of little value in honest evaluation.

Direct Factors

The first thing we need to do in constructing the evaluative cause-and-effect chain is to determine all of the factors that go into it. Then we must develop reasonable methods for measuring all of those factors.

Pre-program crime patterns need to be clearly understood if we are to develop and implement an effective strategy, let alone accurately determine the outcome of that strategy. Thus, for the type of crime and the targets of that crime we wish to deal with, we must obtain historical crime data in at least the following dimensions:

- **Reported versus actual crime.** We must always anticipate that the total incidence of crime will be greater than the reported incidence. We must also anticipate that one of the effects of any crime prevention project may be to increase the reporting rate. In order to make this necessary baseline measurement, some form of citizen victimization data survey is needed as a comparison with police offense report data (both types of information are discussed in Chapter 8).
- **Attempted versus successful crime.** Because the usual crime statistics reports do not discriminate between successful and unsuccessful crime attempts, it is useful to make a special effort to extract this comparison data from offense reports and victimization surveys.
- **Types and amounts of loss.** Also obtainable from a combination of offense reports and victimization surveys, this type of data is useful in before-after comparisons.
- **Methods of attack** may be analyzed from offense reports and victimization survey data and used in before-after crime pattern comparisons.

- **Reporting patterns.** As distinct from the reported versus actual crime comparison, the actual patterns of reports can provide useful comparison data. Police dispatch records can provide information on such things as percent of reports made by non-victims and delay time between incident and report.

Program performance data provides the next major link in the cause-effect chain. As discussed in Chapter 9, such information should be collected as part of the project management function and should include, in addition to simple activity counts:

- **Acceptance rates**, or the extent to which persons in the target population both participate in some way and comply with the recommendations made by project staff;
- **Reporting patterns** directly connected with the project (surveillance and reporting activities in Neighborhood Watch, for example) should be measured in terms of quality, quantity and direct result;
- **Law enforcement response** is another important project performance dimension, particularly for citizen crime reporting types of projects such as Neighborhood Watch. How do police dispatch personnel handle citizen reports? How do patrol units respond? Is feedback provided to project participants? etc.; and
- **Related social and physical changes**, such as modified streetlighting, removal of barriers to visibility, citizen patrol activities and other efforts aimed at securing the general project environment should be carefully documented.

The disciplined collection of program performance data is perhaps the single most important part of impact evaluation. Not only is it a crucial link in the cause-and-effect chain (what happened as a direct result of our project activities?), it is also an excellent way to reinforce the all-important habit of routine program self-examination.

Post-program crime patterns will involve the same kind of measurements described for pre-project crime patterns with one additional feature—displacement. In order to measure displacement as a project outcome (either in its presence or its absence) it will be necessary to conduct pre- and post-project crime pattern measurement in areas adjacent to the project target area, and it will be desirable to perform such measurement in selected areas distant from the project area.

Indirect Factors

As we have discussed, the cause-and-effect chain may be influenced by factors which have no direct relationship to the project itself. Such factors include:

- Changes in police patrol patterns;
- Major physical changes such as city-wide or area-wide installation of improved streetlighting, new commercial or residential construction, and alterations in traffic flow patterns;

- Major economic changes in areas such as unemployment, commercial activity, inflation and recession;
- Seasonal variations in climate;
- Other yearly pattern changes such as school vacations;
- Changes in legal definitions of crimes;
- Major jurisdiction-wide crime scares and anti-crime promotions; and
- Changes in criminal activity patterns in adjacent jurisdictions.

Any such factors which are not part of the project strategy or not under control of project management must be identified and, to the extent possible, their potential effects on the cause-and-effect chain understood.

Some factors, such as changes in police patrol patterns or major physical changes affecting the project area, are best dealt with by anticipation. The practitioner should make it a point early in the project design phase to establish relationship with public agencies and other groups that might instigate physical change, and either allow for such planned change in the project design or persuade those responsible to delay the planned activity until the project can be assessed. Possible changes in police patrol patterns may be handled through cooperative negotiations with the chief law enforcement officer and his patrol commanders so that every effort is made to minimize such change during the project period.

Control Group

Other factors, such as major economic change, climate change and other yearly variations, jurisdiction-wide crime promotions, and changes in the crime patterns of adjacent jurisdictions are best handled by setting up a **control group**. A control group is an area or population group, located at a reasonable distance from the project area or group, which displays social, physical, economic and crime pattern characteristics similar to the project area or group. Pre- and post-measurement is conducted for the control group in the same manner as for the project group, and crime pattern changes in the control group are, in essence, subtracted from the results measured for the project group. Through this technique, major, jurisdiction-wide changes in crime patterns may be isolated from the actual project results.

The use of control groups is a key concept of evaluation, because it may be the only way to conclusively demonstrate that observed effects in a target area or target population can be attributed to program activities and not to any other cause. Back in "evaluation court," we can imagine the conscientious program manager—who has just laid out an excellent cause-and-effect chain linking program activities with specific results—being devastated by the question, "That's very interesting, but how do you know for sure that it wouldn't have happened anyway?"

Ideally, data from a control group that has not been exposed to program activities can be used to answer this question. In the laboratory, for example, a scientist can randomly divide his mice into two groups—one to receive the experimental treatment, and one to be left alone. He can then readily compare the treated to the untreated mice. Unfortunately, such a clean matching of control and experimental groups is seldom possible in the real world. Even more difficult, considering the community-wide thrust of many elements in a crime prevention program, is the matter of finding a control group that can be "left alone" by the program, or by related activity over which the practitioner has no control.

Despite the difficulties inherent in the control group concept, the practitioner-manager should attempt to establish such groups where possible, because even a rough idea of what might have happened in absence of program activities is better than no idea at all.

SPECIFIC IMPACTS

From before-during-and-after measurements such as described above, a number of specific kinds of results can be determined.

Reported crime may increase as a percentage of total crime. While this may be embarrassing to explain, it is a logical consequence of increased citizen concern for and participation in crime prevention programs. If total crime incidence can be measured or estimated through victimization surveys, it may be possible to show increases in reported crime as positive, rather than negative, effects of the program.

Reporting of crime may change in significant ways. Ability to measure such changes can document significant project results such as:

- More reports of crimes-in-progress;
- More reports by observers in addition to victims;
- Less time between the occurrence of thc crimc and the report;
- More feedback and cooperation between citizens who make reports and police who dispatch or respond to those reports.

Crime success ratios are a subtle but useful indicator of program impact. In theory, an effective crime prevention project should lead to increasing proportions of failed attempts compared to total crimes committees. This change may be of more significance than changes in the numbers of total attempts.

Total and average losses from criminal attack may change significantly. The total or average loss might decline more steeply than the crime rate, or even the crime success rate. In any case, loss is as important a dimension of crime prevention program results as crime incidence itself.

Fear and concern for crime may change as a direct result of the program. If citizens feel more secure and comfortable, the program has had a significant impact.

Displacement (geographic, temporal or crime mode) can be a good indicator of program impact, even if there is no net reduction in total crime. The fact that the crime prevention program can significantly change crime patterns is certainly an indication of the success of specific strategies. The next step in such a situation is to follow the displacement pattern with additional specific strategies. On the other hand, if no displacement occurs—or is less in quantity or effect than the target-specific crime reduction that produced it—then the program has resulted in a net crime reduction.

Citizen participation can be related to program impact if care is taken to measure the kind and quality of participation. In the long run, the degree to which people accept and use security procedures and devices and informal social control mechanisms, and participate in organized approaches to altering the physical environment, determines the impact of crime prevention.

Police participation can also be a significant indicator. If interest in crime prevention practice and police/citizen cooperation becomes manifest throughout the local criminal justice structure, the most likely result will be a gradual refocussing of law enforcement priorities toward prevention as a primary means of reducing crime. This also has very high long-range value.

TOTAL IMPACT

As was pointed out in Chapter 8, the beginning community-wide crime prevention program cannot and should not attempt to prevent all crimes for all groups in all places. The strategic approach dictates action priorities which are a reasonable mix of the crime problems themselves, the concerns of citizens, and the resources available for the program. Total impact, therefore, must be carefully defined as that which can reasonably be expected to result from the specific program strategies, not as that which might be hoped for over the life of the program. Crime prevention programs will fail almost by definition if they are forced to prove their worth in a global impact sense during any specific time interval. The crime prevention program can bear fruit, but it must be judged on a strategy-by-strategy, year-by-year basis. If crime prevention works at all, it works in the most specific crime/target situation possible, and it is only by gradually building a wider and wider circle of effective prevention situations over time that crime prevention develops its community-wide impact.

The kinds of specific results described above can be used both to inform program decision-makers and to build support for the program. But it is essential that the crime prevention practitioner condition those to whom he reports to expect a series of specific impact indicators rather than impact statements of global generality.

On the other hand, where the cause-and-effect chain produces enough specific impact indicators to justify statements of across-the-board crime reduction, the practitioner should not hesitate to make such statements.

EVALUATION RESOURCES

True evaluative research, with its emphasis on scientific rigor, extensive statistical analysis and precision of results can probably only be conducted in those few situations where the crime prevention program or some of its projects are deliberately designed to be experimental in nature, and where a large part of the resources available to the program are earmarked for evaluation. However, the information needs and measurement techniques described above can be fulfilled to an adequate degree of accuracy within the range of resources available to the average jurisdiction-wide program.

In addition to project management and staff, who should use every opportunity to learn about crime analysis and relatively unsophisticated evaluation techniques,[2] other resources for both the design and conduct of evaluation processes may be conveniently available. Such potential resources include, but are not limited to the following.

Crime analysis units in many law enforcement agencies possess a significant capability for supporting the crime prevention program. Energizing this resource may require no more than a series of detailed discussions between project staff and crime analysis unit staff through which the specific information needs of the crime prevention program may be identified.

Urban planning units in city government may possess most of the resources needed to design an evaluation process and conduct the analysis of data.

Departments of Business or Social Science at nearby colleges and universities may be an excellent source of evaluation support. In addition to the expertise needed to design the evaluation process and help analyze information, such departments may have undergraduate or graduate students who can directly assist in information collection and analysis through internship programs, required research assignments, and dissertation requirements for advanced degrees. Also, such students may be available to work for nominal sums outside of the formal academic structure.

Marketing organizations in local banks, advertising agencies, insurance companies, or manufacturing firms may be able to help in the design, conduct and analysis phases of crime prevention evaluation as a public service.

Chambers of Commerce can sometimes locate members who have appropriate expertise in the areas needed by the crime prevention program.

Civic groups and volunteer organizations may be able to furnish workers to conduct surveys, extract information from offense reports, and other labor-intensive evaluative applications.

State and local agencies in the criminal justice or human services or housing and urban development areas may be able to provide consulting services, computer services or other resources.

Evaluation consultants may be employed—not so much to conduct the entire evaluation, which can be very expensive, but to provide a few days of professional time during the design phase and to consult occasionally thereafter as the evaluation process unfolds. Consultants can be extremely useful as evaluation program designers and trouble-shooters.

Finally, state crime prevention program agencies, as well as the National Crime Prevention Institute, can provide evaluation training or technical assistance or both. The practitioner should make every effort to use these resources.

CONCLUSION

As was discussed in Chapters 7, 8, and 9, community crime prevention programs can develop and implement a wide range of strategies which can have many different effects on crime patterns. As the program unfolds, evaluation can play a crucial role in guiding selection of the most effective techniques, as well as in providing needed planning and management information and in maintaining and improving the base of community support for the program. While few local programs will have access to the kinds of resources needed to develop complex and sophisticated evaluation approaches, any program can do much to assess its own impact through specific cause and effect linkages, providing that program management develops and maintains an intense critical interest in the results of the program.

Techniques used in evaluation need not be highly accurate, but they must be capable of developing a wide range of measurements—since it is very clear that there exists no simple set of indicators which will provide all the answers. Individual indicators of impact are useful in themselves, and may be, but do not have to be, sufficiently powerful *en masse* to prove significant general impact.

Finally, the resources potentially available in any community to help in the evaluation process may only be limited by the imagination of project personnel, if they are willing to seek such help in a wholehearted fashion.

11 The Potential of Crime Prevention

We have discussed, in admittedly brief fashion, what crime prevention is, where it came from, and how it works at every level from the focussed task of providing crime risk management guidance to individual clients to the complex job of organizing a comprehensive, community-wide crime prevention program. We have showed that opportunity reduction, though complementary with other kinds of crime control activities, nevertheless represents a very distinct break with past theories of crime control.

Crime prevention is, above all else, a management approach to crime control. It deals with the practical, everyday realities of our environment. It says that physical and procedural arrangements and personal and social behavior can either encourage or discourage crime. Since we do have the choice, says crime prevention, why not discourage crime?

Many people still ask of crime prevention that it prove itself workable before they will support it. It is not unreasonable to ask for proof. On the other hand, in order to test the effectiveness of crime prevention one must assume that it can work, for success in crime prevention depends on one's ability to convince others to properly apply crime risk management principles. Crime prevention rests on the activist assumption that potential victims can reduce their own crime risks—if provided with adequate guidance and support. Crime prevention is no passive thing that society can leave up to the police, the courts, the jails or the rehabilitation specialists.

Once we accept the idea of crime prevention, we can begin to develop appropriate strategies and techniques. To paraphrase George Bernard Shaw, some people look at crime and ask, **Why**? Crime preventers look at the potential for reducing criminal opportunity, and ask, **Why not**?

Our country has a magnificant record of achievement based on "Why nots?" Why not establish a constitutionally-base, democratic republic and make it work? Why not develop an almost frightening ability to overcome material problems through a superb technology? Why not put a man on the moon? Why not prevent contagious disease? Why not feed our people and provide them with standards of living unmatched anywhere in the world? So why not roll up our sleeves and tackle the task of reducing crime?

But, we must give the critics their due. Crime preventers, up to now, have gone ahead so powerfully on faith and conviction that they have not often stopped to verify the assumptions, prove the case and in general mold crime prevention knowledge and experience into a comprehensive, reliable technology. Much of crime prevention's current power lies in the feeling of evangelistic fervor that most practitioners and adherents bring to their tasks, and the techniques they use are hardly yet "tried and true", in any sense of the cliche.

On the other hand, crime prevention's grass-roots appeal is probably the best possible indicator of its ultimate validity. People, whether as practitioners, supporters or volunteers, are working nights and weekends all over the country to bring forth crime prevention projects and programs. Governors and other powerful individuals are investing priceless political capital in their support of crime prevention campaigns. An ever-growing number of powerful national associations (The American Association of Retired Persons, The National Exchange Club, Kiwanis International, U.S. Jaycees, Boy Scouts of America, American Bar Association, National Sheriffs' Association, International Congress of Building Officials, American Society for Industrial Security, Service Corps of Retired Executives, Association of Junior Leagues, U.S. Chamber of Commerce, National Burglar and Fire Alarm Association, National Retail Merchants Association, International Association of Chiefs of Police, and The American Management Associations, among others) have adopted crime prevention initiatives, projects and programs as priority activity focusses for their national and local membership efforts.

Practitioners themselves are becoming a powerful force. Thousands of individuals have now received at least basic training in the practice of crime prevention and are operating in law enforcement and civilian-based programs at the local, state and national level all over the country. Recently, a national organization called the International Society of Crime Prevention Practitioners was formed to provide a focal point for professional activities. In addition, more than half the states have statewide crime prevention officers associations in existence or under development.

At least 26 states have a statewide crime prevention program underway. Private industry, too, through the American Society for Industrial Security and other industry-oriented groups is beginning to take an active role in crime prevention. Federal agencies, such as the Department of Defense, Department of Commerce, and, of course, the Department of Justice are also developing specific or comprehensive thrusts in the crime prevention area. The Department of Justice has continued to sponsor the efforts of the National Crime Prevention Council, which conducts a national media campaign and many other services.

Industry, too, is rapidly entering the crime prevention picture. The private security field is developing a host of cooperative arrangements with public crime prevention programs. The insurance industry has made strides in the area of crime insurance premium discounts for clients who apply crime risk management principles. Oil and automobile companies are working to reduce auto theft. Computer companies are concerned with use of the computer to defraud. The construction industry is working to reduce crime at construction sites. The health industry is developing methods to reduce victimization at hospitals and medical complexes. Hotel and motel chains are becoming more security conscious. These and many more such examples indicate the great potential willingness on the part of the private sector to work with crime prevention programs.

Finally, professionals in the social and behavioral sciences and in the physical planning sciences are taking an active interest in the various applications of crime prevention through environmental design.

It is extremely significant that such a volume and variety of interest and effort should have arisen in fourteen years (from the time the National Crime Prevention Institute was established), especially in the absence of a coordinated national campaign. Uniquely among large-scale social change movements of the past few decades, crime prevention has neither been started nor sustained by national political initiatives, nor has it been the object of great outpourings of federal funds such as characterized the War on Poverty or even the national campaign against Swine Flu.

The virtual explosion of grass-roots interest in crime prevention has been the primary factor in the quickening pace with which state and national organizations and government agencies are developing outreach, service and financial support programs. We believe that the American public is demanding crime prevention, and that the state and national organizations mentioned here are quite sensibly responding to that demand.

Still, there are many who wonder if crime prevention is really no more than a passing fad—a will-of-the-wisp that will blow away. And, they have a point. As we have seen in this volume, crime prevention is a simple, practical idea—a great idea, really, but it can only fulfill its promise through hard, diligent, strategic work at many levels. Those who feel that the potential of crime prevention can be realized through promotional campaigns and general application of a few standard types of projects are misguided, to say the least.

The crime prevention field in the United States is a new and rapidly changing area of knowledge. The current state-of-the-art is highly developmental in nature and is characterized by much activity and experimentation and relatively little scientific documentation. As the number increases of local, state and national governmental agencies and non-governmental organizations desiring to establish or participate in crime prevention programs, and as current program managers reach for higher levels of program effectiveness, a great demand is created for usable knowledge. And this is as it should be. At some point in the evolution of any new field of activity, the initial excitement and experimentation begins to give way to demand for reliable performance criteria and standards, for organization of what is known into readily adaptable packages, and for documented proof that recommended methods and approaches will work. It is at this point that the field begins to get organized.

The challenge falls squarely on the shoulders of crime prevention practitioners and organizations such as the National Crime Prevention Institute. We must continue to organize the knowledge of crime prevention and provide proof that crime prevention strategies will work. In no other way will the field get organized, stay organized and develop the powerful, disciplined technology to augment the strength of this existing, creative approach.

It would be unreasonable to hope that we can provide absolute security against criminal attack in American life. However, in time, we can hope to manage crime in the same way that contagious disease is managed through strategies which reduce its current opportunities and contain and limit its new outbreaks. Through this management of crime, we can also hope to increase and improve the well-being of people everywhere. Fulfillment of these hopes is the end product of all of the crime prevention practitioner's efforts. But to even begin the task, practitioners must master the current knowledge and skills of this practice of crime prevention and work steadily to improve the quality of that knowledge and those skills.

This volume presents for the first time, an organized compendium of current crime prevention knowledge and skills. It is our hope that the development and refinement of knowledge in this field will be so rapid as to force frequent updates. It is our intention to keep in touch with the continual discovery of new knowledge, to sift this knowledge, integrate what is of value and discard what is no longer meaningful, to publish this ongoing synthesis, and disseminate it to practitioners everywhere.. To accomplish this aim, we must rely on you, the practitioner, to not only generate and refine knowledge through your own experience but also to share it with us. Please keep us informed of your discoveries as you practice crime prevention.

Understanding Crime Prevention is not the last word, but rather a first step in a continuing effort to assemble, refine, and publish the knowledge of crime prevention.

References

CHAPTER 1

1. C. Ray Jefferey, *Crime Prevention Through Environmental Design*, Sage Publications, Beverly Hills, Calif. p. 20.

CHAPTER 2

1. Walter McQuade, *Cities Fit to Live In,* Macmillan Co., New York, 1971, pp 5-19.
2. F.W. Hudson, "Crime Prevention—Past and Present (Part 1)," *Security Gazette,* Aug 1974, p 292.
3. Edwin N. Sutherland and Donald R. Cressey, *Criminology*, 9th Edition, J.B. Lippincott Co., New York, 1974, p 300.
4. Ibid.
5. Ibid, p 301.
6. Harry Keeney, "Building Security Code," *NCPI Hotline* Feb 1977. (Note original source of Hammurabi's Code provided by the Masonry Institute, San Francisco, Calif.)
7. *Holy Bible*, Book of "Leviticus," Chapter 5, Verse 1 and Chapter 24, Verses 17-20.

8. C. Ray Jefferey, *Crime Prevention Through Environmental Design*, Sage Publications, Beverly Hills, Calif., pp 17-25, 85, 167-187.
9. Op. cit., Hudson, p 292.
10. Ibid.
11. *NCPI Four Week Course Class Notebook* with historical material compiled by Doyle Shackelford, NCPI staff member. Specific reference here from Inspector Ronald Dawson, Home Office Crime Prevention Center, Stafford, England, *History of Police Service*, p 3.
12. Ibid, p 5.
13. Op. cit., Hudson, p 293.
14. Ibid, p 294.
15. Richard Post and Arthur Kingsbury, *Security Administration*, 3rd Edition, Charles C. Thomas, Springfield, Ill., 1977, pp 32-34.
16. "The History and Development of the National Crime Prevention Institute," *NCPI Bulletin*, Jan/Feb 1976, Vol. IV, No. 4.
17. Ibid.
18. *NCPI Four Week Course Class Notebook.*
19. The FBI's Crime Prevention program is illustrated in the FBI publication *Crime Resistance*, USGPO, 1975.
20. HUD's interest in crime prevention is reflected in such exemplary documents as *A Design Guide for Improving Residential Security* written for HUD by Oscar Newman, USGPO, 1973.
21. The National Sheriff's Association was the original sponsor of Neighborhood Watch.
22. Op. cit., *Security Administration*, p 35.
23. Op. cit., Jefferey, p 24.
24. Ibid.
25. Op. cit., Sutherland and Cressey, pp 7, 350, 410, 438, 440-443.
26. Op. cit., Jefferey, pp 98-104; op. cit. Sutherland and Cressey, pp 49, 55-56.
27. Richard Cloward and Lloyd Ohlin, *Delinquency and Opportunity, A Theory of Delinquent Gangs*, Free Press, Glencoe, Ill., 1960, pp 108-109.
28. Op. cit., Jefferey, pp 214-225.
29. Op. cit., Jefferey, p 19; Wilbur Rykert, "Crime is a Thief's Business, Prevention is Yours," in *Deterrence of Crime In and Around Residences*, NILECJ, 1973, pp 66-77.
30. National Advisory Commission on Criminal Justice Standards & Goals, *Report on Police*, LEAA, 1973, p 9.
31. Ibid, pp 9-11.
32. Ibid, p 120; also author's estimate from numerous discussions with police officers attending programs at NCPI.
33. LEAA's commitment to crime prevention was reflected in the continued funding of NCPI for over six years and its funding of such research projects as Crime Prevention Through Environmental Design (CPTED). LEAA spent over $4 million alone on CPTED.

34. Michael T. Farmer, *Police Direct Crime Prevention, State of the Art and Directions for the Future*, The Police Foundation, Washington, D.C., 1977; see also *Assessing Criminal Justice Projects: Findings From the National Evaluation Program (Executive Summary)*, NILECJ, 1977.

CHAPTER 3

1. Interview of Richard Mellard during his teaching visit at NCPI in Dec 1977.
2. Arthur A. Kingsbury, *Introduction to Security and Crime Prevention Surveys,* Charles C. Thomas, Springfield, Ill., 1973, Chapter 1.
3. Michael T. Farmer, *Police Direct Crime Prevention, State of the Art and Directions for the Future*; see also *Assessing Criminal Justice Projects: Findings from the National Evaluation Program (Executive Summary),* NILECJ, 1977.
4. Carl L. Cunningham, et al., *The National Sheriff's Association National Neighborhood Watch Program,* Midwest Research Institute, 1974.
5. Ibid, p 9.
6. Ibid, pp 2-3.
7. Thomas Reppetto, *Residential Crime*, Ballinger Press, Cambridge, Mass., 1974, p 72. Here Reppetto implies a possible relationship between increase in burglary in Boston with increase in number of drug addicts.
8. Jane Jacobs, *The Death and Life of Great American Cities*, Vintage Books, New York, 1961.
9. Discussion between Roy Dixon and El Paso police officers involved in crime prevention.
10. Thomas Reppetto, "Crime Prevention and the Displacement Phenomenon," *Crime and Delinquency*, Vol. 22, No. 2, April 1976, pp 166-168; Arnold Sagalyn, et al., *Residential Security*, NILECJ, Monograph Series, 1973, Chapter 1.
11. Ibid, Sagalyn, p 7.
12. Paul Cirel, et al., *Seattle Study, An Exemplary Project: Community Crime Prevention Program,* Seattle, Washington, NILECJ, Sept 1977.
13. Ibid, p 51.
14. Op. cit., Cunningham, p 10.
15. John Conklin, *Impact of Crime*, Macmillan Publishing Co., New York, 1975, p 249.
16. Ibid, p 141.
17. Westinghouse Electric Corporation, *Elements of CPTED*; "Crime Prevention Through Environmental Policy," *American Political Scientist*, Volume 20, No. 2, Nov/Dec 1976.
18. Op. cit., Farmer, p 20.
19. Ibid.

20. Richard S. Post and Arthur Kingsbury, *Security Administration*, Third Edition, Charles C. Thomas, Springfield, Ill, 1977, pp 6, 35-36.
21. Ibid, pp 6-7.
22. Ibid, pp 7-8; Douglas W. Frisbie, et al., *Crime in Minneapolis, Proposals for Prevention*, Governor's Commission on Crime Prevention and Control, St. Paul, Minnesota, 1977, pp 9-10.
23. Oscar Newman, *A Design Guide for Improving Residential Security*, HUD, 1973, p 3.
24. "The History and Development of the National Crime Prevention Institute," *NCPI Bulletin*, Jan/Feb 1976.

CHAPTER 4

1. *NCPI Class Notebook*. See O.C. Foster's presentation of "Crime Risk Management." See also Richard B. Cole, *Protection Management & Crime Prevention*, W.H. Anderson Co., Cincinnati, Ohio, 1974, pp 13-31.
2. Ibid, O.C. Foster.
3. Ibid.
4. Ibid.
5. Douglas W. Frisbie, *Crime in Mineapolis, Proposals for Prevention*, Governor's Commission on Crime Prevention and Control, St. Paul, Minnesota, May 1977, p. 101.

CHAPTER 5

1. "Building Security Codes," *NCPI Hotline*, National Crime Prevention Institute, Louisville, Ky., Feb. 1977 issue.
2. Thad L. Webber, *Alarm Systems and Theft Protection*, Security World Publishing Co. Inc., Los Angeles, California, 1973, p 179.
3. Douglas W. Frisbie, et. al., *Crime in Minneapolis, Proposals for Prevention*, Governor's Commission on Crime Prevention and Control, St. Paul, Minnesota, 1977.
4. Ibid, pp 232-235.
5. O.C. Foster, *An Introduction to Retail Security*, NCPI Classroom Handout, p 4.

The majority of the material used in the Electronic Security section of this chapter was adapted from classroom material prepared by Carl Kellem, MSEE.

CHAPTER 6

1. National Advisory Commission on Criminal Justice Standards & Goals, *Report on Police*, p 129.

2. Jane Jacobs, *The Death and Life of Great American Cities*, Vintage Books, New York, 1961, No. 3.
3. Lee Rainwater, "Fear And The Home-As-Haven In The Lower Class," *Journal of the American Institute of Planners*, Jan 1966, pp 23-37.
4. Elizabeth Wood, *Housing Design, A Social Theory*, Citizens' Housing and Planning Counsel of New York, Inc., New York, 1961.
5. Schlomo Angel, *Discouraging Crime Through City Planning*, University of California, Berkeley, 1968.
6. Gerald Leudtke and E. Lystad, *Crime in the Physical City*, Final Report, LEAA Grant No. NI 69-078, 1970.
7. Newman-Rand study (1969), published by Oscar Newman, *Defensible Space,* Macmillan Publishing Co., New York, 1972.
8. National Institute of Law Enforcement and Criminal Justice, *Urban Design, Security and Crime*, Proceedings of a seminar held April 12-13, 1972, published by LEAA, p 15.
9. Thomas A. Reppetto, *Residential Crime*, Ballinger Publishing Co., Cambridge, Mass., 1974.
10. John Conklin, *The Impact of Crime*, Macmillan Co., New York, 1975, p 299.
11. C. Ray Jefferey, *Crime Prevention Through Environmental Design*, Sage Publications, Beverly Hills, Calif., 1971.
12. C. Ray Jefferey, "Behavior Control Techniques and Criminology: 1975-2075," *Ecology Youth Development Workshop*, University of Hawaii School of Social Work, Honolulu, Dec 1975.
13. Op. cit., Newman, pp 51-52.
14. Ibid.
15. Oscar Newman, *Design Guidelines for Creating Defensible Space*, LEAA, Washington, D.C., 1976.
16. Edward Perce, "The CPTED Concept," part of "A Special Report: Crime Prevention Through Environmental Design," in *Nation's Cities*, published by National League of Cities, Dec 1977, pp 16-17.
17. Imre R. Kohn, "Crime Prevention Through Environmental Design, Theory and Framework," presented at the *APA Symposium on Crime Prevention Through Environmental Design*, San Francisco, Calif., Sept 1977.
18. John W. McKay, "CPTED in a Commercial Setting," part of "A Special Report: Crime Prevention Through Environmental Design," published in *Nation's Cities*, pp 17-18.
19. Paula Chin Wegner, "CPTED in Schools," part of "A Special Report: Crime Prevention Through Environmental Design," in *Nation's Cities*, p 22.
20. Lynn Olsen, "CPTED in a Residential Setting," part of "A Special Report: Crime Prevention Through Environmental Design," in *Nation's Cities,* p 21. The reader may wish to review the work of William Brill and Associates in public housing. Richard Gardiner and Tony Wiles should also be mentioned as designers in the forefront of this field: William Brill, *Comprehensive Security Planning: A Program for Arthur Capper Dwellings*, U.S. Dept. of

Housing and Urban Development, Washington, D.C., 1977; Richard Gardiner, *Environmental Security Planning: Redesign for Safe Neighborhoods,* Gardiner Associates, Newburyport, Mass., 1977; and Wiles, Tighe, Hawes, and Bass, *CPTED Demonstration Plan for the School Environment*, LEAA contract No. J-LEAA-022-74.

CHAPTER 7

1. John E. Conklin, *The Impact of Crime*, Macmillan Publishing Co., New York, 1975, p 131.
2. Ibid.
3. Ibid.
4. Ibid.
5. Alicia Christian, *The Community's Stake in Crime Prevention: A Guide for Action*, The Center for Community Change, Washington, D.C., 1977, pp 28–30.
6. Ibid.
7. "Developing Citizen Participation," *NCPI Hotline,* National Crime Prevention Institute, Louisville, Ky., Aug 1977 issue.
8. Donald L. Warren and Rachelle B. Warren, *The Neighborhood Organizer's Handbook*, Notre Dame University Press, Notre Dame, Indiana, 1977, Chapter 5.
9. Ibid, Chapter 4.
10. The importance of small groups to local crime prevention efforts is further discussed in these sources: Ed Good, "Citizen Initiative Programs," paper presented at the National Crime Prevention Institute's Program on Community Crime Prevention in Louisville, Ky., June 1977; and Lois Mock, "Citizen Crime Prevention Programs: Some Implications of Past Research," presented at LEAA's Community Crime Prevention Conference, Washington, D.C., July 1977. Also read Sy Rosenthal's "Turf Reclamation: An Approach to Neighborhood Security," *HUD Challenge*, March 1974.

CHAPTER 8

1. *Crime in Minneapolis: Proposals for Prevention*, Governor's Commission on Crime Prevention and Control, St. Paul, Minn., May 1977, pp 11–12.
2. A useful reference on developing a crime analysis capability is *Police Crime Analysis Unit Handbook*, published by the Law Enforcement Assistance Administration in 1973. *Crime in Minneapolis*, referenced above, provides excellent practical information on crime prevention-oriented crime analysis, as does: *An Exemplary Project–Community Crime Prevention Program, Seattle, Washington,* published in 1977 by the Law Enforcement Assistance Administration.

3. Op. cit., *Crime in Minneapolis*, pp 26-27.
4. Ibid.

CHAPTER 9

1. *1974 Criminal Justice Plan for Texas*, Office of the Governor, Austin, Texas, 1974, p 157.
2. *Foundation Directory*, Edition 10, compiled and published by the Foundation Center, New York, 1985.

CHAPTER 10

1. Edward A. Suchman, *Evaluation Research–Principles and Practices in Public Service and Social Action Programs*, Russell Sage Foundation, New York, 1967, p 143.
2. For further information on unsophisticated evaluation techniques, see references cited under Reference 2, Chapter 8.

Index